THE NATURE OF NEW TESTAMENT THEOLOGY

STUDIES IN BIBLICAL THEOLOGY

A series of monographs designed to provide clergy and laymen with the best work in biblical scholarship both in this country and abroad

STUDIES IN BIBLICAL THEOLOGY

Second Series · 25

THE NATURE OF NEW TESTAMENT THEOLOGY

The Contribution of William Wrede and Adolf Schlatter

Edited, translated and with an introduction by

ROBERT MORGAN

ALEC R. ALLENSON INC.

635 EAST OGDEN AVENUE

NAPERVILLE, ILL.

Translated from the German: William Wrede, *Über Aufgabe und Methode der sogenannten neutestamentlichen Theologie*, published by Vandenhoeck and Ruprecht, Göttingen 1897; Adolf Schlatter, 'Die Theologie des Neuen Testaments und die Dogmatik', first published in *Beiträge zur Förderung christlicher Theologie* 13, 1909, 2, pp. 7–82, and reprinted in a collection of his articles, *Zur Theologie des Neuen Testaments und zur Dogmatik*, Christian Kaiser Verlag 1969, pp. 203–55. The publishers are grateful to Dr Theodor Schlatter for permission to translate the latter work.

Published by Alec R. Allenson Inc.
Naperville, Ill.
Printed in Great Britain

CONTENTS

FOREWORD

Some personal acknowledgements are required: first to Dr Ernst Bammel who taught his pupils what is meant by radical historical criticism and introduced us all to Wrede. Secondly to Professor Käsemann who stimulated me to the more difficult, but ultimately more rewarding task of reading Schlatter. Thirdly to Professors C. F. D. Moule and C. K. Barrett whose lecture courses on the theology and ethics of the New Testament have been for many of us the highlights of our undergraduate careers, and who have encouraged me in the preparation of this book by agreeing that publishing some methodological reflections upon New Testament theology might serve the cultivation of its fruits on English soil. Fourthly, and anonymously, to many friends (and a relation) whose critical acumen will enable them to find traces of their collaboration in the translations and the introductory essay. I am extremely grateful.

ROBERT MORGAN

Lancaster 1972

ABBREVIATIONS

ET	English translation
EvTh	*Evangelische Theologie*
HTR	*Harvard Theological Review*
JBL	*Journal of Biblical Literature*
LThK	*Lexikon für Theologie und Kirche*
NF	Neue Folge (new series)
NTS	*New Testament Studies*
RGG	*Die Religion in Geschichte und Gegenwart*
SJT	*Scottish Journal of Theology*
ThLZ	*Theologische Literaturzeitung*
ThR	*Theologische Rundschau*
ThZ	*Theologische Zeitschrift*
ZNW	*Zeitschrift für die neutestamentliche Wissenschaft*
ZSTh	*Zeitschrift für systematische Theologie*
ZThK	*Zeitschrift für Theologie und Kirche*

I

Robert Morgan

INTRODUCTION: THE NATURE OF NEW TESTAMENT THEOLOGY

New Testament theology is a nodal point in contemporary theological debate. Disputed questions of fundamental importance converge here. What is theology and how is it to be done? What are its sources and norms? What is the New Testament and how is it to be read and studied? What is the difference and what the relationship between scripture and tradition? What is Christianity and in what sense, if any, can it be called (a) revealed religion?

The modern debate about New Testament theology is co-extensive with the two hundred years' history of modern theology. Nineteenth-century German Protestant theology was dominated by the effect of the new historical research upon people's understanding of the Christian tradition. After gospel criticism, New Testament theology was the point at which this discipline was experienced most acutely. Since the First World War the 'hermeneutical' debate has waxed more and more strongly, and since the 1950s it has involved Roman Catholic as much as Protestant scholarship. Here, too, New Testament theology is at the centre of discussion.

William Wrede stands at the climax of the nineteenth-century development. The first part of this introductory essay considers his work chiefly in connection with his most important predecessors. His agreement and disagreement with B. Weiss and H. J. Holtzmann, the most important of his conservative and liberal contemporaries to write New Testament theologies, throws some light upon more recent discussion. The twentieth century has added new participants and new points of view, but Weiss, Holtzmann and Wrede represent typical positions which are still maintained.

The second part will inevitably centre on the work of Rudolf

Bultmann, whose place in the twentieth-century debate is at least as central as that of F. C. Baur in the nineteenth. Adolf Schlatter, the greatest conservative of the generation before Bultmann, stands outside the mainstream of the development of New Testament studies. He is included here as an indication that the theological interests of the twentieth century stand in some continuity with those of previous generations. Historical awareness has altered the conditions under which Christian theology is done, but has not fundamentally altered the character of the search of Christian faith for understanding.

I   *Wrede and his Predecessors*

The provocative '*sogennanten*' (so-called) in the title of Wrede's monograph, translated into English here some three-quarters of a century after its original publication, draws attention to the question what the phrase 'New Testament theology' means and whether it is appropriate.[1] The stream of publications using it does not settle the matter; these might be following a traditional misuse of words. The source of the difficulty is the contradiction in method between the historical discipline of New Testament theology (so-called) and the 'normative' activity of the Christian theologian who is not satisfied with saying what Christians *have* thought, but must go on to say what (in his view) they *should* think.

'The name "New Testament theology" is wrong in both its terms', wrote Wrede (p. 116 below). He wanted to substitute the whole of early Christian literature for the New Testament canon as his source material, and to call the discipline not theology but the history of religion. New Testament theology (so-called) would then be recognized in its purely historical character as the history of early Christian religion, reconstructed from all the documentary evidence available. The history would include some history of theology, the earliest chapters of the history of Christian doctrine, but it would itself be history, not doctrine.

Wrede was rightly concerned about the integrity of the historical discipline. For over a century, since J. P. Gabler's epoch-making *Oratio de iusto discrimine theologiae biblicae et dogmaticae regundisque recte utriusque finibus* (A discourse on the proper distinction between biblical and dogmatic theology and the correct delimitation of their boundaries, 1787), 'biblical theology' had been in principle recognized as a historical discipline in contrast to dogmatics. Gabler had demanded that biblical theology be a 'fully independent, historical-critical discipline alongside dogmatics'. Unlike dogmatics, it had a

> historical character in that it hangs on what the sacred writers thought about divine things; dogmatic theology, on the other hand, bears a didactic character in that it teaches what every theologian through use of his reason philosophizes about divine things in accordance with his understanding.[2]

But after more than a century, the discipline was still not, in Wrede's view, a truly historical one in practice (p. 69 below). His first substantive point concerns the boundaries of the discipline. This issue is returned to and treated positively in the light of subsequent discussion; the programme Wrede is advocating can be seen to *demand* the wider view of the task; historical method requires that all available sources be considered. But here the question is treated from the negative side; historical methods and results must not be restricted by dogmatic prejudgments. To confine one's attention to the canonical writings of the New Testament is to allow theological considerations to determine one's conception of the historical task. The historian is interested in the past as it was, and 'no New Testament writing was born with the predicate "canonical" attached' (p. 70 below).

Wrede was in fact clearly wrong to say that 'where the doctrine of inspiration has been discarded, it is impossible to continue to maintain the dogmatic conception of the canon' (p. 70 below). The *theological* problem of the canon stands at the centre of contemporary debate amongst scholars who share Wrede's general critical position.[3] It is by no means obviously true either, that 'anyone who accepts without question the idea of the canon places himself under the authority of the bishops and theologians of those [second to fourth] centuries'.[4] But Wrede's point is that the dogmatic category of the canon must not be allowed to influence a historical account of early Christianity. This is certainly correct. The surviving literature must be evaluated as source material without regard to its ecclesiastical status. It must be classified according to historical criteria. The separation of the New Testament from other early Christian literature would only be justified if it were indeed (as it has traditionally been thought to be) the literature of the 'apostolic

age', distinct from that of the 'sub-apostolic age'. But this is not
the case. In date and in content the later writings of the New
Testament overlap with those of the Apostolic Fathers. The
'death of the last apostle' is of no more importance for defining the
boundary of primitive Christianity than it was for the composition
of the New Testament writings.[5]

Wrede's rejection, for historical purposes, of the dogmatic conception of the canon was not primarily directed at traditional
views of biblical inspiration and revelation. In Germany at least,
Protestant orthodoxy's pre-critical view of the Bible had long since
succumbed to the blasts of historical criticism, at least so far as
academic theology was concerned. Even a fairly conservative
scholar like Bernhard Weiss could fully accept in principle what he
considered a historical approach to New Testament theology.[6]
Weiss was not prepared to abandon supernatural 'facts of salvation', but he accepted that the different authors, writing at different
times and in different situations, would offer a 'variety of religious
ideas and doctrines' (p. 3). And,

> This could not be the case if the revelation of God in Christ
> consisted, as to its nature, in the supernatural communication of
> a sum of religious ideas and doctrines, whose correct trans-
> mission must also have been secured by an absolutely super-
> natural influence of the Spirit of God upon the writers of the
> New Testament. On this assumption the biblical theology of
> the New Testament would have nothing else to do than to
> collect those ideas and doctrines which are scattered in a very
> inappropriate manner in the heterogeneous writings of the
> New Testament, arranging them systematically, and, since a
> certain variety unquestionably presents itself at the first look,
> showing their unbroken unity and conformity. The theology
> of the New Testament would, in that case, be no longer a purely
> historical, but a systematic discipline (which) we should more
> naturally call biblical dogmatics (pp. 3f.).

The older *unitary* conception of scripture, in which *dicta pro-
bantia* or proof-texts for Christian doctrines could be selected at
random from the Bible, had been abandoned. Following Gabler's
distinction between biblical and dogmatic theology, his colleague
G. L. Bauer separated the two Testaments when he carried out the
programme of biblical theology in *Die Theologie des alten Testa-*

ments (1796) and *Die Theologie des neuen Testaments* (1800–02). In the latter work he treated the theologies of different authors separately, so that not even the New Testament could be seen as a doctrinal unity in the older way. But that did not guarantee a truly historical conception of the discipline. Gabler read his own rationalism into the New Testament. This can be seen especially in his theory, inherited from J. S. Semler (1725–1791), that Jesus and the apostles 'accommodated' their real enlightened views to the primitive ideas of their hearers. It was only gradually during the nineteenth century that New Testament scholars learned not to impose their own doctrinal schemes upon the New Testament writers, but to present the theology of each in his own terms. B. Weiss gave clear expression to this requirement:

> The representation of the several doctrinal systems will have to start from the central point around which the doctrinal view of each individual writer moves, and from that point, following the lines of thought which are found in the writer himself, it will have to describe the whole circle of his ideas and doctrines (p. 17, §4).

However, both his conception of the subject-matter of New Testament theology as essentially doctrine, and his presentation of it, show how little Weiss had advanced beyond the old doctrinal use of the Bible towards the historical conception of early Christianity which Wrede advocated. This is particularly clear in the distinction Weiss draws between New Testament theology and 'the history of theology in the apostolic age', and in the reasons he gives for his refusal to 'present a progressive development of the religious ideas and doctrines' (p. 20). He acknowledges that:

> nothing seems more natural than to adopt a different method, and to give biblical theology (which, indeed, professes also to be a historical discipline) itself the form of a history of the development of theology in the apostolic age, in so far as it can independently bring out such a development from its own sources.

However, he objects to this that:

> 'apart from the circumstance that the inner history of the apostolic age can never be adequately represented without attention

being paid to much which belongs to the outer history, and which must therefore be borrowed from some other quarter, no historical development can be described without historical criticism, and biblical theology is not a historico-critical but a historico-descriptive discipline (p. 10, n. 3).

This last distinction shows how far removed Weiss's *Biblical Theology of the New Testament* is from what Wrede could accept as a truly historical conception of the task. To critical scholarship, 'historical' means 'historical critical'. According to Weiss, 'biblical theology has to refrain from every criticism as to what appears essential or non-essential; it has to represent, with equal carefulness, the whole contents of the religious ideas and doctrines' (p. 11 n.). It merely 'furnishes the history of that (apostolic) age with the material for the representation of its inner development'. It is merely what Schlatter calls 'statistics', and Weiss himself an 'auxiliary science'. Weiss fears that to let New Testament theology be more than this will 'only drag foreign matter into the discipline'.[7] That is correct. A historical view cannot accept the total isolation of the New Testament world of thought from its background, especially in Judaism. What Weiss has in fact done is merely to 'attempt to defuse the work of the critical school by taking up and making its own the elements of this which can be assimilated'.[8]

The critical edge of biblical theology which the Enlightenment and pietism had brought to bear against orthodoxy in the early days of the discipline has entirely disappeared here. Weiss will not allow New Testament theology to disturb traditional Christian doctrine. The unity of the New Testament revelation is shifted from the vulnerable text to 'the saving fact of the perfect revelation of God in Christ' (pp. 20f.). This allows diversity in the doctrinal systems contained in the New Testament, but not antitheses and contradictions, though admittedly the Tübingen school 'gave people a sharper eye for the differences of the apostolic tendencies, since it conceived them as contradictions'. For Weiss,

the representation of the biblical theology of the New Testament will be a continued proof that the Spirit which ruled in the apostolic church and secured the preservation in its purity of the saving revelation of God in Christ, was always guiding it more and more into all truth (p. 32).

The main object of Wrede's attack, however, was not B. Weiss, whose position had long been abandoned by liberals, but H. J. Holtzmann, whose monumental *Textbook of New Testament Theology* had just appeared. This classic of historical-critical scholarship rejected Weiss's conservative views about authorship, his isolation of the New Testament from the surrounding world of thought, and especially his view that revelation could be presupposed by the discipline. Modern historical method questions all traditional views about the sources of the New Testament; it sets them in a larger historical and causal context; and it excludes on principle dogmatic presuppositions such as the notion of revelation, since it is methodologically uncommitted to any particular theology.

However, Holtzmann retained the traditional name 'New Testament theology', and he restricted himself to the canonical documents. He did so on pragmatic grounds rather than as a matter of principle, and in fact defined New Testament theology to mean the history of religion and ethics. He had no objection, either, to anyone taking a wider view of what source material should be used. But Wrede saw both as serious faults and symptoms of a failure to break completely with the modified orthodoxy of B. Weiss's conception of the discipline. The main characteristics of that had been a presentation oriented upon the New Testament documents rather than upon the history to which they witness, and an assumption that the content of the New Testament was (revealed) *doctrine*. New Testament theology was therefore for Weiss the

> representation of the various doctrinal systems . . . (by) finding the central point around which move the principal lines of thought and circles of ideas of each . . . (and) as far as possible connecting with this point everything else . . . until at last the whole extent of his ideas and doctrines is described (p. 18).

To allow the presentation to be shaped by the material was an advance upon the pre-critical imposition of the scholar's own dogmatic framework upon the documents. But the literary and doctrinal orientation, reflected in the arrangement of the material by 'doctrinal concepts' or theological topics, remained the source of all the distortions which Wrede wished to eradicate from the historical reconstruction of early Christianity. For all his advance over Weiss in historical criticism, and his properly historical attempt to trace the development of thought, Holtzmann had found little to object to *methodologically* in Weiss's orientation upon the New Testament documents. Despite an excellent chapter on 'The Theological Problems of Primitive Christianity' (ch. 3), not even Holtzmann was free of this survival from the old doctrinal use of the New Testament.

Wrede rejected absolutely the suggestion that the needs of the church could influence the historian's presentation of New Testament theology (so-called) and justify the restriction to the New Testament documents. Historical research has its own goals and demands methods appropriate to these. That restriction to certain documents could even be contemplated was proof that Holtzmann's New Testament theology, too, was oriented upon documents rather than upon the history. This would be correct in a history of New Testament literature, but was a mistake in New Testament theology if this was to be seen as the history of early Christian religion and theology.

The literary approach led to distortions of the history. For example, it was always tempted to detect more literary relationships than actually existed. Consider how many verses from contemporary Jewish literature would have been labelled 'Pauline' if they had appeared in the New Testament (p. 187 below)! Literary dependence was not the main channel for the history of New Testament ideas. If occasional documents are ransacked for the material they happen to contain instead of being treated as the sporadic witnesses to a history lying behind them which happen to have survived, distortions are inevitable. Unimportant matters receive undue prominence, and important matters (such as the doctrine of God) which are taken for granted by the document are ignored by the historian. The purpose and practical character of the documents are likely to be under-emphasized, and the subtleties of tone ignored, when they are pressed for theological information instead of being heard in their own terms (pp. 75ff. below).

All these observations on historical method contained perceptive criticism of contemporary practice in Wrede's time. The same must be said of the matters of 'style' which Wrede raises. The historian's art is most evident in the selectivity with which he uses his material. Weiss was not prepared to leave anything out, because this would involve making judgments about what was important.[9] But the same striving after completeness was a fault in Holtzmann's work. It is important for New Testament theology not to lose sight of the wood for the trees. A history is not a reference book; it must let its subject live. In discussing a particular author it is important to single out what is *characteristic* of him. In a full and undifferentiated account this is liable to be lost (below, pp. 77, 107).

Throughout the essay Wrede is arguing for the consistent recognition in the field of New Testament theology of the intellectual revolution of nineteenth-century liberal theology in which the old dogmatic method of deduction from revealed data had been replaced by historical induction from human evidence. The old dogmatic theology was thought to have been replaced by the history of religion. The reason why his monograph is generally so convincing is that his chief opponent Holtzmann agrees with him on the fundamental question of theological method: that all that is required is the history of religion. Granted this presupposition, Wrede is able to show that Holtzmann does not carry the programme through consistently. He is not arguing about theological presuppositions but about historical method, and as an account of what is demanded by the historical investigation of early Christianity his essay is unsurpassed. Historical research in this area is still sometimes perverted by theological interest. Wrede's account of what 'purely historical' means in such a context is therefore still worth pondering.

It is, however, Wrede's theological presuppositions which are crucial in considering the implications of what he says for the nature of New Testament theology. These motivate the claim that the subject-matter of New Testament theology is not theology or doctrine, but religion, and that therefore the method of presentation in terms of 'doctrinal concepts' is misguided. The contrast between a 'literary' orientation on the sources and a more truly historical orientation on the subject-matter in turn supports the 'not theology but religion' thesis. However, before the legitimacy of Wrede's exclusivist claims for his history of religion programme is examined, it is important to recognize the consistency of the programme itself and the correctness of the points made against Holtzmann. This debate within liberal Protestantism about the practice of historical method in the field of religion, and especially in that part of the field occupied by the Christian tradition, must now be clarified before the limitations of the entire programme are explored.

Wrede was a member of the little study group of young scholars in Göttingen in the late 1880s who became famous as the 'history of religions school'. The group consisted also of Albert Eichhorn (who published very little, and so did not become a full professor), Wilhelm Bousset and Hermann Gunkel (who was a New Testament scholar before the job situation forced him into the Old Testament field). Ernst Troeltsch and Wilhelm Heitmüller came in later, and Johannes Weiss (son of B. Weiss) was associated with the group, and had similar aims.[10] One thing which united the Göttingen group was opposition to the Göttingen master, Albrecht Ritschl (1822–1889), whose theology was built upon historical foundations, but who arbitrarily abandoned these at the point where they conflicted with his doctrine, especially his belief in the canon. They believed that if historical methods are applied in theology (and it was agreed that this was inevitable), then they must be consistently applied, even if this meant the destruction of the older dogmatic method of doing theology.

The theological implications of this historical approach were worked out by Ernst Troeltsch, who came to be known (with his approval) as 'the dogmatician of the history of religions school'.[11] Wrede, Bousset and Gunkel, on the other hand, were biblical scholars – i.e. historians, not systematic theologians or philosophers of religion. Their work in the narrower field of historical theology both continued and *corrected* the great liberals of the older generation.

These giants of critical theology, Harnack, Wellhausen and Holtzmann, had themselves advanced a long way beyond Ritschl. They were now outflanked by the younger advocates of a purely historical theology. The older historians were among the chief teachers of the younger ones.[12] Both groups were in fundamental agreement that the subject-matter of the Bible and church history was human *religion*, and both were theologically interested in religion rather than doctrine. But the younger historians drew more methodological conclusions and criticized the literary orientation of their teachers' historical practice. They assumed that the biblical literature was the result of literary processes. But religion is a matter of traditions and popular conceptions, often handed down orally. Its history, therefore, cannot be treated like the history of philosophy or literature. The canons of literary relationships and dependence are inadequate to account for the background and meaning of religious documents.

For about a generation, research had concentrated upon the documentary sources. Great advances had been made in the science of New Testament critical introduction, and this was necessary for accurate historical reconstruction. But however correct such documentary hypotheses might be, to give them more than secondary importance was to project scholarly attitudes on to popular material. The history of religions school was interested in both the origin and the history of traditions. This involved both the often pre-literary history of motives contained in the documents, and also the historical processes leading to the composition of the documents. Unlike Gunkel and Bousset, Wrede did not examine the mythic origins of the biblical traditions. But in his own New Testament area he studied their history prior to the composition of the documents more perceptively than anyone else, and contributed significantly to the reconstruction of the history of the tradition between the subject-matter and the sources, the two poles between which the historian's eye must move.[13]

The new history of religions approach has led New Testament scholars up many blind alleys as each new piece of evidence from the ancient world has been tested for its possible importance for the history of early Christian thought. But the correctness in principle of the new interest in history and religion is confirmed by the extent to which the study of the history of traditions has dominated biblical research throughout this century. Wrede's chief work, *The Messianic Secret in the Gospels* (1901), inaugurated an epoch in gospel criticism. That monograph applied in a limited area the principles which according to this earlier methodological essay of 1897 should govern the task and methods of the historical study of early Christianity. It restored the gospels to their position in the history of early Christian religion and theology first explored systematically by F. C. Baur. The methodological essay, which is also reminiscent of Baur, demanded that the implications of a consistent historical approach be taken seriously in New Testament theology (so-called). This led him to criticize Holtzmann's continued use of the method of doctrinal concepts.[14]

The full impact of Wrede's work was not immediately felt outside Germany. English New Testament scholarship was not greatly influenced by the main organs of history of religions study,[15] and continued to be dominated by literary (source) criticism.[16] A serious gulf developed between English and German scholarship, which was aggravated by the political history of the first half of this century.[17]

Wrede died in 1906 at the age of forty-seven without fulfilling the programme he had outlined by himself writing a complete history of early Christian religion and theology. P. Wernle, *The Beginnings of Christianity*,[18] was a mediocre attempt to meet Wrede's demands, and Bousset later fulfilled the history of religions programme for the christological centre of New Testament theology (so-called) in his great work *Kyrios Christos*.[19] J. Weiss, *Primitive Christianity*,[20] reflects the same ideals. But the most impressive fulfilment of Wrede's historical programme is contained in Bultmann's *Theology of the New Testament*.[21] This work is guided by theological interests which Wrede would not have endorsed and which enabled Bultmann to omit the '*sogennante*' of Wrede's title. But since its greatness consists in part in its synthesizing of Wrede's historical interest with other theological concerns, it must be mentioned here amongst Wrede's successors.

Bultmann agrees with Wrede and Holtzmann that New Testament theology consists in the history of early Christian thought and nothing else. His novelty consists in conceiving this history-writing in such a way as to be able to do his own theologizing in and through it. He thus does what Luther and Calvin did when they wrote much of their theology through biblical exposition. Bultmann does the same thing in the changed conditions of modern historical consciousness presupposed by Wrede. Whether the project succeeds and what it should be called will be discussed below. It is mentioned here by way of contrast to Wrede's purely historical enterprise.

The chief emphasis of Wrede's essay, for which the sharp distinction between the literary sources and the historical subject-matter sets the stage, and the arguments about the proper name of the discipline and the extent of its sources are supports, is that *the historian is concerned with what lies behind the sources*, in this case the history of religion. The theological motive for this shift of emphasis in New Testament studies was that the old authority of the biblical text as revelation had disintegrated in the light of historical research. The documents appeared to have value only as sources for the history of Christianity. If Christianity was to be defended now, it could not be on the basis of an appeal to the New Testament as revelation, but only on appeal to the religion visible in history.

The harsh alternative between revelation and religion reconstructed from historical sources had been avoided by the father of historical theology, F. C. Baur of Tübingen (1792–1860). Baur's Hegelian metaphysics allowed him to see the totality of history as itself revelation. For him the subject-matter of Christian history, and so too of New Testament theology, conceived as the history of early Christian thought, was the movement through history of the divine or infinite spirit; this could be apprehended by the historian's finite spirit or intellect. Baur saw the history of primitive Christianity as dominated by a single (ecumenical) theme: the gradual reconciliation of an originally opposed Jewish and Gentile Christianity. He located each New Testament document according to its position (determined by its 'tendency' or slant) on this bilinear development. There was nothing wrong in Baur's judging each document from its content and placing it in the overall framework of development; every historian does this. But historians have to be ready to modify their provisional picture of the framework in the light of the detailed pieces of evidence supplied by each source. Baur's scheme had to be abandoned in the light of further research because it failed to do justice to the complexity of early Christian history. Since his locating of each document depended upon his over-simplified view of the whole, his chronology was also mistaken. But the grandeur of his conception should not be under-emphasized. It was the first time that a New Testament theology had been presented on the basis of a fully critical evaluation of the sources and reconstruction of early Christian history.[22]

Two features of Baur's reconstruction are especially important. Firstly, his idealist philosophy of history led him to see the subject-matter of New Testament theology in *intellectual* terms. For all its modernity, it therefore bore some resemblance to the traditional type of New Testament theology which regarded its essential content as doctrine. The name 'New Testament theology' was appropriate in his case, as in Bultmann's, though for different reasons. It was above all in the *doctrine* of each New Testament writer that each new stage of the Spirit's advance was reflected. Secondly, his location of each document according to its place in the historical development meant that he could relate the history as he saw it by simply taking one document after another.

In both characteristics, Baur's *Lectures on New Testament Theology* bear closer superficial similarity to Weiss's work than to Wrede's programme. In fact, however, the opposite is the case. Baur's structure is based formally upon the succession of documents, but materially upon the history which these were thought to reflect. The structure of B. Weiss's account, on the other hand, is based solely upon his ordering of the documents. Baur's Hegelian content is the spirit in the history; Weiss's is the traditional doctrine. When Hegelianism lost favour in Germany, what remained of Baur's work was not doctrine, but history without the Spirit; and not a mere succession of documents, but a historical framework in need of revision. Wrede was the true successor of Baur, even though a Baur shorn of his Hegelian fleece is not immediately recognizable. His criticism of Holtzmann, that the latter concedes too much to the modified orthodoxy of Weiss, is entirely consistent with Baur's historical-critical method.

Despite its use of Christian doctrinal language and the conviction that the same reality was being spoken of in both cases, Hegelianism had little in common with traditional Christian theology. When the metaphysical bubble burst, therefore, there could be no question of a return to traditional views. Liberal theology had to be content with a somewhat de-divinized history which it proceeded to analyse minutely.

This concentration upon questions of detail, together with the climate of historical positivism and ecclesiastical reaction, was not conducive to reflection upon New Testament theology. That requires philosophical and theological intelligence as well as a comprehensive grasp of history. The period between Baur and Wrede produced little methodological reflection and less creative ideas, despite its abundance of historical detailed research and its significance as the period in which moderates came to accept historical criticism. Wrede's essay signifies an important advance and is a landmark in the history of the discipline – even if it looks more like a tombstone upon any theological conception of it.

Wrede recognized the central importance of historical understanding for the whole field of New Testament studies. Judgments made here about the total picture are often decisive for settling individual critical problems. One's always provisional conception of the whole development provides the framework or outline sketch which determines the range of possibilities within which each piece of evidence is tried out in historical hypotheses. The necessity for such a sketch and the considerable difficulties in the way of filling out the picture can be described by the analogy of a jig-saw, or series of jig-saws.

Historical work always demands that a particular piece of evidence be seen in the context of one's provisional view of the whole development. One might have to modify one's hypothesis of the overall development in the light of a particular bit of evidence, or the evidence might have to be interpreted differently to fit into the pattern formed by other evidence. In practice the historian has an eye to the whole range of possible interpretations of the evidence (so far as he can see them) and also to the whole range of possibilities for the shape of the total framework. As the jig-saw is gradually pieced together a picture begins to emerge, but in the process individual pieces are tried out in different places. The operation is difficult because in all historical work some pieces are missing, and in this case of ancient history the vast majority of the pieces are missing. Nothing is more important for the historian than recognizing and defining the gaps in his knowledge (p. 97 below). The temptation to obscure these by making forced connections between two pieces of available evidence is to be resisted. Missing links must be respected, and measured.

A further complication is that New Testament theology (so-called) is a matter of piecing together not one but a series of jig-saws which, when placed together, may be expected to form a coherent sequence. Uncertainty about date and authorship of some of the documents means, in terms of this analogy, that the pieces of the different jig-saws are somewhat mixed up together. Uncertainty about the meaning of some of the evidence we possess is analogous to the pieces of the jig-saws which are available being more or less faded.

This description of New Testament theology (so-called) or the history of early Christian thought as a sequence of tableaux to be pieced together, shows the difficulties confronting the New Testament historian. One central tableau, Paul, is especially clear, though able to be understood in many different ways. Another,

John, is complete and self-contained, but requires a background before it can be understood. As regards the remaining pieces available, the most important question raised by Wrede was how *many* tableaux one should attempt to reconstruct. It was here that the break with the literary approach had most important consequences, and Wrede made some most important suggestions. Whereas Holtzmann, like Weiss, produced a tableau for each author, Wrede recognized that the evidence was too fragmentary for these to constitute accurate reconstructions of the history. He defined the conditions under which an author like Paul and even Ignatius could be considered worthy of independent treatment, and insisted that works which are little more than pamphlets should not constitute separate tableaux but be combined to provide a wider range of source material for a single tableau (pp. 81ff. below).

The historian is assisted in his reconstruction of primitive Christianity by possessing several clearer and more complete tableaux in the same sequence at later stages of the development. He can draw some lines backwards from these and propose hypotheses which may make sense of the earlier evidence he possesses about first- and early second-century Christianity. He also has various jig-saws (again sadly defective) of the background out of which the scenes in which he is most interested have developed, and others from the same period which form no part of the chain of development, but which may be in some ways analogous and so provide suggestions for understanding the early Christian evidence. In these ways the difficulties arising from lack of evidence, and from the obscure or faded character of some of the surviving evidence, can in part and provisionally be overcome. How far they can be overcome is a question which still divides optimistic and sceptical historians of early Christianity.[23]

The viability of Wrede's project depends upon the quality and quantity of the evidence we possess. There can be little doubt that it enables historians to write at least a fragmentary history of early Christian religion and theology, though perhaps this amounts to even less than Wrede and his successors hoped for. Whether the sketch which emerges will have much positive theological value is rather doubtful. If this were all that Christianity could expect from New Testament theology, historical criticism would have dealt it a serious blow. A theological response to this suggestion will be given below. At this point a caution about Wrede's position must be raised from his own standpoint of purely historical research.

This concerns Wrede's sharp distinction between the literary sources and their historical subject-matter, and the insistence that the historical subject-matter is religion, not doctrine. In 'life of Jesus research' both distinctions are readily intelligible. The sources (the gospels) can be clearly distinguished from the subject-matter (Jesus), and it is perhaps misleading to call Jesus' proclamation 'doctrine'. Baur called it 'religion' in contrast to the church's 'theology'. But in the history of early Christian thought, both distinctions are more difficult. Wrede is concerned, for example, in his monograph on Paul[24] with the *historical Paul*, and the greater part of that work could be included as it stands in a New Testament theology (so-called). In practice, however, his exposition of Paul's theology scarcely differs from a document-oriented account of the theology of the genuine epistles. Wrede himself cannot be criticized here. He recognized more clearly than other liberals that 'the religion of the apostle (Paul) is theological through and through: his theology is his religion' (p. 76). The history of religion framework advocated by Wrede allows theology in principle to occupy its proper place within the history. If the climate of the last twenty years accords the label 'theology' to more New Testament writers than either Wrede or Bultmann did, this need not cause any fundamental alteration to Wrede's framework. Nevertheless, the 'religion not theology' thesis can only be accepted as a corrective to a too-narrow view of the content of the New Testament, and the 'historical subject-matter, not literary source' orientation as a prescription about the total framework, rather than something which necessarily affects the content of the presentation at every point. Part of Wrede's greatness is that he (unlike most liberals) did not let his theological or apologetic disinterest in doctrine and preference for religion prevent him from recognizing that the New Testament writers were less modern.

It is a further question, and no longer a historical one, which account of *Christianity* is better: one based upon texts and doctrine, or one based upon the history of the religion which lies behind the texts. The liberals retreated to the history following the collapse of orthodoxy's view of the texts as inspired and their doctrinal content as revealed truth. Renewed emphasis upon the *text* in New Testament theology since the First World War has been associated with a renewal of doctrinal or systematic theology which has learned again to speak of revelation or 'word of God' in connection with the biblical text, though without naïvely identifying the two. It has been the combination of a history of traditions approach in biblical criticism with a kerygmatic theology which has led to the new flowering of the discipline called New Testament theology, at the centre of which stands Bultmann's work.

It will be seen that the new theological movement in the 1920s was able to raise some pertinent questions about Wrede's project – above all how far he can claim to have *understood* his authors from his allegedly neutral standpoint. But it will be argued that the history of religions approach to Christianity (like any other religion), supported by recent methodological advances in the phenomenology of religion, can defend its right to exist provided that it does not usurp the title 'New Testament theology' or claim that it is the only intellectually defensible way of using the New Testament.

Wrede's important suggestions about how the historian of early Christianity should arrange and delimit his discipline did in fact prevail among critical scholars.[25] At individual points subsequent research has suggested further refinements.[26] But the direction has generally been along the lines pioneered by Wrede and his contemporaries. They lived in the heyday of New Testament criticism.

Wrede's great importance as a landmark in New Testament *criticism* gives his account of New Testament theology a special value. It is clear from what has been said against Weiss about the development of early Christian thought being a necessary aspect of New Testament theology (if not the only one) that any New Testament theology presupposes the results of historical criticism. Holtzmann provided Wrede with an excellent partner in dialogue for discussing the question of historical *methodology*, because both were in substantial agreement on questions of New Testament critical introduction. Since content is necessary to elucidate methodological issues, agreement about this prevented unnecessary side-tracking. There is today a much greater critical consensus about questions of authorship and date, and the views of Wrede and Holtzmann have been largely vindicated. Matters on which

Wrede would agree that the evidence is closely balanced, such as the authenticity of II Thessalonians (which he denied), are still disputed, as he expected them to be (p. 95 below). But when he wrote, serious scholars still defended the apostolic authorship of the Fourth Gospel. B. Weiss considered every New Testament document authentic, and even Harnack, speaking of a 'return to the tradition' could say that, 'In the whole of the New Testament there is probably only one single writing, II Peter, which is to be called pseudonymic in the strictest sense.'[27]

If the discipline is conceived in a historical way, as it has been now for almost two hundred years, every presentation is bound to be determined by the critical position of its author. In comparing different New Testament theologies, consequent differences of structure are particularly obvious. Scholars like B. Weiss, W. Beyschlag and A. Schlatter, who accepted the traditional authorship of James and I Peter, placed chapters on these before their accounts of Paulinism.[28] These structural differences do not in themselves involve methodological disagreement about the nature of New Testament theology. They can, however, lead to it. B. Weiss's conception of the task itself was dependent upon his conservative view on questions of New Testament introduction:

If, indeed, it were possible to prove that the majority of these books belong, as to their origin, to the post-apostolic age, it would be altogether unreasonable to treat of the contemporary non-canonical Christian writings apart from them, and so to make the latest of the New Testament writings the boundary line of the first period of the history of Christian doctrines (p. 2 n. 1).

The supposedly early date and apostolic (or near apostolic) authorship of the New Testament writings was also a part of Schlatter's justification for treating them separately (p. 148 below), though he, unlike Weiss, denied the authenticity of II Peter. What can be seen here are the traditional, supposedly historical grounds for the New Testament canon surviving awhile in a historically critical age, until the weight of critical opinion finally destroyed them. Though all that was immediately at stake was the boundaries of the discipline, the subject had wider implications. Similar argumentation had, in the early days of historical criticism,[29] caused the idea of the canon itself to be tied to the sinking mast of traditional apostolic authorship.

The dependence of New Testament theology upon the results of New Testament introduction, and the considerable room for disagreement here, was recognized by Wrede to constitute a problem. He saw this as most serious in connection with the reconstruction of Jesus' preaching, where critical judgments about particular sayings have to be made even though the ground is so uncertain that scholars whose general critical position is similar reach very different conclusions (p. 104 below). This difficulty still exists seventy-five years later, though now it is an open question whether the teaching of Jesus belongs in a New Testament theology. Less serious difficulties arise about how many Pauline epistles are authentic. Someone who accepts Ephesians, or even Colossians, not to speak of the Pastorals, will have a very different picture of Paul from someone who does not. Those who expected these difficulties to subside as research continued have been proved mistaken, despite the critical consensus on such major issues as the Johannine question. As investigation of the history of traditions has developed, more possibilities for disagreement have emerged; and as our knowledge of the history of religions background increases, so too does the scope for possible interpretations. This spells destruction for biblicism (even for the most sophisticated sorts), and gives ample scope for cynicism. But it also contains new possibilities for theological method which will have to be explored below. The waxen nose of New Testament theology may yet prove to be theologically significant.

II   *The Theological Problem*

Wrede insisted on describing the task and methods of his historical discipline without reference to the interests of Christian theologians. What the systematic theologian does with the historian's results is his own business (p. 69 below). The historian's goals are given him by his discipline and his material, not by interests external to these. Wrede's sole concern is to rid his discipline of the remnants of such heteronomy. Everything he says could be endorsed by a non-Christian historian.

He is, of course, aware of the difficulties his own work makes for theologians. But these have to be solved by theologians. His duty is to do his own historical work honestly and regardless of the predicament of theology. He defines the church's difficulty succinctly:

> The church rests on history, but historical reality cannot escape investigation, and this investigation of historical reality has its own laws (p. 73 below).

The real problem for theology rests in the third clause and was defined most carefully by Troeltsch.[30] These 'laws', which have proved themselves over a wide field, do not allow historians to speak of supernatural causality. A purely historical account of Christianity does not require that its author believe in God. One can talk about the Christian religion from a neutral standpoint, whereas talk about revelation (as opposed to talk about other people's belief in revelation) presupposes a theological position.

Wrede restricts himself to the clarification of what his historical discipline demands. But his rigorous exclusion of the theological question does presuppose something of the answer he would give to it. His attention to the historical discipline regardless of the theology claims autonomy for it. Whatever way theology solves its own problems will have to involve coming to terms with the historical discipline, the integrity of which must not be infringed. The worst crime that the historian can be accused of is modernization; theology, looking for a contemporary meaning in the sources, continually tempts him in this direction. Many, like Beyschlag (p. 83, below), succumb.

In discussing the task and methods of the historical study of early Christian thought, Wrede is sensitive to the relationship between sources and subject-matter, the two poles upon which the historian's attention is concentrated. The point at which questions may be posed about his understanding of historical method concerns something he did not discuss: the relationship of the historian *himself* to his source and subject-matter; that is, the hermeneutical question about the conditions of historical understanding. The most significant contribution here is that of Bultmann, but Schlatter's essay translated in this volume is interesting on account of its grasp of the problem. The discussion is still open. Wrede would, with some justification, have dismissed much of the existentialist reaction against historicism as modernization. On the other hand, the truth in the reaction may prove to be more important for Christian theology than has yet been generally recognized.

This debate within systematic theology is relevant to discussion of the nature of New Testament theology. Wrede could simply *assume* that New Testament theology (so-called) is the history of early Christian religion and theology because his own liberal Protestant systematic position involved the substitution of the history of religion for the traditional orthodox theology. There was no need for him as a Christian to take dogmatic theology seriously. He will always find support not only from historians of all persuasions for his incisive remarks on historical procedures, but also from Christian theologians whose theological position does not require a biblically-based dogmatic theology. Nothing but a certainty deriving from theological presuppositions regarded as self-evident can explain the brevity with which Wrede dismisses the suggestion that the word 'theology' in the phrase 'New Testament theology' might imply a theological discipline (p. 116 below). The subject determines the name, not vice versa; and we all know what the subject is. We know this, Wrede implies, from the history of the discipline. He appeals, in fact, to his reading of the history of New Testament scholarship as a process of historical research, cutting itself loose from dogmatic prejudgments. The history of biblical criticism does indeed reveal such a process, and nowhere is this clearer than in the history of early Christian thought. Wrede's own contribution is one of the most important. His monograph may be called the classic expression of what 'purely historical' means in this field.[31]

Nevertheless, the history of New Testament theology has two aspects. It may be viewed from one perspective as historical work becoming gradually more conscious of itself. But it may also be viewed in the context of the development of theological method, with which it has always, in fact, been associated. The word 'theology' in the phrase is no accident. Most people's interest in the New Testament, including their historical interest in it, has been engendered by its significance for Christian faith. The discipline has been developed in the interests of traditional Christian faith and also out of hostility to it, but not with indifference to it. Such disinterest is possible and one might, like Wrede, for the sake of the integrity of historical investigation, practise it. But it would be absurd to deny that the theological problem exists. Both the name and the history of the discipline invite an approach to the question of New Testament theology from this other side, as theologians.

Christian theology had to take seriously modern historical work on the Bible because this established a convincing claim to open up a new avenue to the truth about Christianity by showing what it *had* been. Its answer to the question of what Christianity essentially *is*, by reference to its *history*, inevitably came into competition with answers based upon claims to revelation. As the central locus of revelation, and the most important sources of the history, the New Testament naturally became the main battleground. The outer bastion of verbal inspiration soon crumbled under the rationalist advance, and D. F. Strauss's *Life of Jesus* (1835–6) went straight for the citadel with a damaging assault upon the christo-logical centre of Christianity. On the assumption that it had fallen, Strauss offered an alternative home for christology,[32] but since this did not house *Jesus* it was not attractive to Christians. Later liberals defended Jesus, but a Jesus driven from his old dogmatic citadel.

The main controversy about the work of Strauss's teacher F. C. Baur concerned the origins of Christianity: were they supernatural or not? While the defence was occupied at this point, Baur made important advances elsewhere and established a historically critical view of Christianity which has long survived the abandonment of his Hegelianism and the correction of his chronology. Since the heart of this history was for Baur intellectual, his historical achievement was nowhere more effective than in the sphere of New Testament theology. Wrede represents the reaction against this too intellectual view of Christianity. In his more sociological concentration upon *religion* rather than doctrinal theology, he therefore inevitably brought into the open the tension between the historical approach to Christianity and traditional views of reve-lation. This had been partly concealed by Baur's quasi-theological theory about the nature of history as the progress of the divine spirit. Baur's history of early Christian *religion* could still take the form of lectures on New Testament *theology*, and his *Church History in the First Three Centuries*[33] likewise could be largely history of doctrine. For Wrede, the rest of the history of religions school, liberal Protestants generally and emergent sociologists of religion, on the other hand, religion and theology were juxtaposed. This opposition originated in the Enlightenment criticism of Protestant orthodoxy; its embers are still burning, even though the phenomenological study of religion has meanwhile left the controversy behind.

It is always tempting to see a historical development from the perspective of the victors. The intellectual dominance of the liberals in the nineteenth century, and the subsequent assimilation of most of what they stood for, makes it very easy to accept uncritically, say, Troeltsch's brief account of the either – or which exists between historical and dogmatic method. Theology used to proceed deductively, by rational argument from agreed revelational premises, in both Catholic and Protestant scholasticism; now it has to proceed historically, and for a historicist that means exclusively historically. There could be no question but that New Testament theology means the history of early Christian religion and theology. If the choice were really as simple as that – Protestant (or Catholic) orthodoxy, or liberal Protestantism – there would be little to discuss. But in fact, as Troeltsch was well aware,[34] the real problem for *theologians* is to find a theological method properly based on historical research. When the old dogmatic method of doing theology has been destroyed by historical research, the question which remains is how to do theology now. It may turn out that one's answers are not very different from those of one's favourite predecessors after all.[35]

Though Wrede does not discuss the matter here, it is fair to ask him how he would see the theological task which he has rightly excluded from his historical work. It was the weakness of the liberal Protestants' answers here which led to the reaction against them and the theological revival of the 1920s. When the conflict between historical and dogmatic methods is seen in the context of a new awareness of the task of theology, the question is no longer which is to be chosen, but rather how one's theological methods can do justice to the legitimate claims of historical research. It is clear that in the light of this new knowledge, Christians cannot use the Bible in the same ways as their forefathers, because this would conflict with their modern consciousness of truth. But it may be possible to do justice to their forefathers' concerns without violating modern canons of historical truth. The historian would then be seen as simply defining the conditions under which Christians can use the Bible with integrity. He would no longer be seen as possessor of the only key to understanding it. There may still be the possibility of something justly called New Testament theology: a theological interest in the New Testament which is not identical with Wrede's historical interest, yet which does not conflict with this.

The New Testament has always been a uniquely important source of Christian theology, and the concept of revelation used in association with it reflects this fact. But the character of this source has been understood in different ways. Sacred text and historical source represent sharp alternatives posed by modern historical study; but both can be associated with various ideas about revelation. The answers given to this question of revelation have naturally reflected answers to the christological question about how one regards Jesus and the theological one about what one means by 'God'. The reason why hermeneutical discussion has occupied the forefront of Protestant theology for half a century[36] is that the interpretation of the New Testament has related to these two basic issues of Christian theology. It has been thought that the way in which Christians use the New Testament might help to make sense of what they mean by God and show something of the way in which they evaluate Jesus.

There is some confusion in the theological disciplines at present, and at no point is this confusion more marked than on the boundaries between New Testament studies and dogmatic or systematic theology. The ambiguity of the phrase 'biblical theology', which generally means the theology to be found in the Bible and specifies a historical discipline, but which has also in the past meant a theology which is true to the Bible,[37] reflects the difficulty. It is widely agreed that Christian theology should be (broadly) biblical in the second sense, but it has generally been found necessary to go beyond biblical theology in the former sense. This posed no problem as long as the church's doctrine was assumed to be biblical, but when a distance between them was ascertained, the question of *interpretation* became important as the only way of bridging the gulf. The question about the nature of New Testament theology is in part whether, or how far, or in what ways, it should be involved in the enterprise (a historical or theological enterprise – or both?) of bridging this gap.

The great virtue of Wrede's contribution is the clarity with which he defines his own historical task, and repudiates bridge-building. His criticisms of other historians for allowing theological interests to prejudice their historical work, and not attaining methodological consistency, are in part justified. But in view of the declared *theological* interests of B. Weiss and Beyschlag, his brusque criticism of them inevitably gives the impression that there is no room for any interest in the New Testament other than a historical one. Wrede would probably have shared Harnack's impatience with Barth (p. 173 below). But it is one thing to say that theological interest in the New Testament must not contravene the canons of modern historical method, and quite another to imply that these prohibit any theological interest in it or interpretation of it by a historian while he is wearing his historian's hat. No doubt some types of theological interpretation do contravene historical methods. Perhaps, too, the rules of historical method are less absolute than Troeltsch suggested. But in any case the possibility of a new synthesis must not be ruled out in advance, and theologians at least will be concerned to explore it.

New Testament theology in the twentieth century has been and still is dominated by the synthesis between historical research and theological concerns achieved by Rudolf Bultmann. His Meyer Kommentar on *The Gospel of John* (1941) and his *Theology of the New Testament* (1948–51) are the slowly ripened fruit of more than half a lifetime's study. A series of articles in the 1920s and 1930s had already established his dominance of the critical wing of German New Testament scholarship, and especially of New Testament theology, in which Germany has indisputably provided the leadership. The demythologizing controversy and the wider hermeneutical discussion of faith and history which have centred on his work have not generally been directly concerned with detailed exegetical questions, but with larger issues concerning problems of interpretation. For Bultmann himself, however, these have always been rooted in the study of the New Testament; the theology of the New Testament is the place where historical and systematic questions converge. Wrede might deliberately ignore this; anyone who is interested in the New Testament as a theologian, as well as being a historian, cannot.

One reason for Bultmann's enormous impact has been the

patience with which he has plotted his position in relation to his predecessors.[38] As a direct successor to the history of religions school his critical position is close to that of Wrede, Heitmüller, Bousset and J. Weiss. But Bultmann also has other predecessors, and amongst these, a scholar to whom he makes deliberate and detailed reference is Adolf Schlatter.[39]

If recourse is to be had to the generation prior to Barth and Bultmann in order to elucidate the nature of New Testament theology, there are several reasons why Schlatter should be chosen as the natural counterpoise to Wrede. Certainly the two men could scarcely be more different. Wrede is a striking example of the critical wing of New Testament scholarship. Not only Harnack, but even his friend Bousset appears conservative alongside him.[40] No one is more obviously Bultmann's mentor in historical scepticism.[41] Wrede might disown D. F. Strauss and give only 'very limited' credit to Bruno Bauer,[42] but in critical acumen he has something in common with both, as well as with his most obvious critical predecessor, F. C. Baur. Schlatter, on the other hand, was considered a conservative, and is perhaps the only 'conservative' New Testament scholar since Bengel who can be rated in the same class as Baur, Wrede, Bousset and Bultmann.

A more important difference between Wrede and Schlatter, and one which places Schlatter with Baur and Bultmann and in the opposite camp to Wrede, is that he was self-consciously a Christian theologian and approached the New Testament as such. He was professor in Berlin (1893–8) with responsibility for the church's doctrine[43] before moving to Tübingen, and wrote important works on dogmatics and ethics.[44] While he regarded New Testament studies as primarily a historical discipline and himself as a historian, there could be for him no question of setting aside the theological question, except momentarily for methodological reasons (p. 125 below). On the contrary, whereas most New Testament scholars have allowed their world-view and historical method to be given them by their culture, Schlatter saw it as his theological duty to work these out for himself, and passionately rejected the methodological atheism of modern historical method.[45] The extent to which he forged his own metaphysical basis is one factor, together with his difficult style and avoidance of explicit debate with his contemporaries, which make him difficult to read and have led to his comparative neglect.[46] Whereas Wrede can be read today and sounds almost contemporary, Schlatter very clearly belongs to an older generation. (In fact, though born seven years before Wrede, he outlived him by thirty-two years.)

The first edition of Schlatter's *New Testament Theology*[47] appeared in 1909–10, and since it extended beyond the limits of a foreword, the methodological essay translated here was published separately in 1909.[48] *Das Christliche Dogma* followed in 1911. He tells us that he 'wondered whether a unitary summary of the historical and the dogmatic material were not the more correct procedure', as not only Calvin but more recently Hofmann in his *Schriftbeweis* (1852–55) had assumed. He says that he 'decided finally that separate treatment of the two tasks was today valuable for the correctness of our thinking, but [was] not certain whether the decision was not a concession to the spirit of the time'.[49] The justification for the separation which for most New Testament scholars since Gabler has been axiomatic is provided in this essay; but Schlatter's hesitation is interesting. An example of his thought is provided here as the work of a New Testament scholar who considers the nature of New Testament theology in the light of the systematic or doctrinal task of Christian theology. All the issues that Wrede discusses are posed by what the historian discovers about the nature of his material. Schlatter, on the other hand, is guided by his view of what the material has meant and means for the Christian church. If New Testament theology is the acutest point where historical and theological questions converge, it seems sensible to listen to New Testament scholars perched (with astonishing self-assurance) on the two different horns of what we continue to experience as a dilemma.

Subsequent research has rarely sounded so confident as Wrede and Schlatter. One reason for this has been an honest concern to do justice to what both these scholars, both so right in their own ways and yet so very different, stood for. In a state of methodological confusion it is generally wise to look to history to find one's bearings.[50] The generation prior to Bultmann may still have much to teach us. The *theological* concern, exemplified by Schlatter, has now dominated New Testament studies for fifty years, and this has resulted in the recent appearance of a crop of New Testament theologies.[51] But many of Schlatter's own suggestions have still not been taken seriously. Bultmann could welcome his existential emphasis,[52] but that is all. Käsemann can see in him a forerunner of the new quest for the historical Jesus,[53] and can learn from his interpretation of the Pauline formula, the righteousness of God.[54] His emphasis upon the church, and upon the theology of individual writers, especially Matthew, is widely appreciated as pointing the way for subsequent New Testament research. Nevertheless, he has not been as influential as might have been expected. The main reason for this is perhaps that certain of his emphases, above all his emphasis upon nature and upon history, ran counter to the prevailing currents in Germany during the 1920s. At a time when some reaction against Barth and Bultmann is being felt, and neither history nor natural theology (p. 34 below) are any longer considered unimportant, Schlatter's demand for *observation* of the past, and for *reasons* for believing,[55] are worth reconsidering. He also provides salutary evidence that attention to nature and history does not necessarily involve denigration of 'the word'. There are more than two ways of believing in revelation. For him both history and the word are the ground of the Christian's existence (p. 157 below).

Schlatter was conservative, if not in his attitude at least in his critical conclusions. He upheld the authenticity of all the New Testament books apart from II Peter (the exception suggests that this was not the result of dogmatic prejudice), and argued strenuously for the priority of Matthew.[56] These historical conclusions would be almost universally rejected today, and that makes certain of Schlatter's views about New Testament theology untenable. This has to be said against Schlatter, just as it may have to be said against Wrede that New Testament theology does involve theology. But critical conclusions apart, it is striking how far Schlatter is in agreement with Wrede about the necessity for historical method in theology and the way it must operate, unhampered by the historian's own personal viewpoint.

His argument for separating the New Testament from later ecclesiastical writings, like that of B. Weiss, can only be maintained on the assumption of the traditional views about its authorship (pp. 146ff. below). The same mistake leads Schlatter to place too much weight upon particular personalities, on the grounds that they were founding fathers of the church. But contrary to what one might have expected, this does not lead to a static view of New Testament theology. Unlike Weiss, within his restricted time range he is willing to see movement and development (p. 142

below). He recognizes the problem of the differences between the
Paul of the earlier epistles and the Paul of the Pastorals, between
the synoptists' Peter and the first epistle bearing his name, between
the synoptists' John and the Fourth Evangelist. He raises the
question of how much personal development is possible, even if
his answers are probably wrong. He does not think that acceptance
of apostolic authorship obviates the possibility of a development
in the thought of the New Testament, nor does he simplify the
problem of how a New Testament theology should be structured.
This is a complicated issue, and oversimplified views of the
development (such as Hegelian ones) are as unsatisfactory as the
traditional position which denies all development. The emergence
of an idea cannot be accurately located by the date of the document in which it first appears (p. 143 below). The transition of
Christianity to the Greek world marked a watershed, but Jewish
Christianity continued to develop and was influenced by what it
saw of the Pauline mission (p. 143 below). This sensitive and flexible
approach to the historical data went some way towards neutraliz-
ing the wrong answers given to critical questions.

A particularly striking point at which Schlatter's use of historical
methods in New Testament theology can be compared with that of
Wrede is in the use of parallels from the history of religions. The
history of religions school (so-called – it was not really a school) is
generally associated with the discovery of Hellenistic and oriental
parallels to biblical statements. The Hellenistic emphasis was pursued in the early years of the present century. In the earlier period
the main and only direct influence upon the New Testament considered by these scholars was Judaism. The Göttingen group
reacted against Ritschl's restriction of the significant New Testament background to the Old Testament, and extended it to the
apocryphal and pseudepigraphical writings, especially apocalyptic.[57] There are signs that the wheel has turned full circle and that
Judaism, especially apocalyptic and sectarian Judaism, a Judaism
admittedly strongly influenced by Hellenism, is now again considered the all-important background to the New Testament.[58]
Wrede was cautious about Deissmann's observation that attention
should be paid to the Hellenistic background. He agreed, but
insisted that this does not have quite the same kind of importance
as Judaism (p. 115 below).

Since history of religions work is generally associated with the radical wing of New Testament scholarship, it is worth remembering that Schlatter was a pioneer in this field. The scathing, yet well-judged remarks he directed against the unhistorical excesses of some of the parallel hunters (pp. 144f. below) must be considered together with his appreciation for the contribution of sober and responsible work in this area. Much of his own historical research sought to illuminate both Palestinian and Hellenistic Judaism.[59]

Like Wrede, Schlatter is aware that the historian is limited by the fragmentary character of his sources as he attempts to trace the development. He knows, too, about the inter-relationship of the development of thought and the external history; and he recognizes that the account of Jesus must involve more than his thought.[60]

It would, therefore, be a mistake to minimize Schlatter's importance as a historian. Yet the most interesting features even of his historical attitude are grounded in his theology. That is to say, they are grounded in his view of reality, which he declined to accept as something 'given' by a secular culture independently of Christian faith. He expected 'observation' to disclose God's revelation in the biblical history, and he considered dogma to be no less 'knowledge' than the results of historical investigation. The discussion is obscured by the line of demarcation which Schlatter draws here between history and dogma (pp. 118, 126 below). Much that might be called historical interpretation is called dogma, and history is in danger of being reduced to chronicle. In a pluralistic world it is necessary to distinguish 'what Christians believe' from 'what every rational person knows', and to recognize that dogma is the historically conditioned interpretation of the Christian tradition. It may be no less true than a historical report, but it certainly has a different epistemological status.

Nevertheless, Schlatter's conviction that his theism was bound to affect his view of the world must surely be taken seriously. The test case for this matter in recent years has been discussion of the resurrection of Jesus, where it can be argued that faith leaves a door open, even in the physical world, for the possibility of something which is scientifically and historically inexplicable actually to have happened. To say this is at least as persuasive as most liberal Protestant speculations about what happened to give rise to the Easter faith of the disciples.

Schlatter, like most good theologians, was having to fight on two fronts. As well as criticizing liberalism, he was defending the viability of New Testament theology as a historical discipline against conservative objections. The core of his argument, and the heart of his own view of revelation, was that 'the New Testament utterly repudiates the thesis that revelation and history cannot be united' (p. 152 below). This statement places Schlatter closer to the liberals than to either the older conservatives or to the subsequent 'theology of the Word'. It can equally well be turned against the latter, and in fact Pannenberg's formidable critique of kerygmatic theology has much in common with Schlatter's conception of revelation and faith.

The theological question which Wrede ignores and Schlatter takes very seriously concerns the Christian's relationship to the New Testament. Christians have normally regarded the New Testament as a uniquely important source in their theological work of trying to reach a better understanding of their faith. This assumption has traditionally been enshrined, however inadequately and misleadingly, in the doctrine of inspiration. When this collapsed in the eighteenth century, it appeared at first as though the whole fabric of traditional orthodoxy were undermined. What was at most a bulwark appeared to many people to be the foundation of the church's faith in the divinity of Christ. Schlatter's work was an original and illuminating, if ultimately unsatisfactory contribution to the church's theological struggle to do justice to both the traditional faith and the new historical method, with its concomitant modern apprehension of reality. Both of the harsh alternatives, *either* the old orthodoxy *or* a historical account of Christianity which non-Christians could accept, failed to give an account of Christianity which was rationally defensible and true to the tradition. If the liberal solutions conceded too much to the modern spirit and failed to do justice to the Christian tradition,[61] Schlatter conceded too little and failed to do justice to the claims of historical reason. Since Christian theology, as contemporary interpretation of the Christian tradition, consists always in this ongoing argument between conservatives and liberals or modernists, the study of liberal Protestantism can usefully be balanced by some consideration of Schlatter.

In the second edition of 1921–22, Schlatter called the two volumes of his *New Testament Theology* 'The History of the Christ' and 'The Teaching of the Apostles'. Together these led to the formation of the church (p. 120 below). In his view the New Testament canon is founded on the historical fact that this 'history and the word which witnesses to it' are the ground of Christianity's existence: 'Christianity is based upon the New Testament.' He thought that the christological judgment that Jesus is the Christ, implicit in his title, was the result of historical observation; in fact it clearly followed from an admitted doctrinal prejudgment which would generally be considered illegitimate in modern historical research. It may be argued that the liberal 'lives of Jesus' were also based upon 'dogmatic' presuppositions, and that their authors were less aware of theirs than Schlatter was of his (pp. 125ff., 154 below). But however fair criticism this is of liberal Protestantism, it does not justify Schlatter's procedure.

Schlatter's doctrinal prejudgment makes his solution to the problem of a New Testament theology unacceptable to anyone who wishes to see it as a purely historical discipline to be undertaken by the methods shared by all historians. But even apart from this, his account of his own relationship to the New Testament as a Christian rests upon historical premises, and if these are falsified his theological view of the New Testament is undermined. If Wrede was substantially right about the origin and historicity of the documents, then Schlatter's historical view of them was wrong and his theological use of them undefended. Some other account of the Christian's theological use of the New Testament would have to be found which was not thus vulnerable to the results of historical criticism.

Some such new account was offered by the neo-Reformation 'theology of the Word' which emerged after the First World War. Its chief literary monument is Barth's *Epistle to the Romans* (second edition, 1921). The form in which this new theology became most important for discussion of New Testament theology was in Bultmann's radical version of it as a 'theology of existence'.

The solution offered by the new theology to the problem of how Christians should use the New Testament was to locate divine revelation not in the biblical history but in the *kerygma* or proclaimed word of God. This involved a sharp break with the liberalism in which its proponents were educated; it also contrasted strongly with Schlatter's solution. The biblical word was seen as no longer witnessing to a revelation in history but to a revelation which touched history only as a tangent touches a circle. This revelation was said to take place in and through the apostolic proclamation of Christ. It had been and would be reactualized, where and when God wills, through Christians hearing, interpreting and continuing the scriptural witness. Schlatter's theology had centred upon God and the earthly Jesus in a way which was formally similar to, but materially very different from the liberal theology. The 'dialectical theology' of the 1920s, like its ancestors Paul and Luther, centred rather upon the risen Christ made present through proclamation. Luther would not have said with Schlatter that Christianity is based upon the New Testament history and word. It is based upon the word of Christ alone.

The flight from history, including the historical Jesus, characteristic of dialectical theology was a natural reaction against the loss of the category of revelation traditionally associated with the Bible, which resulted from liberalism's emphasis upon history. As they fulfilled the requirements of modern historical methods, the liberals could see only human religion as the subject-matter of the New Testament. There was an inevitable hiatus between their talk about God (in whom they generally still believed) and their scientific study of the New Testament. Barth's intention was to re-unite theological talk about God with the interpretation of the New Testament. As a Christian theologian he was convinced that its subject-matter was God, and he was not satisfied with treating it merely as a historical source for human religion.[62] A theological interpretation of the New Testament which communicated its divine subject-matter was needed.

Since God is not a part of the world, his self-revelation could not, in Barth's view, be communicated directly through metaphysical or historical knowledge. He can only be apprehended in faith. Christian theology must therefore be connected with evoking faith.[63] This was also the concern of the New Testament writers themselves, and by interpreting these texts Barth hoped to continue their work of Christian witness. Theology is *ministerium verbi divini*, and Barth's 'sole aim was to interpret scripture'.[64] He sought to communicate its subject-matter by using it as the starting point for Christian proclamation or verbal witness to Jesus as decisive for human existence. Revelation occurs in the act of proclamation when the message is 'got across' and a hearer 'gets the message' and acknowledges Jesus as his Lord in faith. It is therefore no longer located in the documents (or tradition), nor in the history, but in the event in which, on the basis of the tradition, the Christ (who touches history only as a tangent touches a circle) is represented.[65] This event is not within human control, but the human activity of proclamation sets the stage for it. God will enter the stage or speak to the hearer, evoking faith or rejection, where and when he wills.

Proclamation always depends upon tradition, the raw material which it interprets in order to witness to Jesus. This interpretation of the New Testament with a view to proclamation is able to accept its historical character as tradition, subject to whatever judgments historians make concerning it. It is compatible with sceptical views about the historicity of the gospels[66] as well as with the non-apostolic authorship of the New Testament, because this is all mere tradition. Only when actualized in proclamation can it become a vehicle for the word of God. A dialectic is therefore proposed between the biblical word which is mere *tradition* and part of this world, and the *revelation* or transcendental act of God in addressing the hearer, which might take place when the tradition is interpreted in proclamation.

This theological interpretation of the New Testament can claim to be a more appropriate way of doing theology than the liberals' historical reconstructions of the religion, because it is rooted in and does justice to the intention of the New Testament texts, which are themselves the product of Christian witness. Historians may try to learn from their sources other things than these mean to relate. Their interests often differ from those of their sources. But the tension between the liberals' legitimate modern historical interest and that of the texts themselves places a question mark against the claim that this is the sole legitimate interest of academic theology in the New Testament.

Pursuit of the new aims and methods of historical science independently of dogmatics had in the eighteenth century led to a breach between the academic study of the New Testament and Christian God-talk – an unprecedented situation for the Christian church, whose theological method had always involved the believing study of scripture. F. C. Baur had been able to overcome the breach and view history and theology as a unity, because for him the course of world *history* was the progress of the infinite *spirit* in its successive manifestations. By reconstructing the history through a critical use of the sources, he was able to show its theological meaning. But when this Hegelian vision of reality collapsed, historical-critical work on the New Testament pursued its own positivist path without reference to classical theological concerns. Human *religion* was the object of the liberals' enormous intellectual effort, and the category of revelation was ignored. However correct their historical procedures (so far as they went), and however fruitful their work seemed at the time for Christian apologetics, a reaction or corrective was inevitable.[67]

Barth's insistence upon the theological subject-matter of the New Testament marked an epoch in the history of theology, and inaugurated the contemporary absorbing interest in hermeneutics. But it is Bultmann rather than Barth whose life-work in New Testament theology[68] has done most to recover the unity of historical and theological uses of the New Testament. The problem posed by what Christians believed about the subject-matter of the New Testament was how to express it in human words. Barth's solution was to 'assume that Paul is confronted with the same unmistakable and immeasurable significance of that relationship with which I myself am confronted' (between a God and man infinitely qualitatively distinct but related in Jesus Christ), and to 'speak with' the text 'till I stand with nothing before me but the enigma of the subject-matter; till the document seems hardly to exist as a document; till I have almost forgotten that I am not its author; till I know the author so well that I allow him to speak in my name and am even able to speak in his name myself'.[69] Then perhaps the Word will be exposed in the words, and the subject-matter which historical-critical commentaries studiously avoid will find expression. Barth's book therefore looks more like an extended sermon, proclamation *in actu*, than 'scientific' New Testament scholarship.

Bultmann was able to retain the indirect speech appropriate to a historical presentation without losing sight of the transcendent character of the New Testament subject-matter on account of his definition of theology as 'the conceptual presentation of man's existence as an existence determined by God'.[70] God, the kerygma and faith – the complex involved in the event of revelation – could not be analysed historically; but the statements in which faith expressed its understanding of God, the world and man disclosed by the kerygma could be so analysed. If he could understand these statements correctly, the historian would understand the faith of his authors and so do justice to the subject-matter of the New Testament. New Testament theology, 'the scientific presentation of the theological thoughts of the New Testament, has the task of pointing them out as the unfolding of believing self-understanding'. By 'interpreting the theological thoughts as the unfolding of the self-understanding awakened by the kerygma', the historian can do full justice to their character.[71]

Like Gabler, Wrede and almost all New Testament scholars,[72] Bultmann regards New Testament theology as a historical discipline. But like F. C. Baur's, his presentation of the history is accompanied by a philosophical and theological position and a fully thought-out view of their relationship. Historical discussion of his exegetical judgments might ignore this; consideration of his method, however brief, cannot. Bultmann's conclusion is 'that theology and exegesis – or systematic and historical theology – fundamentally coincide',[73] because the 'relation of the interpreter to the subject-matter that is (directly or indirectly) expressed in the texts'[74] is the same for theology as for history. Behind this stand views of theology and of history which make his work important for both historians of the New Testament and systematic theologians, but especially fascinating and significant for New Testament scholars interested in theology, and Christian theologians who consider that their work should be rooted in the rigorous historical study of the New Testament.[75]

What connects history, philosophy and theology, according to Bultmann, is that all three are concerned with human existence – one might almost say: with *nothing but* human existence. The concern with human existence found in philosophy differs from that of theology, but 'theology's theme also is existence in faith, . . . man is the object of theology'. Theology therefore depends upon philosophical anthropology for the clarification of its concepts: '*Every* theology is dependent for the clarification of its concepts upon a pre-theological understanding of man that, as a rule, is determined by some philosophical tradition . . . always the concepts that must guide the interpretation are concepts in which the 'natural' man understands himself and his world . . . (because) what is being talked about has to do with man . . .'[76]

Since theological statements relate exclusively to human existence,[77] and that is also what historical work is interested in,

Bultmann can do his theology *through* historical research. Theology is essentially man's self-interpretation, and this can only be pursued through the interpretation of history,[78] i.e. through the interpretation of texts or tradition. Like theology, 'historical knowledge is at the same time knowledge of ourselves'.[79] Bultmann does not have to say much in defence of his theological method, apart from establishing the identity of historical and theological exegesis.[80] It is enough if his account of historical method is accepted, because 'genuine historical exegesis rests on the existential encounter with history and therefore coincides with theological exegesis, provided that the justification for this too is just that'.[81]

The existentialist historiography which helps Bultmann to combine Barth's theological with Harnack and Wrede's historical concerns owes most to Wilhelm Dilthey (1833–1911).[82] It sees the historian's task not in reconstructing a panorama to view but in entering into dialogue with the past. Its material consists above all in human 'life-utterances' which cannot be treated with the same detachment as the material of the natural sciences. It has to be listened to and taken seriously, and may call the interpreter himself into question, and help him to understand himself and his place in the world. This can no longer be assumed to be known in advance by the historian with the arrogant self-confidence or easy optimism typical of some Enlightenment and late nineteenth-century thinkers.

Bultmann explains that every interpreter approaches a text with some prior understanding of what it is about. As an (existentialist) historian he is '*interested in history as the sphere of life in which human existence moves*, in which it attains its possibilities and develops them, and in reflection upon which it attains understanding of itself and of its own particular possibilities'.[83] Religious texts (such as the New Testament) are good specimens for this sort of questioning about their understanding of existence. The interpreter's own provisional understanding of human existence is to be 'critically tested' by the witness of the texts themselves in the process of interpretation. The interpreter who questions the text must at the same time let himself be questioned by it; he must listen to its claim.[84] 'This *existentiell* relation to history is the fundamental presupposition for understanding history.'[85]

If it is agreed that New Testament theology is a *historical* discipline, the crucial question about Bultmann's union of the historical and theological interpretation of the New Testament is whether it illuminates the history. The project may be deemed to have failed if it can be shown *necessarily* to lead to a distortion of the history. Since it is the *method* of New Testament theology which is under consideration, *actual* distortion of the history by Bultmann would not finally discredit it. Someone else might apply the same method to achieve greater historical accuracy. Only if it *necessarily* distorts the history will this way of doing New Testament theology have to be rejected or modified.

It is only possible here to indicate briefly the point at which the identification of historical and theological work breaks down, leading to a distortion of the history by Bultmann, and to say whether this is inevitable. But it must first be conceded that, considered purely in historical terms and without reference to theological interests, Bultmann's interpretation of Paul and John constitutes a quite enormous advance. If he is in fact wrong about Paul at certain points, as Käsemann argues, Käsemann is nevertheless able to correct him without using different methods.

Secondly, it is necessary to distinguish in Bultmann's critical interpretation of the New Testament authors between what is legitimate in theological interpretation and what is possible for historians. In arguing for a distinction which Bultmann does not make, and claiming that what he does goes beyond the limits of historical interpretation, I do not wish to deny the legitimacy of what he does as *theological* interpretation of the New Testament. Again, his actual theological conclusions may be mistaken. But this can be argued, and Bultmann corrected, by the same methods which he himself employs.

The argument between Bultmann and Käsemann about the correct interpretation of Pauline theology which I shall take as a concrete example to illustrate the methodological issues is not just a historical argument, though the battle-ground is that of historical exegetical debate. Opposing systematic theologies are in conflict here, and the mode of argument, as always in theology, is a debate about the correct interpretation of the tradition. Theological argument over the tradition in a historically conscious age which recognizes the variety in the tradition is inevitably a matter of historical argument about the correct interpretation of various *parts* of the tradition. Theological construction is a matter of

weaving the pattern of one's own convictions with the various
threads of tradition in the web of one's own experience. A person's
historical situation influences what threads he receives, and the
structure of his own life has some effect upon what in the tradition
makes Christian sense to him. But as he listens to the tradition and
gives prominence to parts of it and discards other parts, it is his
own (continually changing) mental image of the complete picture,
his current apprehension of Christianity, which guides his selection
and criticism of the pieces of tradition. That might equally be
modified by the tradition as he realizes that something which he
had not taken seriously before truly speaks of Christ. Either way,
whether his faith-understanding corrects or is corrected by a piece
of tradition, it is the unobjectifiable revelation which is the
criterion of the piece of tradition in the event of interpretation.
But having rejected a piece of tradition in the light of his apprehension of Christianity, a theologian must justify himself by appealing to the tradition as a whole, and to contemporary experience,
and show that these support his view rather than that of the offend-
ing piece of tradition.

In his best known work on theological criticism which he
referred to provocatively (and misleadingly) as 'demythologizing'
the New Testament, Bultmann appealed especially to contemporary experience in justification of his new interpretation of the
tradition. 'The purpose of my existential interpretation of myth is
precisely to enquire into the possibility of a valid meaning for the
mythical picture of the world, and in this I am trying to proceed
methodically.'[86] He did also appeal to the tradition in support of
his procedure, notably to the Fourth Gospel,[87] but he could have
strengthened this by reference to Luther's theology of the cross,
which is his chief ancestor in theological criticism.[88] Bultmann
uses historical methods to understand the tradition, but for him
this includes more than Wrede, for example, was prepared to
recognize. He includes in the question of interpretation the 'relation of the interpreter to the subject-matter that is (directly or indirectly) expressed in the texts'.[89] Every historian approaches the
text with some 'pre-understanding' of what it is about, and this
guides his questions.[90] Unlike many of his liberal predecessors
(but like Schlatter), Bultmann was concerned to give account of
his prior understanding. He assumed that the New Testament
texts speak of human existence, and this fundamental conviction

about the nature of theological language guides his interpretation, which is therefore 'existential interpretation'.

To be guided by a particular pre-understanding is perfectly proper, and since Bultmann's view of the subject-matter as relating to human existence does not exceed the bounds of the historian's vision, he can defend his procedure on grounds of historical methodology. It is more problematic, however, when Bultmann assumes that human existence remains constant throughout changing views of the world, so that provided the interpreter asks about *this*, he will get at the real meaning of the text. That is a postulate which historians will have to test by reference to the evidence. They must be prepared to acknowledge that their author may have understood human existence very differently from the way they do, and to say that his view is not a live option for them.[91]

But Bultmann's seemingly doctrinaire approach to history, or what has been called[92] the rather schoolmaster-ish way that he questions each writing about its understanding of existence, can be understood in the light of his theological motives. A theologian does not have the same freedom as a historian. He cannot say that this was how the tradition understood Christianity, but that it is not a live option for him. If he is to remain a *Christian* theologian, he *must* be able to claim continuity with the tradition, and that means weaving the pattern of his own position with threads received from the past. He must understand each piece of tradition in the original context where it made sense to someone, but must then go further and either agree with it or reject it, in the light of his own apprehension of Christianity. The theologian's judgment upon the piece of tradition he is interpreting thus goes further than the historian's, because for him everything depends upon the correlation he is trying to establish between his own position and the tradition as a whole.

Bultmann's existential interpretation of a part of the tradition is a matter of theological criticism, in which some of the tradition is rejected in the light of his own position at the moment of interpreting it, dependent as this in turn is on parts of the tradition. His own theology reflects the Kantian and Ritschlian restriction of theology to the human ethical sphere. This position can in turn appeal to the tradition, particularly to the Reformers' reaction against scholastic metaphysical speculation. But it goes further than that in reacting to the rise of modern science, by excluding the *world* from serious consideration by theology. Other theologians may consider that this was a bad move by theology in the modern period, and feel that the traditional belief in God as creator demands that the debate with the natural sciences be kept open.[93] Perhaps Schlatter's theological emphasis upon nature remained more true to the Christian tradition than the Kantian and Ritschlian bifurcation of reality. But whether Bultmann's systematic theology is good or bad, his method is the same as that of all theologians: he interprets the tradition in the light of contemporary experience. He claims, too, to avoid the liberals' error of reducing the tradition to the size and shape of his own experience.[94] In fact it is difficult to find instances of his apprehension of Christianity being expanded or modified by the witness of the tradition; that may be because he did not rush into print before he had studied the tradition for a long time, and because his own experience has perhaps been less tempestuous than that of many of his contemporaries. For whatever reasons, he has changed his mind astonishingly little; but in principle he accepts that his pre-understanding must be 'critically tested' by the text.[95]

Reference has been made to the demythologizing project because this is very clearly a theological activity; it is interpretation of the New Testament part of the tradition for the sake of Christian proclamation. Although Bultmann's essay 'The New Testament and Mythology' did not appear until 1941, it contained nothing new; what is said there was implicit in his earlier methodological essays of the 1920s, particularly in what was said then about *Sachkritik*. This topic is crucial for consideration of his attempt to unite historical and systematic work in his conception of New Testament theology.

Sachkritik has been variously translated into English as 'content criticism', 'material criticism of the content', 'objective criticism'(!), 'theological criticism', 'critical interpretation' and 'critical study of the content'. It refers to the interpreter's criticism of the formulation of the text in the light of what (he thinks) the subject-matter (*Sache*) to be; criticism of what is said by what is meant. The disagreement between Barth and Bultmann about whether this is necessary in the theological interpretation of the New Testament marks a parting of the ways which has been fundamental and fateful in the history of twentieth-century Protestant theology.[96] Barth's apprehensions about a method which gives so much scope to the subjectivity of the interpreter are well founded, and may be read as a warning against premature application of a method which is all too likely to do violence to a historical text in making it correspond to the interpreter's own view. But if the aim of theological interpretation is to achieve some correlation between the theologian's apprehension of Christianity and what he finds in the tradition, then some method for rejecting tradition is inevitable, and there is no reason why it should not be used on biblical tradition, once it is agreed that this is not itself revelation. Whether or not Bultmann's defence of *Sachkritik* as a necessary part of *historical* method can be maintained, there is little doubt about its necessity in *theological* method, where theology is understood as the interpretation of the tradition anew in every age, in the light of contemporary experience which includes rationality.

The necessity for content criticism can be reinforced by seeing it as the appropriate means of theological criticism in a historically conscious age. As such it succeeds allegorical interpretation, which is no longer possible because it conflicts with rational or historical experience. Since it is impossible to accept all the tradition, some methodically controlled procedure for criticizing it has always been necessary if the tradition is still to be taken seriously. Where there is no such safety-valve the tradition will be arbitrarily disregarded. Marcion rejected allegory – and also rejected the Old Testament part of the tradition, parts of which could at that time only be considered Christian with the help of allegorical interpretation which effectively concealed everything in these Christian scriptures that was un-Christian. Liberalism rightly rejected allegory, as incompatible with modern historical consciousness, but with nothing to put in its place,[97] it arbitrarily eliminated much of the tradition as theologically worthless.[98] *Sachkritik*, like allegorical interpretation, allows the tradition to remain intact; it 'gets around' obstinate pieces of tradition by re-interpretation, instead of removing them. This allows the argument about its meaning to continue. What one generation finds irrelevant and even offensive might become profoundly meaningful for another generation in another historical context.

To use a topical analogy: a chess player has a definite aim, and the strategy behind his moving pieces around the board is dictated by that. Similarly, in interpreting the whole tradition to reach a cogent theological position a theologian must so marshal the evidence of the tradition that an opponent has to admit the superiority of his position. The tradition, like the chessmen, dictates what is possible and provides the means through which the battle is fought. But it is human minds that are being exercised and alternative conceptions of Christianity which are in conflict. During the game a player will have to sacrifice some pieces. Theological criticism is analogous to that. Luther found Paul his most valuable piece of tradition for expressing the gospel, and for the sake of keeping this queen was prepared to abandon an epistle of straw and various bishops and pawns of ecclesiastical tradition.

Two important features of *Sachkritik* are evident in this analogy. Firstly, after every game of theological interpretation all the pieces of tradition come back on to the board. The set would be impaired if a part of the tradition were destroyed.[99] Theological criticism does not mutilate the tradition by annihilating what is thought to be unacceptable. It simply renders this innocuous for the moment so that a theologian can correlate his own theology with the tradition. Secondly, the necessity for this drastic move, in which a piece of one's own tradition is removed from the board, or a thread not included in one's tapestry (see above p. 40), can only be gained as the game proceeds. It depends upon the state of play at a given moment, i.e. the state of one's understanding of the tradition and of the revelation that one is trying to express through it. It is impossible to know in advance that one will surrender a castle at the thirtieth move. That can only be seen to be the most strategic move out of a variety of possibilities at a given time in the light of one's overall aim to express the Christian message.

The criterion by which a piece of tradition is judged cannot be given in advance because it is supposed to be the revelation itself. This is said to be heard in the act of interpreting the tradition. The Christ, made present in proclamation and apprehended in faith, is the measure of 'what (in the tradition) proclaims Christ' and what is misleading.

The tradition is necessary raw material for the proclamation in which revelation might occur. But it consists of fallible human formulations, which sometimes need correction in the light of the revelation event – i.e. in the light of the believer's apprehension of Christianity at the particular moment. This dialectic between the tradition and the non-objectifiable revelation accounts for the 'peculiarly ambiguous and even contradictory situation [of *Sachexe-*

gese], since it comes to what is meant only through what is said and yet measures what is said by what is meant'.[100] The danger of *Sachkritik*, as of allegorical interpretation, is that as a means of gagging a piece of tradition it can be used to suppress elements which should have been taken more seriously by the modern theologian.[101] Bultmann's rejection of futurist eschatology through reinterpreting the mythological imagery of the New Testament to refer to the present historical existence of believers and their openness to the future is one example. However, we are not concerned here with the rights and wrongs of Bultmann's systematic position, but with the way he finds it in the New Testament through the *historical* discipline of New Testament theology. His key move is to claim that the *Sachkritik* which has been defended here as necessary for theological argument about the tradition is a necessary element in *historical* interpretation.

The historian of the New Testament has a large number of variables to contend with, and these may affect his judgment about what an author meant. Questions of authorship, redaction, sources, interpolations, background situation and the history of the tradition generally, as well as textual critical, philological and grammatical issues, hover in the background of any interpretation. A part of the strength of Bultmann's theological interpretation of the Fourth Gospel is that its historical foundations are so thoroughly laid. It is far more difficult to dismiss it as arbitrary than it is Barth's New Testament interpretation. If Bultmann's theological appeal to the Fourth Gospel is to be disallowed, historical chipping at its historical foundations is necessary. The difficulty is that in areas where the evidence is as fragmentary as in the New Testament, subtle historical hypotheses are difficult finally to refute. The areas of uncertainty are large enough for various theological proposals to claim a textual basis in New Testament theology if they so wish. The battery of historical scholarship can be used (in all good faith) by a theological interpreter to draw an author closer to his own position. The historical argument itself often turns on a scholar's reconstruction of the author's theology,[102] which is what is in dispute, making an account of this difficult to refute. Reconstructions often have to be judged persuasive or implausible rather than demonstrably true or false.

But Bultmann's interpretation of the New Testament goes

beyond judgments which can find support in this type of straightforward historical analysis, while still claiming to be historical
interpretation. His view of the historian's duty to enquire about
the text's understanding of existence, coupled with his view of the
anthropological character of theological statements, allows historical and theological exegesis to coincide. In his pre-understanding about the human subject-matter of the texts he has an anthropological key with which to open the doors to their interpretation, to disclose their meaning. There is no doubt that the key is
very helpful. Bultmann's interpretation of Paul and John is a landmark in the *historical* understanding of these authors quite apart
from his own theological interest in them. The question is whether
Bultmann's anthropological key fits all the theological statements
of the New Testament, or completely fits any of them. Does it
open all the doors to their interpretations? Even if all theological
statements have (as Luther thought) an anthropological basis, it
does not follow that Bultmann's understanding of existence coincides with that of the New Testament writers. If there is a
conflict of anthropologies, Bultmann is surely right that a modern
theologian cannot drop his own and opt for that of a New Testament writer. Rather, he must interpret the New Testament critically, allowing it to illuminate his own understanding of existence,
but letting this guide his interpretation of the New Testament.
However, the *historian* is less interested in correlating his own
views with those of the New Testament writers. He can therefore
be content to point out the differences. The theologian who is
anxious to claim continuity with the tradition cannot let the matter
rest there, and must therefore strive for a critical interpretation
which can claim to be true to the author (perhaps understanding
him better than he understood himself),[103] and yet be valid for the
modern reader. The question at issue here is whether in doing this
the theologian's interpretation goes beyond what is legitimate for
the historian, or whether it distorts historical research.

In addition to the anthropological key with which Bultmann
hopes to disclose the historical and theological meaning of the
texts, he has in his technique of *critical* interpretation or *Sachkritik*
what can only be called a crowbar, to be used when his key fails.
The justification for using an interpretative key is that where a text
expresses its meaning in mythical form it is unintelligible to modern
readers. The myth bars access to genuine understanding. This

barrier can be removed by using the appropriate key, i.e. existential interpretation. But sometimes New Testament authors, in their human fallibility, failed to say adequately what they meant. In these cases the lock is jammed and the historian must use a crowbar if the author's real meaning is to be reached. It is fair to use the simile of the crowbar, because there is an admission of doing violence to what is said for the sake of getting at what is meant.

It is true that historians are sometimes critical of some of their sources' formulations, and have to correct these, despite the danger that they may have misunderstood the author. They will proceed with the utmost caution, and normally justify their correction of what is said on a basis of what they think is meant by reference to what the author himself says elsewhere. If they correct an author on the basis of their own understanding of his subject-matter derived from elsewhere, the dangers of reading their own views into the text are magnified. Correction of the New Testament authors in the light of their theological content is especially hazardous, because the interpreter's apprehension of this is in- evitably dependent upon more than the text being considered.

Some of Bultmann's *Sachkritik* can be justified as demanded by historical work. It is arguable that his interpretation of the Fourth Evangelist, or the major theologian standing behind the text as we have it, is historically convincing and that John emphasized 'the presence of eternity' as strongly as Bultmann himself, despite a few traditional egg-shells of futurist eschatology. If that is right, these can be 'interpreted away' without distorting the historical picture. Similarly, it is not improbable 'that Paul is betrayed by his apologetic into contradicting himself' in I Cor 15,[104] in which case the historian may criticize one of Paul's formulations in the light of what Paul himself says elsewhere.

In these cases *Sachkritik* can be said to 'stem from the text itself'[105] and to be necessary in historical work. The historian no less than the theologian is interested in 'what Paul really meant or what he wanted to direct our attention to',[106] namely, human existence. Since historical exegesis 'is concerned not with explain- ing nature but with understanding history, to which we ourselves belong', the historian must 'confront history in such a way that we acknowledge its claim upon us, its claim to say something new to us'. He must ask 'what is the content of what is said and to what kind of reality does it lead?'[107] But when Bultmann's *Sachkritik* corresponding to this *Sachexegese* claims to 'take the central intentions of the text itself as the standard of criticism',[108] an ambiguity enters his all too sketchy argument. For where does Bultmann's knowledge of the 'central intentions' of the text being criticized come from? And what is the character of 'this criticism (which) is much more radical than philological historical criticism?'[109]

Bultmann claims that his criterion for criticizing the text comes from the text itself. It does, but in the sense that the criterion for an act of theological criticism is the revelation which occurs when the text is being interpreted. That is a theological claim. If a historian were to describe what is happening here, he would not at first sight identify it with his own procedure of correcting one formulation by what the author says elsewhere. Rather, he would have to say that the interpreter is disagreeing with the text on the basis of his own apprehension of Christianity. Such criticism is sometimes necessary (though always dangerous) in theological argument. But it is not historical method, and if Bultmann wishes to claim that what he is doing is what historians normally do, he will need more arguments than are given in his very brief accounts or notices of *Sachkritik*. This is a procedure appropriate to theology, and transferred to history without sufficient attention being paid to the differences of the relation between interpreter and tradition in the two cases.

That Bultmann has a *theological* procedure in mind is confirmed by his references to Luther's canon criticism,[110] which is a theological procedure lacking any reference to historical method. The topic habitually arises when Bultmann is primarily concerned with theological method and the integration of historical method within this, rather than when he is discussing historical method in its own terms.[111] This confirms the suspicion that Bultmann has assumed too easily that a procedure which is legitimate as theological interpretation is also valid as historical method.

All that is being argued is that Bultmann makes the identification of historical and theological method without sufficient justification. It may be possible to maintain it on other grounds. It may well be that a *Sachkritik* which goes beyond the correction of an author's formulation in the light of what he himself says elsewhere is permitted in the writing of history. Such a correction is bound to be risky, but Bultmann accepts and even emphasizes this risk.[112]

Bultmann sometimes corrects what an author says in the light of his own grasp of the subject-matter which may be derived from elsewhere, despite the risk of reading his own views into it. He is even prepared to emphasize the audacity of this (still allegedly historical) procedure: 'It is no small matter that the ideas of Paul which at first sight are the most prominent and which were certainly important to Paul (the whole "closing scene of history", for example) are so to speak explained away (*weginterpretiert*) – whether it be by re-interpretation (*Umdeutung*) or by critical analysis (*kritische Scheidung*).'[113]

Paul can thus be interpreted in the light of what Bultmann himself believes to be the subject-matter, even though Bultmann's apprehension of this probably owes most to the Fourth Gospel[114] (itself critically interpreted).[115] This is without any doubt legitimate as theological interpretation, where the believer has a greater freedom to criticize a piece of the tradition, as he interprets the tradition as a whole in such a way as to correlate this with his own view of Christianity. For theologians, the tradition is relativized by being secondary to the revelation, and especially because revelation is a matter of speaking the unspeakable.[116]

But is it legitimate as *historical* interpretation?

Imagine the following conversation: Bultmann, having critically divested Paul of his futurist eschatology, says to Paul, 'You were wrong about the future, of course, but on the whole I agree with what you taught about God and man. Though I am doing Christian theology as I interpret your epistles, I am actually a historian and I claim that my interpretation is historically true even though it is a a critical one, removing the egg-shells of traditional futurist eschatology which you did not realize were inessential to your position.' Now Paul might reply: 'Well, actually, I *was* wrong about the date of the parousia, and you are right to look for ways of getting around that, so that you can continue to take my witness seriously. I agree, too, that what I taught about God and man remains valid regardless of the date of the parousia; so if your account of my theology ignores that aberration it may still be true to the substance of what I was saying. Unfortunately, however, you have thrown out some of the baby with the bath water. You have misunderstood me in making me say the same thing as your hero John, who did not accept any future perspective. I disagree with that heresy and approve of the ecclesiastical redactor who made John acceptable. The truth is that Käsemann, Moltmann and

Co. have understood me better than you, though of course they owe more to you than to anyone else since brother Martin!'

Bultmann claims to know Paul better than Paul knew himself, and the question raised by the dialogue is whether Paul would recognize himself in the interpretation. As an experienced theologian himself, Paul can appreciate Bultmann's interest in *Sachkritik*. The suggestion is also made, however, that whether the conversation took place in AD 60 or in 1960, Paul might concede that his expectation of the imminent parousia was not essential to his position, though some belief about the future of the world was. If such a conversation can be imagined, then even though Bultmann may have been wrong about Paul at an important point, and this show the danger of *Sachritik*, nevertheless the procedure itself is appropriate. In presenting his author's thought the historian must go for what is central and essential. *Sachkritik* is here a way of doing justice to the heart of Paul's position. The same method is used as by theologians, but for a different purpose: for the sake of doing justice to *Paul*, not for the sake of correlating Paul with one's own theological position. However, the suggestion here is that everything depends upon the author being able to acknowledge the interpretation. This would rule out Bultmann's 'so to speak interpreting away, whether by re-interpretation or by critical analysis, the ideas of (for example) Paul which at first sight are the most prominent and *which were certainly important to Paul*'.[117] In fact, of course, since Paul is dead, it is never possible to be certain what he would have accepted as true to what he was saying; it is necessary to be satisfied with the opinions of other historians arguing on the basis of the evidence available to all. And historians will continue to argue about the evidence. Bultmann is correct to insist that historians should be concerned with the subject-matter; but they are finally concerned with *Paul*'s understanding of it. At the point where an interpreter's concern for the subject-matter leads him to take leave of *Paul* (as opposed to some of Paul's formulations), he is doing something other than history. The question what Paul should have meant is not the historian's business. It is, however, precisely the theologian's business, because he must 'apprehend the subject-matter, which is more important even than Paul'.[118] But since the theologian can only know the subject-matter at all through the witness of the tradition, it is important for him to be able to claim continuity with this, and that demands historically plausible interpretation. He is bound to argue that his interpretation of the tradition, or at least of that part of it to which as a Christian theologian he appeals, is true to it.

The notion of 'true interpretation' of a piece of tradition is, of course, notoriously ambiguous. Many literary critics would say that a true interpretation of *Hamlet* does not depend on understanding Shakespeare's intentions. A work of art or literature has an independence over against its author. Should not the same apply to the New Testament? In suggesting (against one sentence of Bultmann) that the interpretation should (hypothetically) be acceptable to the author, it is being claimed here that New Testament theology is a historical discipline and that the interpreter of the New Testament has less freedom than a literary critic. This is not to deny that unhistorical interpretation may be profoundly Christian and therefore good theology. In that case it would be able to appeal to other parts of the tradition. But the Christian tradition is not simply a body of literature claiming to interpret human existence. It is that, but it also claims to interpret a particular contingent historical event, and must therefore always be referred back to that. The peculiar status of the collection of traditions called the New Testament is connected to its proximity to that event. This does not guarantee its theological or historical reliability, but it does mean that on the whole it contains the nearest that any surviving part of the Christian tradition provides to a norm for the guidance of the expanding tradition. As a matter of fact it has functioned in this way; it therefore makes sense to measure the subsequent tradition by reference to it.

Bultmann's phrase about 'the ideas . . . which were certainly important to Paul' has been criticized, and what Paul might have found acceptable proposed as the limits of historical interpretation. In fact, however, when his actual practice is considered, one is confronted by profound new interpretations of Paul and John which are based on historical exegesis and claim to be historical interpretations. It is possible to set aside his own theological motives, and also the material issue of whether one agrees with the interpretations themselves, and simply ask whether what is presented here has the form of a historical presentation.[119] Answers will vary according to how the task of history of thought is conceived. How far can the presentation of a position be cut loose from its historical form? Is a 'distillate'[120] allowable? Is the result not inevitably 'a certain ultra-Pauline one-sidedness, since the specifically Pauline ideas are put on their own in the centre . . .?'[121] The methodological question opened up through a discussion of *Sachkritik* is not how adequately Bultmann has in fact understood his authors' intentions, but how far it is legitimate to criticize formulations on the basis of these. In practice, if the result is considered correct, the method will be blessed; and if the result is considered historically faulty, the admittedly risky method will be blamed. That means that in historical work the procedure is useful for framing hypotheses, but that these then have to be tested by the evidence. If the proposed critical interpretation makes the best sense of the evidence, historians will be prepared to accept it. In other words, the risk involved in *Sachkritik* is a necessary element in historical research. But when a hypothesis has been thus framed, historians' debate follows. In Bultmann's case the hypotheses and the constructions based on them have been severely criticized by his fellow-historians. Before considering the point at which Bultmann's presentation of his 'theological interpretation' in the form of a complete 'theology of the New Testament' *does* seem inevitably to conflict with historical aims, it will be useful to give an example of such criticism. As well as confirming the legitimacy of the daring hypothesis in historical work, this will clarify further what is involved in the legitimate activity of *theological interpretation* of the New Testament, or doing one's own theology through a theologically motivated historical interpretation of certain texts.

It has already been noticed that the historian of the New Testament has a large number of variables to settle when he proposes an interpretation. This means that there is considerable scope for disagreement among specialists about the meaning of the New Testament. It has also been noticed that theologians are interested in claiming the support of certain parts of the tradition for their own views. When Bultmann interprets the Fourth Gospel, he is not simply doing history; he is also advocating his own contemporary theology. When Käsemann recalls Luther's *crux sola nostra theologia*[122] and Kähler's 'the cross, basis and criterion of christology',[123] it is his own theology which is being expressed through the interpretation of Paul. What Schlatter saw happening in his own generation is happening here (p. 124 below). Historical argument has become the battleground for opposing systematic theologies.

It is worth choosing our examples from the field of Pauline interpretation, because this is where Protestant theologians since Luther have generally heard the gospel 'clearest of all'. This is, therefore, the point at which their interpretation of the tradition and their own theology are most likely to coincide. In saying what Christianity *was* for Paul, they are often saying what it *is* for themselves.

In an important essay on a 'theme (in which) the central problem of Pauline theology is concentrated', Käsemann declared his aim of 'identifying the unitary centre' of Paul's thought before saying 'whether it is possible – and perhaps obligatory – for us to pursue this same dialectic in our own day'.[124] He considers that 'the problem attacked here . . . (in which the whole of the apostle's theology has to be subpoenaed in order to reach the correct translation of a single word and, conversely, the correct translation of this one word determines the whole of the apostle's theology . . .) is at least just as important as that of the historical Jesus, and ought perhaps even to take precedence over it'.[125] And he adds, confessing the theological motives for posing this particular historical question from New Testament theology: 'It would help our theological situation if the fire that has been kindled (i.e. by his criticism of Bultmann) were not extinguished too quickly.'

The argument with Bultmann about Paul is at the centre of Käsemann's theological and exegetical achievement. Its interest for the methodology of New Testament theology is increased by the quite substantial exegetical agreement between the two historians. Both see Paul as a theologian and can talk of the centre of his theology. Both see this centre in the doctrine of justification. They even agree that 'Paul's teaching on justification is, it could be said, his real christology'.[126] But Bultmann at once takes this to mean that christology is subordinate to soteriology and anthropology,[127] whereas for Käsemann it supports the claim that christology forms the centre of Paul's thought.[128] This combination of substantial exegetical agreement and fundamental systematic disagreement means that the argument about the interpretation of this piece of the tradition hinges upon a few apparently minor exegetical nuances. These are argued about with a vehemence which is quite perplexing to observers who do not realize how much is at stake. But these nuances determine which interpreter's perspective is more true to the historical Paul, and therefore who can appeal to him with most justice in support of his own theology. The question has more than historical interest, if that be reduced to mere reconstruction of the past.[129]

The different perspectives on Paul are the result of different theological positions. Bultmann's anthropologically oriented theology can appeal to Schleiermacher and Melanchthon. It is unequivocally stated in his answer to the question, 'Does he help me because he is God's Son, or is he the Son of God because he helps me?'[130] The important truth and apologetic value of Bultmann's existential emphasis is not denied. No theology worthy of the name can be without it. But Käsemann, following Barth and Iwand, is convinced that for a theology to be truly Christian, its centre must be constituted by christology.[131] The Reformers had struggled to reassert the lordship of Christ against a Catholicism which was subordinating christology to ecclesiology, and the subordination of christology to anthropology in neo-Protestantism from Schleiermacher to Bultmann and his successors is taken to be an outbreak of the same disease.[132] We are not concerned here with the doctrinal dispute itself, but only with how the battle is waged:[133] by historical exegetical interpretation of a piece of the tradition, in this case of Paul.

There are other points at which Bultmann's interpretation of Paul is guided by his theological interests, and where Käsemann, no less guided by theological motives, attacks him on historical exegetical grounds. Bultmann's Kantian-Ritschlian exclusion of the world from serious concern by theology has already been mentioned. Käsemann stresses that for Paul Christ is destined to be cosmocrator,[134] and interprets the Pauline concept *soma* to mean man as a bit of the world.[135] Since theology is interpretation of the tradition in the light of contemporary experience, Bultmann has to defend his interpretation of Paul (for example – but always the most important example) by reference to these. He has to refute exegetically the charge that his concept of self-understanding is narrower than the Pauline account of man in the world;[136] that the exaggerated individualism of his existentialist theology is untrue both to this part of the tradition and to experience; that the resulting view of ethics in which the Christian is thought to be 'out of this world' is similarly untrue to both Paul and to contemporary experience.[137] In each case the evidence is somewhat ambiguous; alternative theologies continue to argue about the correct historical interpretation of the tradition. Even historical arguments which have been thoroughly laid to rest have a habit of rising again in the third generation.

In this example both theologians appealed to Paul. Their theological interpretation shows a profound understanding of what Paul is talking about, but this interest also involves the danger of modernization. The critical task of the historian is to stand guard against such violence being done to the tradition.[138] This critical task can sometimes be more easily done by someone with less sympathy for the text's viewpoint.[139] But such hostility can also bar the way to genuine understanding. It is necessary to beware of the optical illusion by which an unsympathetic interpretation which stresses the difference and distance between the text and the historian's own standpoint, or emphasizes the past in its pastness, looks more genuinely historical than one which tries to understand the past in the present.[140]

Bultmann and Käsemann belong to the neo-Reformation theological revival of the 1920s, and naturally appealed, like the Reformers themselves, to Paul. The liberal Protestants against whom they reacted could expect less support from this piece of tradition. But theology for them, too, was a matter of interpreting the tradition in the light of contemporary experience, even if the emphasis here was more upon what was new in the modern apprehension of reality than upon the abiding validity of the tradition as a whole. It is instructive to see how they coped with the counter-witness of what had normally been considered a rather authoritative part of the tradition.[141]

A popular gambit was to deny that Paul was a theologian, and to concentrate upon him as a hero of the religious life of man. In this more congenial role it was possible to claim him as 'one of us'. It is to Wrede's credit as a historian that, little as he personally (as a theologian) liked Paul's theology, he recognized that Paul's 'religion is theological through and through'.[142] But he weakened the force of Paul's counter-evidence by driving two wedges between Paul and the rest of the tradition. By denying that justification formed the centre of Pauline theology,[143] he undermined the powerful alliance between Paul and Luther which formed the backbone of traditional Protestantism.[144] More important still for his own liberal Protestant position, he drove a historical and theological wedge between Paul and Jesus, and could thus appeal (like de Lagarde before him)[145] beyond the 'second founder of Christianity' to a higher authority, the authentic (historical) Jesus.[146] When later Bultmann (with Barth and Schlatter) wished to reintegrate Paul's witness as central in his own theological picture, he had to argue that Paul had interpreted Jesus correctly (though from a post-resurrection standpoint),[147] and also to restore justification to the centre of Pauline theology, *and* deny that Jesus could properly be called 'the founder of Christianity'.[148]

Fluctuation in the theological evaluation of Paul is not confined to the modern period. Throughout church history he has generally been more respected than understood.[149] In the 120 years following him, 'Marcion was the only Gentile Christian who understood Paul, and even he misunderstood him'.[150] Even Augustine, who owed more to Paul than most of the Fathers, presents an interesting amalgam of Paul and Platonism.[151] Theologians from Marcion to Käsemann who have found Paul most congenial have generally found it necessary to reject other parts (even scriptural parts) of the tradition.[152] Thus modern 'radical Protestants' such as Käsemann have a strong distaste for Lucan theology. They can appreciate its necessity at a particular point in the history of the early church, but it does not form the centre of their own apprehension of Christianity. If Luke makes a salvation-historical perspective the framework of his thought, whereas these theologians can at best give it a subordinate role, they will disagree with Luke, and appeal to Paul and John, and argue furiously with a theologian like Cullmann who tries to claim these witnesses as well as Luke for his scheme of salvation history.[153] It is not denied by Käsemann that Paul and John have ideas of salvation history, but it is denied, again through historical exegesis, that these form the centre of their thought. The argument is exegetical, but behind the scenes stands a systematic theological rejection of salvation-historical frameworks as a basis for contemporary theology. The reasons for this rejection are that salvation-historical ideas are mythological and drastically conflict with modern experience of reality; that they conflict with a Lutheran existential conception of faith; and that they lead to a triumphalist view of the church which ill-befits followers of the crucified one.[154] Here, too, an interplay between the tradition and contemporary experience is involved in making theological judgments.

The legitimacy of this theological criticism of Luke, an aspect of theological interpretation of the tradition (which is a way of doing Christian theology), is not in question. It contains the danger of distorting historical work, but this can be guarded against. All historical work involves the danger of misinterpreting the evidence, and every proposal must be subject to the scrutiny of other historians. Theology done through interpretation of the tradition must meet the condition that it does not contravene what historians can say about the tradition. This is why allegorical interpretation is no longer acceptable. It conflicts with the canons of truth and rationality generally accepted today. Wrede's essay is a brilliant statement of the conditions imposed by historical methods upon theological interpretation. Wrede himself is not interested in doing theology, but he rightly protests against theologians' distortion of the history. Bultmann's New Testament theology respects the limits imposed by the historian, even though what he is doing through his historical research is theology.

The recognition that what some theologically motivated authors are doing under the title 'New Testament theology' is in fact theological interpretation of the New Testament accounts for some of the perplexing work done in this field. It enables us to make sense, for example, of what is at first sight a particularly opaque statement of Dr Alan Richardson. In the Preface of his *Introduction to the Theology of the New Testament* (1958), he referred to Gore's theology of the New Testament (?) as 'orthodox' and Bultmann's as 'heretical'.[155] If New Testament theology is a historical discipline, how can examples be deemed orthodox or heretical? But when one recognizes that Richardson, Gore and Bultmann were all engaged in theological interpretation of the New Testament, then Richardson's theological (and therefore inevitably polemical) statement is intelligible. It is perfectly reasonable for Richardson to judge the New Testament interpretations – i.e. the modern theologies – of his fellow-theologians in this way. It was perhaps misleading of Bultmann and Richardson to call their works New Testament theologies, since this term generally (however inappropriately) refers to a purely historical discipline. It is a further question whether Richardson's own theological interpretation of the New Testament keeps within the bounds of historically allowable interpretation. The work could be defended in principle as not a New Testament theology, but an introduction to, or 'sub-structure' of this, as implied by the title and opening reference to C. H. Dodd's work *According to the Scriptures. The Substructure of New Testament Theology*.[156] But Richardson goes on to speak of 'the underlying theology of the New Testament documents', which is problematical. It is one thing to speak of an underlying unity and quite another to find this in a particular theology which can be spelled out like a textbook of dogmatics. In fact Richardson's work looks in some ways like a return to the pre-modern, unhistorical textbooks of biblical dogmatics which failed to distinguish between the theologies of different authors. Schlatter allowed that these works had some value, but his historical conscience forced him at once to kill the concession with qualifications (p. 161 below). That many people have found Richardson's work so helpful is an indication that a genuinely historical understanding of the New Testament is still not widespread.

Another most attractive work which has been found edifying in the best (Pauline) sense of the word is E. Stauffer's *New Testament Theology*. This work also makes no pretence to fulfil Wrede's programme. Its aim is rather to 'provide an introduction to the thought world of the New Testament'. The book contains a brief account of 'the development of primitive Christian theology' from Judaism to Ignatius, but its main part is 'the christocentric theology of history in the New Testament'. A better title for this theological interpretation of the New Testament might have been *New Testament Theology of History*.

To revert to an earlier example: if Wrede's historical programme and that of theological interpretation are two different, but both legitimate enterprises, W. Beyschlag can be rescued from some of Wrede's criticism. He is admittedly rather confused about the relationship of his historical work to the theological interest which he professes.[157] But in answering the charge of 'modernization' he shows an awareness of the hermeneutical problem which one might have expected in a theological descendant (through C. I. Nitzsch) of Schleiermacher. He 'seeks to revive the past and bring it into the present', having 'learned from Schleiermacher that criticism is an art, which above all seeks by thought to restore life to the writing that is to be judged, and to judge it only from the basis of this living reproduction'. If this is the nature of the historian's art it is necessary to insist that:

the translation of what we find in the Bible into our own modes of thought and speech is indispensable. For we are to endeavour to understand what we find in the Bible; and as we are neither Jews nor Greeks of the first Roman Empire, but Germans or Englishmen of the nineteenth century, how are we to understand without a translation in the widest and deepest sense of the word? A translation of the biblical speech, in the ordinary sense, into German or English of the present day, is itself a kind of modernizing process. But a mere dictionary translation would help us very little, would give us only words without intelligible meaning. There must be added a mental translation, a transference not merely into our vocabulary but also into our mode of thought, as speech and thought cannot at all be separated. No doubt this procedure may be abused, and lead to a voluntary or involuntary importation of one's own ideas, but *'abusus non tollit usum'*.[158]

Wrede dismissed this as modernization, and he would probably have dismissed some of Bultmann's theological interpretation of the New Testament done through historical interpretation in the same way. It is true that a historian must be able to appreciate historical distance, but it does not follow that those who emphasize the distance have necessarily understood best.

A theological function has been proposed for Wrede's historical (and by intention atheological) enterprise. It provides a criterion against which all theological interpretations must be tested. If these conflict with what historians say about the sources, they cannot be accepted. Since historians have no professional interest in whether the texts witness to something or someone who transcends human reality, their writ does not extend to the evaluation of theological interpretations. Their role here is simply the negative one of ruling out those which conflict with historical truth. Since theologians interpret the tradition in the light of contemporary experience, they can welcome this condition, imposed by their culture. They wish to talk sense to their contemporaries.

The restriction of valid theological interpretation to what is historically admissible, and the theological method of interpreting the tradition by historical methods, means that an actual account of an author may be identical when done by a Wrede or a histori-cally-conscious theologian. There would seem, therefore, to be no objection to New Testament theology being considered a purely historical discipline, yet also used in a theologically loaded way. Käsemann, for example, often chooses to write on a topic from the New Testament which has implications for the current theo-logical debate. It is clear enough where he goes beyond historical judgments.[159] He does not conceal his disapproval of those parts of the New Testament which suit Catholic theology better than Lutheranism, and he does not pretend that his judgment that Paul is a better theologian than either Matthew or Luke is made quite independently of his own systematic position, though he does defend it by reference to Jesus. The New Testament authors dis-agree in their theologies. The theological interpreter must make choices within the tradition and defend his choice by reference to his understanding of the tradition as a whole, and to the appre-hension of reality that provides the web in which threads of tradi-tion are woven to represent a theological pattern corresponding to his apprehension of the Christian revelation.

A difficulty, however, arises when a particular author or topic is no longer under consideration. Where Paul is being interpreted, and the theologian agrees with Paul, the historical task may over-lap completely with that of theological interpretation, and New Testament theology function simultaneously as a historical and a theological or doctrinal discipline. Or a single theme, such as freedom, may be selected as an organizing theme for a 'polemical (theological!) survey' of the New Testament which does not claim to be a complete theology.[160] The *genre* of a complete theology of the New Testament, on the other hand, leads to a conflict between a Wrede-like historical presentation of the development of New Testament thought, and theological interpretation which involves making out a case about the nature of Christianity. The choices made by the theological interpreter of the tradition involve his own apprehension of Christianity, and therefore go beyond the decisions made by the historian.

History is not value-free, and the historian also makes decisions about what in his sources is important. Bultmann's strategy for combining the historical and theological tasks is, as has been seen, to refer both to the same subject-matter, human existence, which is of concern to historian and theologian alike. The historian of literature makes judgments about what does and what does not illuminate human existence. Why should not the historian of a religious tradition do the same?

Käsemann's theological interpretation takes Paul as a norm and defends this 'canon within the canon' theologically.[161] If Bultmann is to defend his theology of the New Testament purely as history of ideas, he must give some other account of his procedure. If he is really doing what Käsemann admits to doing, he would have to disguise this. His strategy is to make the combination of Paul and John his norm, and to justify this by a definition of theology which allows only these to be considered self-conscious theologians.[162] This involves a theological claim about the anthropological character of theology, which may or may not be accepted, and some historical claims about Paul and John which are open to exegetical debate. If Bultmann's account of the eschatology of Paul is historically less convincing than his John, and his account of both their christologies defective; if the authors of Hebrews and Ephesians and the synoptic gospels are worth more consideration as theologians than Bultmann allows; if themes such as salvation history and the Old Testament are more important to Paul and John than they are to Bultmann; then his basis for his theology of the New Testament can no longer be defended on purely historical grounds. It is brilliant theological interpretation, constructed entirely from the materials of a historical presentation, but in its conception it is something more than a 'purely historical' account of New Testament theology. Bultmann would agree that it is more than what Wrede meant by 'purely historical', but would add that Wrede's conception of history was defective. The argument of this essay is that Bultmann's theological interpretation goes beyond any valid account of what is meant by 'purely historical' – and that it is none the worse for that. Behind this argument stands the theological and philosophical (or metaphysical) postulate that theological statements do more than overlap with historical ones, if the realm of the historical is restricted to human existence.[163]

The position reached so far is that a distinction must be made between Wrede's history of early Christian thought and the theological interpretation of the New Testament part of the tradition. Neither is appropriately called New Testament theology, and the use of this label for both obscures what New Testament scholars are doing. The next step is to enquire whether the distinction made here can be bridged and thus lead to something more appropriately called New Testament theology.

Some such move might be expected from scholars whose view of theology, tradition and revelation differs from that of Bultmann and Käsemann and (in their view) Paul and Luther.[164] H. Schlier and H. Conzelmann are instructive examples. Both were pupils of Bultmann and continue to bear signs of their past. But both have moved away from kerygmatic theology, and prefer to find a more concrete foundation for New Testament theology in primitive credal formulations. A part of the tradition is more tangible than the unobjectifiable event of revelation. Schlier became a Roman Catholic in 1953, and his position is consistent with the traditional Roman Catholic devaluation of dogma (authorized ecclesiastical tradition) over kerygma or proclamation.[165] Conzelmann wants to emphasize the pastness of (for example) Paul in contrast to Bultmann's 'distillation', and considers that the best way 'to avoid the danger of historicism [is] by regarding theology not only in general terms, as the interpretation of the faith made at a particular time, but in a more special sense as an exegesis of the original *texts* of the faith, the oldest formulations of the creed'.[166] It is difficult to believe that Conzelmann changed his mind about what theology is just to avoid the danger of historicism. One must assume that his own theological position has more in common with Barth's element of scriptural positivism than with Bultmann's consistently maintained dialectic between tradition and revelation.[167]

It is difficult to see any significant advance on Bultmann's synthesis here. A new approach to the problem of New Testament theology from the side of theology must probably await a creative new development in systematic theology.[168] It is perhaps not yet the *kairos*. But meanwhile more advances could be made from the historical side. Wrede's clarity of mind has scarcely been surpassed. But he was a man of his time, and some of his limitations ought by now to be overcome.

The history of religions scholars were more aware than their contemporaries of the importance of the historian's sensitivity to the religious phenomena being studied. Their empathy has since become commonplace in the study of religion. But this study has made further advances, particularly with the emergence of the phenomenology of religion.[169] The phenomenologist's subject-matter is still man and his religion, not God. But an adequate treatment of this subject-matter involves doing full justice to what the participant or believer thinks the subject-matter of these texts is. 'The believer is always right' is a typical dictum. Barth's protest about contemporary historical study of the Bible was an indict-ment of a failure here which has not yet been adequately met by historians of the New Testament and of Christian doctrine. They rarely succeed in communicating to a non-Christian reader what it felt like for Paul or Athanasius to believe in God in Christ.[170] Barth had his own remedy, but that was only relevant for New Testament scholars (like Bultmann) who happened also to be Christian theologians. What was valid in his strictures on the his-torians has also to be met from the historical side.

The phenomenological standpoint takes Paul's beliefs more seriously than the liberals were able to do. Both their polemical situation of opposition to the dominant orthodoxy and the anti-metaphysical climate in philosophy made it difficult for them to treat theology or doctrine sympathetically. Religion was often proposed as the antithesis of theology, and the central place of theology in a developed religion was not appreciated. Since the theological revival of the 1920s, the scientific and historical study of religion has been better placed to understand its subject-matter, except where it is still preoccupied with fighting old battles. Those who study their own religion historically have little excuse now to be blind to the systematic implications of their work.

The massive labour of men like Bousset, Gunkel, Reitzenstein and Bultmann on the religious source material of the ancient world was itself important prolegomena for the phenomenology of religion. Phenomenologists take a cross-section and study, for example, rites of initiation in several religions. Early history of religions research upon the New Testament was probably wrong in some cases to suggest direct influence upon early Christianity from, for example, mystery religions. But the material they ex-plored may well throw an indirect light upon how early Christian writers thought. This is less than a causal explanation and by no means an explaining away, but it is relevant for historians of the New Testament as well as for the history of New Testament inter-pretation and for the formulation of Christian doctrine today.[171]

The history of interpretation is itself another area through which the historical study of New Testament theology can be enriched. Where the subject-matter is, even in historical terms, so difficult to locate precisely, different perspectives upon it gained by reading a series of interpreters who have been more or less in tune with the documents are a valuable help to the historian. They are, of course, absolutely indispensable to the theological interpreter of the New Testament, whose entire debate with this part of the tradition is largely conditioned by the intervening tradition.[172]

Wrede has perhaps said the last word about the impossibility of limiting the historical discipline to the New Testament texts. It has to be asked whether there is any justification for limiting theological interpretation of the tradition in the same way. Bultmann is often said to be a 'scriptural theologian'. Writing about theological exegesis 'with faith as its presupposition'[173] he does touch on the question 'whether, for example, Augustine, Luther, Schleiermacher or even the Bhagavad-Gita should be interpreted in the same way as the New Testament'. But his answer is to side-step the issue: 'Insofar as I reflect theoretically, and put myself in an abstract, traditionless situation, there will be no difference. But whether in such an interpretation the [revelation] event will happen and my hearing be the hearing of faith (echoing Gal. 3.2, 5) cannot be answered as a matter of principle' [but only in the actual event].[174] The sort of exegesis which has faith as its presupposition cannot be established and justified. It can only be *done*, and done in full knowledge of the risk involved. This is because the presupposition (faith) is not something objective, over which control can be exercised, but is something which happens, in the event of revelation, and is occasioned by God.[175]

Bultmann might as well have admitted that any piece of tradition could in principle be used as a springboard for proclamation. An 'occasionalist' view of revelation follows from Bultmann's distinction between the event of revelation and all tradition. It is inevitable in a theology which emphasizes so strongly the distinction between God and the world. In principle anything might trigger off a Christian revelation event. But a bird singing or an Oxfam advertisement or the Bhagavad-Gita could only do this if it were understood in the light of some specifically Christian tradition. The distinction within the Christian tradition between canonical and extra-canonical material is more difficult to justify.

It is all tradition and it is all (more or less) Christian. The New Testament documents are not the best of Christian literature, and they can no longer be defended as a whole as the literature of the apostolic age. They are nevertheless generally the earliest specifically Christian tradition we possess, and their proximity to the contingent historical events which Christians consider fundamental[176] has something to do with their special status.[177]

The notion of a canon, however, means a 'norm', and in this context must refer to a theological norm. The historical reference is insufficient to justify it. It has been argued that strictly speaking only the revelation event, the Christ, can be the criterion of tradition, and that he is the criterion of the scriptural traditions also. On the other hand the *de facto* authority which these early traditions have enjoyed in the church is such that it makes sense to speak of 'church history (or the history of doctrine) as the history of the interpretation of scripture'.[178] Since these traditions have in fact been used as the basis for most subsequent proclamation, the traditional distinction between scripture as *norma normans* and subsequent ecclesiastical tradition as *norma normata* is meaningful. The important practical implication of this is that modern interpretation of doctrinal formulations should understand these in the direction of the biblical theology they were trying to interpret in their own age. For most of Christian history the reverse has happened. The Bible has been understood in the light of subsequent doctrinal decisions.

Defence of the canon by reference to the historical effects of what has in fact been done in the church demands recognition of the fact that the scriptural canon itself has only been an approximation and outer limit to the early tradition which has actually functioned as a major source and guide of later developments. In practice, Christians have always used a 'living centre of scripture'.[179] Whether clarity is served by calling this a 'canon within the canon' may be doubted. That slogan makes a point, but it might be taken to suggest that the rest is to be rejected. In fact, even tradition (including scriptural tradition) which is not found helpful is preserved.[180] Another generation might hear the voice of Christ through it. Since the word 'canon' suggests a rather formalistic use of scripture as a norm, it is paradoxical that those who see the gospel as the real norm should continue to give currency to it by the use of the phrase 'canon within the canon'.[181]

Discussion of the canon inevitably raises the question of the Old Testament. There never has existed a New Testament canon on its own. It is often argued that discussion of New Testament theology must eventually expand into a discussion of *biblical* theology.[182] Since we have avoided the phrase New Testament theology, there is no need to follow that route directly. But both activities described here, theological interpretation of the tradition and history of early Christian religion and theology, demand that our discussion of the tradition extend back into Judaism[183] as well as forward into the post-canonical material. The overlapping relationship between Christianity and Judaism is certainly an important theme of New Testament theology. The two are generally considered different religions now (just as vulgar parlance considers Roman Catholicism and Protestantism to be different religions). The historian, and so too the theologian (who must always be a historian nowadays), must emphasize that they share the same tradition.

The tradition which they share is not simply the Hebrew scriptures. Neither historians nor theologians can restrict themselves to the pieces of tradition which have been most influential. The ever-expanding tradition and the history of its critical interpretation is very complex indeed. It included matters such as the Christianization of the Testaments of the Twelve Patriarchs. Or the Christianization of some Jewish apocalypse which (probably) led to the Book of Revelation. This example is a reminder that the historian of the tradition must investigate the pre-history which lies behind certain New Testament documents, especially the gospels. This information (almost always hypothetical – but sometimes fairly securely established) is of interest to the theological interpreter of the tradition. A theological interpretation of the Fourth Gospel need not be limited to the text as we have it. Anything the historian can say about the stages in its formation might be grist to the theologian's mill. This is simply another point at which historical research has profoundly affected the discipline called biblical theology.

This account of the twofold task – history of the tradition and theological interpretation of it, often coinciding but logically distinct – offers an approach to the vexed question of whether the historical Jesus belongs within New Testament theology. A direct answer to this ambiguous question results in the same confusion which is caused by asking whether Jesus was a Christian or a Jew.[184] There is obviously something wrong with saying that the historical Jesus is 'theologically irrelevant',[185] since Christians assert his identity with the risen Christ, upon whom the Christian tradition centres. On the other hand, the historians' Jesus results from a means of access to the past developed modern rationalism.

It is necessary to ask about the place of historical investigation of Jesus in both activities discussed. A history of Judaeo-Christian tradition would have to show what it was about Jesus which led to his execution and the subsequent bifurcation in the tradition. Christian theological interpretation of the tradition (including interpretation of the so-called Old Testament)[186] centres on the Christ of faith. If the Jesus of history and the Christ of faith are one and the same, it follows that anything the historian can say about Jesus might function as a criterion of Christian theological statements.[187]

This does not answer the practical question of what a theology of the New Testament should look like. But that is no more than a practical problem. One may argue about where a history of the Reformation should begin and end, and also about how much a theology of the Reformers should contain. The hardness of men's hearts and the weakness of their minds and the awful complexity of history means that specialists on the Reformation are necessary. The same goes for primitive Christianity. But neither Reformation nor New Testament studies is a subject. The subjects which both involve, involve more than both: history and theology.

II

William Wrede

THE TASK AND METHODS OF 'NEW TESTAMENT THEOLOGY'[1]

Everyone knows that the emergence, growth and development of biblical and especially New Testament theology is one of the most important features of theology in the past century. Everyone knows, too, how deeply New Testament theology penetrates the central problems of theology in the present. It goes much deeper even than historical-critical work on the New Testament documents, though admittedly since Strauss and Baur it has been closely bound up with that. For New Testament theology is decisive for the question of the essence and emergence of original Christianity.

An account of the task and methods of this discipline can therefore reckon on general interest. That is, provided that it does not remain at merely an abstract and formal level.

I

It may be asked just how fast the theology of the New Testament has developed since the year 1787, i.e. since Gabler's programmatic address *De justo discrimine theologiae biblicae et dogmaticae regundisque recte utriusque finibus* (On the proper distinction between biblical and dogmatic theology and the correct delimitation of their boundaries). But it cannot be doubted that the development has brought considerable general advances.

That is clear from many matters which have only recently become self-evident. For example, the Old and New Testament are to be treated separately. Today it is self-evident not only that the teaching of Jesus is to be distinguished from that of the apostles, but also that the different views of different groups have to be distinguished within the latter. It is self-evident that somehow a historical development of the ideas of the New Testament has to be demonstrated, and also that one must try to present these ideas not in line with a dogmatic scheme which is alien to the biblical writers, but according to their own points of view.

Can it also be claimed as self-evident[2] that New Testament theology must be considered and done as a purely historical discipline? Formally and in theory most people would say yes.[3] When the material is contemplated, however, a different view emerges. So long as New Testament theology retains a direct link with dogmatics as its goal, and people expect from it material for dogmatics to work on – and that is a common view – it will be natural for biblical theology to have an eye to dogmatics. Biblical theology will be pressed for an answer to dogmatic questions which the biblical documents do not really give, and will endeavour to eliminate results which are troublesome for dogmatics. The writings which contain the material are burdened with definite dogmatic predicates like 'normative', which say nothing about their character as documents. So long as this continues to be the case, it is at least psychologically probable that New Testament ideas which go contrary to expectation will be worked on and arranged till they fit those predicates. On these presuppositions some things, such as, for example, serious contradictions within the New Testament, are not allowed to emerge.

I do not intend to dwell on this question of principle for long, but I must state from the outset that my comments presuppose the strictly historical character of New Testament theology.

The old doctrine of inspiration is recognized by academic theology, including very largely the conservative wing, to be untenable. For logical thinking there can be no middle position between inspired writings and historical documents, although in fact there is no lack of partial doctrines of inspiration about the place. Biblical theology has to investigate something from given documents – if not an external thing, still something intellectual. It tries to grasp it as objectively, correctly and sharply as possible. That is all. How the systematic theologian gets on with its results and deals with them – that is his own affair. Like every other real science, New Testament theology has its goal simply in itself, and is totally indifferent to all dogma and systematic theology.[4] What could dogmatics offer it? Could dogmatics teach New Testament theology to see the facts correctly? At most it could colour them. Could it correct the facts that were found? To correct facts is absurd. Could it legitimize them? Facts need no legitimation.

The first thing which must be required of anyone who wishes to engage scientifically in New Testament theology is, accordingly, that he be capable of interest in historical research. He must be guided by a pure disinterested concern for knowledge, which accepts every really compelling result. He must be able to distinguish between the alien modern ideas of his own thought and those of the past. He must be able to keep his own viewpoint, however precious, quite separate from the object of his research and hold it in suspense. Then he will indeed know only what really was.

One might say that this account of New Testament theology entirely surrenders its specifically theological character. It is no longer treated any differently from any other branch of intellectual history in general or the history of religion in particular. That is quite correct. But in what should the specifically theological type of treatment consist? It would always result in a mixture which included the personal theological viewpoint of the scholar, and that could only obscure things. Or can a specifically theological understanding of the discipline guarantee some kind of knowledge that goes beyond the knowledge of the historical fact that such and such was taught and believed by the men of the New Testament? Can it add anything to the factuality of this? It is not true, either, that the purely historical view of the discipline tends to rob the New Testament of its profoundly religious thinking or noble ethical outlook. An extra theological something would have to be demanded for exegesis, too, and for history of doctrine and church history, if this something were considered necessary before New Testament theology could be considered a theological discipline.

If the New Testament writings emerged in the course of a history and are the witnesses and documentation of this history, then we are faced with a question: why should our discipline be concerned just with these and no other writings? The normal answer is that only these belong to the canon. But that is not a satisfactory answer. Where the doctrine of inspiration has been discarded, it is impossible to continue to maintain the dogmatic conception of the canon.

No New Testament writing was born with the predicate 'canonical' attached. The statement that a writing is canonical signifies in the first place only that it was pronounced canonical afterwards by the authorities of the second- to fourth-century church, in some cases only after all kinds of hesitation and disagreement. The history of the canon is sufficiently instructive in this respect.

So anyone who accepts without question the idea of the canon places himself under the authority of the bishops and theologians of those centuries. Anyone who does not recognize their authority in other matters – and no Protestant theologian does – is being consistent if he questions it here, too.[5]

It is not necessary to doubt that on the whole the early church put together what was religiously most valuable and also oldest and so historically most important, not only of what we know but also of what was then in circulation. They made a collection worthy of all praise. But this judgment involves us in saying that the boundaries between the canonical books and the extra-canonical material closest to them fluctuate at every point.[6]

So unless one is prepared to consider the New Testament writings from the point of view of a 'subsequent experience' that had nothing whatever to do with their original character, they are to be seen not as canonical but simply as early Christian writings. In that case, of course, one's historical interest insists on taking together everything from the totality of early Christian literature that historically belongs together. The borders of the material of the discipline are to be drawn where a real break in the literature can be observed. This is not, of course, decided on a basis of religious value. The question is simply which writings are most closely related in ideas and outlook, or at what point the ideas take on a noticeably different character.

Is it possible to say that in this sense the New Testament writings constitute a special group, distinctly separate from the neighbouring literature? If only one could say that the New Testament is the literature of the apostolic in contrast to that of the sub-apostolic age! And if only the idea of a sort of decline were tenable, in which this apostolic period were followed by a lower level of thought! But this idea is legend. The New Testament can by no means be temporally located in the apostolic age. The Gospel of John, the Catholic Epistles, the Pastorals and other books lie outside its limits. Some of these writings belong chronologically in the middle of the group we call the Apostolic Fathers. I Clement is certainly older than several New Testament writings, and II Peter and

James are probably later than several of the Apostolic Fathers. Others of these New Testament writings stand close to them. Altogether they are no further (or not much further) in time from even the latest Apostolic Fathers than they are in the other direction from the Pauline epistles.[7]

The main point, however, is that their content accords with their date. In comparison with the older parts of the New Testament, writings like the Gospel and Epistles of John, the Pastoral Epistles, James, Jude and II Peter, and also Matthew, confront us with essentially new questions and phenomena. There is a christological dogma and it is defended; the struggle against gnostic heresy has flared up; there is the concept of orthodoxy in opposition to heresy; the formula of belief, the confession, begins to play a role; the ministry is beginning to become normative in the expanding church and the spirit is now associated with this; the church's break with Judaism is a fact of the past – it utters polemic against Judaism as an alien religion. Nor are these the only changes over against primitive Christianity. All these traits, on the other hand, are characteristic of the Apostolic Fathers. There are, of course, also new characteristics there. But no clear line of demarcation can be drawn between them and those New Testament writings. The similarities are more obvious. Even the noticeable increase in Hellenistic ideas yields no complete division. Consider, for example, the specially close relationships between Hebrews and Barnabas, between James and I Clement or the Shepherd of Hermas, or between John and Ignatius. It is at least certain that the distance in ideas and outlook between these early Christian writings and the latest New Testament writings is by no means greater and in many ways smaller than the distance between these New Testament writings and the genuine epistles of Paul.[8] Since our discipline cannot easily stop at Paul, and since it cannot make much use of the concept 'apostolic age' as its boundary,[9] then it must extend outside the New Testament, as Krüger has recently quite rightly demanded.[10]

Against this demand it might be said that the church has, in its history and its theology, as in its practice, a quite peculiar relationship to the New Testament writings, and that theology 'must serve the church'. However, this formula, so frequently used and going back to Schleiermacher, is – at least for everything in theology which belongs to history, and so for the whole field of biblical studies – either totally untenable or utterly devoid of content.[11]

The service to be rendered to the church would still have to be either the results of research or the way in which the material is treated or the tasks which are set. Striving to serve the church says absolutely nothing about results or method. Both are determined solely by the nature of the historical object. The tasks set come also in the main from the subject-matter. The questions and needs of the church can be a legitimate influence only in a limited sense – and probably least of all in the biblical field. On the whole it is not within the historical researcher's power to serve the church through his work. The theologian who obeys the historical object as his master is not in a position to serve the church through his properly scientific-historical work, even if he were personally interested in doing so. One would then have to consider the investigation of historical truth as such as serving the church. That is where the chief difficulty of our whole theological situation lies, and it is not created by individual wills: the church rests on history, but historical reality cannot escape investigation, and this investigation of historical reality has its own laws.

The motive of having to serve the church therefore breaks down. It is, then, impossible to make the special value placed on the New Testament by the church of the past or the present, or any other account of its special historical importance, into a reason for a particular delineation of biblical theology, if this contradicts the nature of the subject-matter.[12]

Then how far beyond the New Testament should we go? A provisional answer is sufficient here; we must stop before the Apologists, because these can be recognized to have an essentially different character from all the preceding early Christian literature. But we shall come back to this point.[13]

II

The dominant method of New Testament theology may be labelled the *method of doctrinal concepts*.

It proceeds in this way. It sets out to reconstruct as exhaustively as possible the thoughts of every individual writer – i.e. his 'doctrinal concepts'. Related authors or writings are grouped together, but treated separately within the groups. In the case of

Paul, the doctrinal concepts of different periods are sometimes further distinguished. The individual parts of the whole are, so far as possible, arranged in a historical way. The individual doctrinal concept is obtained by working out what the main characteristic ideas of this writer are and arranging accordingly what has to be said on this and every other point. In each case the individual concepts of a writing are carefully, meticulously analysed and maybe defined by combining all the passages which contain a reference to them.

The merit of this method is that it has grasped the individuality of each writer much more precisely than earlier attempts had done. Against the unhistorical and superficial mixing together of every possible New Testament view it has to be thanked for taking so much trouble to make differentiations. But at the same time one can only hope that the method has just about had its day. There are several objections to it, and I must now spell them out.

First, this method does considerable violence to the New Testament writers and documents. Writings like I Peter, II Peter with Jude, and James, are simply too small to extract doctrinal positions from. Their authors were not trying to write compendiums, so it is unreasonable of us to expect from a few pages any clear idea of their world of thought. At best they give us a characteristic touch of their religious thinking, but it is equally possible that what is most characteristic of them lies in the background – if they even have any leading characteristics. Finally, it is true of even a writing like Hebrews, though less acutely, that we possess only extracts from its world of thought. That applies even to Paul and must never be forgotten. The method in question, on the other hand, simply presupposes that an author's ideas are more or less completely present in his work or snippet. At every point it claims the right to put the views and ideas it has in front of it in every combination that is logically possible, drawing conclusions where necessary, but without much attention to the question whether the author himself ever thought of such combinations and conclusions.[14]

It therefore continually falls a prey to the danger of regarding as characteristic what in fact is not. If an author chances to utter an idea which is not found elsewhere, this is made into one of his characteristics. The concepts are sharply isolated from their historical background.

The concrete aim of the piece of writing and the individual circumstances of its origin are also completely ignored. Yet the New Testament authors' pronouncements are very strongly influenced by them. It would be possible in many cases for the same writer to treat the same theme in a quite different, almost diametrically opposite way, in different circumstances, for different readers, or having a different practical slant. How then can one abstract from the particular conditions which affect a document? Consider I Peter. It talks a good deal about hope. Peter is therefore called 'the apostle of hope'.[15] Whether we are dealing with Peter or some other author, one thing is certain: the epistle has a practical paraenetic purpose, not in a general sense but with reference to a particular point – suffering, to which readers are exposed from the non-Christian world. The whole matter is then clear. It is almost inevitable that the author will point to the one thing that can lift his readers above suffering – the glorious hope of the incorruptible heritage which does not pass away, which is reserved for them in heaven and which does not have to be waited for much longer. It is quite simple to assert that absolutely every Christian at that time in the same situation would be able to speak of hope in the same way,[16] and that in another position the author of Peter would be able to write a letter in which hope was virtually never mentioned. Instead of seeing this, it is customary to credit him with a kind of special taste for *elpis* (hope), just as others preferred *pistis* (faith) or *agapē* (love). That does violence to the document.

A second crime committed by this method is indicated by the name 'doctrinal concept'. It rests on the assumption that the New Testament writings contain 'doctrine'. In a sense, of course, they do. But on closer inspection the expression is inappropriate. It is only justifiable to speak of doctrine when thoughts and ideas are developed for the sake of teaching. That happens only rarely in the New Testament. Most of it is practical advice, direction for life, instruction for the moment, the stirring up of religious feeling, talk of faith and hope for believers and hopers. Ideas, notions and credal statements play a part here, but are touched on in passing or presupposed, rather than consciously developed. Where there is deliberate development this normally happens under the control of some practical impulse or purpose. New Testament theology makes doctrine out of what in itself is not doctrine, and fails to bring out what it really is. The after-effects of the old way of doing dogmatics are clearly visible here. Every passage used to be asked what it teaches and 'by religion in general a doctrine was assumed to be meant'.[17]

This procedure has to be condemned especially because it forces the material into a mould which does not fit the historical reality and robs it of its living colours. One cannot help seeing that the intellectual level of the different authors and documents varies considerably. It is necessary to distinguish between those which are already formulated in theological terms and those which are not.[18] The difference is a relative one, but it exists and is significant. Paul is not, of course, a theologian or systematician in the modern sense. He never writes treatises with formal sections, and it is important in his case also to do justice to the movement and liveliness of a spirit which cannot be forced into the fetters of technical theological language. But his epistles do contain a strong theological element. He is a Christian thinker, and reflects like a theologian. It makes some sense in this case to work out a 'doctrinal scheme', or sketch of his theological viewpoint. The authors of writings like Acts, the Apocalypse or the Pastorals, on the other hand, are not theologians, however many elements of theology are found here. Writings like this must therefore be treated differently.

But even apart from this sort of difference between writings – what is the use of a New Testament theology that lacks any feel for the variety and special character of all the elements of what we call religion and Christianity and which were there in the primitive period, as later? What is the use of a science which has nothing to say about the significance and power of the religious tone as well as ideas and concepts, but which in the grey monotony of its 'doctrine' mixes up every real difference between the living conception and what is merely taken over and has become half meaningless, or between the formula which is shared by all and the home-grown theological idea which bears the mark of an individual, between the mere pictorial idea and the credal statement affirmed in full consciousness, between simple faith and religious speculation?

This process of flattening out often goes with making individualizing distinctions between numerous doctrinal concepts.

Thirdly, mention should be made of something which is closely related to the preceding errors.

Concepts must no doubt play a leading role in New Testament

theology. They are the easiest part of early Christian religion for us to grasp, and most of the results of the religious development are summed up in them. Our discipline,[19] however, is not concerned with every single concept, but only with the normative and dominant, and hence the characteristic and indicative ones. In both cases, again, these concepts are not to be considered wholesale and from every angle provided by the material. It is only the historically important and typical aspects which are relevant.

The trouble with the usual method is that it has a wrong idea of what is to be done with the New Testament concepts and often approaches them in an incorrect way.

As regards this incorrect approach, I do not intend to discuss how wrong-headed it is to squeeze as much conceptual capital as possible from every single phrase and every casually chosen expression used by an author. Something else needs emphasizing here. People think they have mastered concepts when they have given an exact philological account of every passage in which they occur, have shown how they are related to other ideas in the passage, and have expressed the result in a logically correct definition which covers all the aspects discovered. Take, for example, the treatment given to the Pauline concepts of *pistis* (faith) or *sarx* (flesh). This procedure would be appropriate if the author had developed his concepts systematically and applied them precisely and with full awareness of their content and range of meaning. This can reasonably be expected of an academic dogmatic theologian. To presuppose the same thing of the religious writers of the New Testament is to allow one's own dogmatic habits to saddle them with a dogmatic procedure which is alien to them. There can be no question here in the New Testament of marking off the meaning of a concept according to every possible individual passage. The sense has rather to be oriented on a few decisive conceptions of the author, so that the main lines of its meaning can be given. In the case of the concept *pistis*,[20] this will involve the characteristically Pauline view of its object and in the case of *sarx*, what he says about *hamartia* (sin), *dikaiosunē* (righteousness), *nomos* (law), *thanatos* (death), *aiōn houtos* (this age), *pneuma* (spirit), etc. Otherwise one will discover all sorts of things, even correct things, but not what is essential. Or perhaps one will find the essentials, but they will be mixed up with what is secondary.[21]

But this is just what is wrong with the false view of the task mentioned earlier. This is what I regard as most important. People feel obliged to be complete. They have to show every concept and every colouring of the main concepts (instead of leaving that to exegesis). Or they register every little deviation from the sense which another author gives them.

One might with some justification call New Testament theology the science of minutiae and insignificant nuances. That is bad. It means that the main things are obscured. It also means that New Testament theology is an arid and boring subject. It also means that the thought of the New Testament is not reaching us in the living freshness which belongs to it.

One example which will illustrate a number of earlier observations may suffice to show how New Testament concepts can even today be discussed in widely read textbooks. B. Weiss heads a paragraph in his treatment of the theology of James 'Election'.[22] One is led to assume that for James this concept has some special significance. Now the expression 'election' in fact occurs once, in the passage: 'Has not God chosen the poor of this world rich in faith and heirs of the kingdom?' (2.5). One might also bring in 1.18: 'According to his will (*boulētheis*) he has begotten us through the word of truth.' On this material Weiss builds the following definition: 'Election is that act by which God makes his own the poor in Israel who love him.' And further: 'He does this partly by begetting them through the word, the purpose of which is to produce a specific consecration to God, and partly by effecting faith. . . .' (cf. *en pistei*, 2.5). He then goes on to express, among other things, his surprise that the condition of salvation brought about by election is not designated as being God's children.

What can you say to this? The word *eklegesthai* (to choose) could not be used in a more neutral way than by James. Weiss uses it for constructing a definition. It does not occur to James to indicate that election must be thought of in connection with 'effecting faith'. Weiss provides this combination. It now looks as though the author had reflected upon how election takes place. Hence the actual definition: as though James had a sort of dogma, and a special dogma at that, that God has chosen the poor! The whole section, over three pages long, can be dismissed by the simple observation that at that time, if not every Christian, then at least all those who could speak like this of election, were angry about the pride and luxury of richness. Think what it would be like to analyse the concepts in Paul Gerhardt's hymns or Spurgeon's sermons in this way!

This false procedure is nourished in the first place by people's interest in what the biblical concepts are worth for dogmatics. With this, as already indicated, goes the unspoken assumption that these concepts must be of similar character to those of dogmatics. But other factors come in.

The custom of using texts, and that means every single word of the text, in sermons, plays a part. As a result of this, texts easily come to look different to us from the way they were meant. They have been given an aura making every phrase look significant and every word intentional and specially chosen, whether or not it was. How differently we read and respond to a story like the prodigal son from the way its first readers did! Think what the *Didache* would look like to us if it had served for centuries as texts for sermons and had had to be learned off by heart in confirmation classes!

The hair-splitting glosses of our commentaries are partly responsible, though perhaps it ought to be said that what we find in exegesis is only the same thing as turns up in biblical theology. It is far more tolerable and to some extent even necessary in exegesis.

There is, at any rate, one more thing that strongly favours the method I am attacking and will continue to give it support for a long time yet. It is particularly important to bring it up here because the critical camp itself (though not only the critical camp) has a special interest in it.

What I mean is the widespread type of literary criticism[23] which finds connections of thought and expression between the documents at every point and tries to establish literary influence and dependence in matters great and small.

This phenomenon cannot be thoroughly assessed here. It must be freely acknowledged that such criticism has done valuable work in establishing chronological relationships between particular writings, in grasping their peculiar character, in the question of authenticity and other problems of 'critical introduction'. On the other hand, it has been all too often over-hasty and too clairvoyant in assuming literary connections or in saying that a writer could not have said such and such. It is above all deeply enmeshed in the view that early Christian phrases, formulae and ideas generally travelled from one person to another by literary channels. It follows, however, from the nature of the subject-matter that then, as indeed now, there existed a rich unwritten community tradition in the wider (and again in the narrower) group, from which even literary Christians must have received by far the greater part of their ideas and religious language. This makes it quite natural that numerous similarities and points of contact exist. It is impossible to estimate the extent of literary influences correctly and to see what is possible for an individual author and what is not, unless this fact is borne in mind. It is necessary to have a definite conception of that shared material or community tradition. In other words, one must always keep in mind the course of historical development. Literary criticism, on the other hand, usually isolates the documents being compared and so sees them in a very narrow perspective. It then easily finds, of course, what it is looking for.

This results in a number of corresponding errors in New Testament theology which need to be pointed out. Quite neutral statements about faith (I am not thinking here of James) by later writers are immediately understood as an effect or an abandonment or a half-rejection of Paul's teaching about faith. Similarly, as for example in Luke, mention has only to be made of divine grace and mercy for Pauline influence to be seen. As though there was not enough about faith and grace in Jewish writings which generally sound just as Pauline! In other cases, where definite ideas are derived wholly or in part from individual passages, we are not given any intelligible account of *how* the idea came from the passage. Psychology, which should have something to say here, seems to have been totally suspended.[24]

But let that pass. Much more important than recognizing examples of careless and premature conclusions is, I think, understanding that literary criticism has been given[25] a role in New Testament theology that does not belong to it.

Even when the literary-critical observations are correct, that says nothing about their significance. It does not even say how much significance such borrowing and dependence has for an author. For example, an author who gets a lot from Paul may still be less closely related to him than another who takes over less. Nor does it say anything about its general historical significance. Only an evaluation made from the perspective of the history of religions can decide that. But it is with just this significance that

New Testament theology is concerned. Similarities and differences[26] which are unimportant for the history of ideas – and that means most of the ones which can be traced – are irrelevant to it. Minute comparison and distinguishing between different authors is just as bad as making trifling distinctions between the concepts of a single author. Here, too, what is unimportant can be disregarded. Literary criticism all too easily sidetracks one into a false attention to and overvaluation of these details.

This does not mean a treatment which skims over things and is confined to large vistas and superficial sketches. Where the matter of detail is characteristic and significant it cannot be utilized too thoroughly. The minute hair-splitting I am attacking is only the undifferentiated attention to detail which is unable to recognize, as it should, the difference between what is historically important and what is not.

One more thing. In a living religion, almost every significant change of outlook is conditioned by processes in the history of religion and only very slightly by the influence of what is read. It therefore requires in addition a proper religious explanation and not simply a literary one. Literary criticism conceals this. Quite apart from the inadequacy of many of its own explanations, by continually pointing to the dependence of later upon earlier authors, it easily gives the impression that it has made an important contribution towards the historical explanation of the conceptions and the way in which they have changed.

The method of literary comparison plays a positive and by no means insignificant part in New Testament theology. It helps decide, for example, a number of important preliminary questions about the character and relationships of the literary documents, and contributes towards weighing up the historical influence of a man like Paul. In individual cases it is able to draw attention to characteristic variations in the ideas. None of this, of course, is being questioned in any of these comments.

A *fourth* error of the method under discussion is, finally, that it sees New Testament theology as a succession of individual doctrinal concepts, or so to speak a conglomeration of clear little biblical theologies. The most that is done to relate them to each other is to place them in chronological succession, make a few comparisons and glance at what has gone before. Although people like to see the truly scientific character of the procedure here, it must be stated that, far from meeting the demands made by a really historical presentation, this is by no means adequate, and even signifies more or less the abandonment of any such project.

This point needs thorough discussion to itself, since it is of decisive importance. But first it may be worth going back over what has been said so far.

Consider the following: suppose that we are living two thousand years from now and are interested in the social democratic movement in our nineteenth century. Most of the literature of social democracy is lost, but we do still have a reasonable number of sources – two popular biographies of Lassalle, an academic treatise of Marx, a few letters of Lassalle, Engels and one or two unknown workers active as agitators; then a few pamphlets two or three pages long and finally a socialist inflammatory writing describing the socialist picture of heaven upon earth, – i.e. a collection of literature something like the New Testament. Now suppose we want to use these documents to get a picture of the outlook, ideas and earliest development of social democracy. We proceed as follows: we establish the order in which they were written. We then treat each one on its own. Marx and Lassalle rank alongside all the rest, only are dealt with more fully. The same procedure is adopted in each case. We naturally ask what Marx understands by labour, production, surplus value, etc. But we also ask what the pamphlets and letters mean by the concepts bourgeoisie, proletariat, by the idea of its 'disinheritance', and by the variation in the concepts of labour or co-operative. Perhaps we manage to establish that in one of the papers the concept of ownership means just the same as that of property, and that some of Lassalle's ideas and phrases can no doubt be found in the inflammatory writing, and also – remarkably enough – traces of Darwin's influence, and a little Nietzsche. There are four occurrences of 'struggle for existence', two of 'adaptation', and one of 'master morality'. Another author has a special preference for the idea of agitation – so he is clearly 'the socialist of agitation'. In this way we carefully catalogue the ideas of each writing, stolidly piling one investigation upon another, arranging it all attractively according to the main points of view. Then we call the whole thing 'The Ideas of Social Democracy in its Period of Origin'.

Now is that a caricature? Opinions may differ. It is enough to concede that the method of doctrinal concepts *provokes* caricature.

I have spoken of the 'dominant' method. That needs some explanation. I wanted to describe a kind of average specimen of this method such as we have in B. Weiss's textbook.[27] But the method cannot in this form be called dominant now. Many of its peculiarities have been criticized for a long time.[28] There are monographs on biblical theology which are quite free of its aberrations. The description I have given would certainly not fit a presentation like that of Baur's posthumously published *Lectures on New Testament Theology*. Yet certain of the basic characteristics and errors of the method reach far into the list of those works which, because they take quite seriously the separation between dogmatics and biblical theology, are most free from its crimes.

It is natural to think here of H. J. Holtzmann's recently completed two-volume textbook. The announcement of this work can be thankfully welcomed. Until now learners have had to be directed to the widely-used work of Weiss and the more recent one by Beyschlag. One cannot withhold praise for the careful and thorough work of Weiss, and we can gladly acknowledge that it contains a good deal that is correct and instructive on particular issues. But – if the comment is still necessary – it must be said quite plainly that no one can learn 'New Testament theology' from it. A New Testament theology must show us the special character of early Christian ideas and perceptions, sharply profiled, and help us to understand them historically. The textbook of Weiss blurs what is characteristic and special at almost every point, so that it is impossible to recognize the decisive issues. Individual chapters are linked in purely external fashion, and no real connections are made. The New Testament conceptions are put into a number of separate baskets, and, not to mention the critical basis and the scholastic pedantry of the presentation – what has happened to the fresh air of real life?[29] The supple, fresh and warmly written book of Beyschlag is rid of some of the ballast – in a biblical theology to have a lot of exegetical detail is ballast – and moves altogether more freely than that of Weiss. But in other respects it is inferior to Weiss, and equally fails to give a true reproduction of early Christian religion and theology. The author brings far too many of his own ideas into the New Testament. He modernizes,[30] and smooths things over, too often passing by the most important historical problems with complacent ease.

In contrast to these books, Holtzmann's work is without doubt a very welcome enrichment of the literature. As regards historical sense, illumination from many sides of the wider and the immediate historical context, sharp and adequate grasp of the imagination and thought peculiar to early Christianity, sensitivity for the difference between teaching and edification, between the religious and the theological – in all this Holtzmann's work is superior to the other two at almost every point.

Nevertheless, I cannot see in it an ideal New Testament theology. Leaving aside results which seem to me open to criticism, and also questions of form – for example, I consider the presentation determined far too much by its attention to all sorts of extraneous views – my reservations are largely on the lines of these methodological considerations. I cannot allow that Holtzmann has really broken sufficiently with the method of doctrinal concepts and posed the task of New Testament theology correctly. In some parts of the work the characteristics of the literary-critical approach as described above are clearly evident.[31] Corresponding to the excess of literary criticism is a shortage of really historical grasp and reflection that is truly history of *religion*.[32] It has to be emphasized here that Holtzmann, too, has treated every single writer separately.[33] This brings us back to the theme already posed.

III

Holtzmann gives New Testament theology the task of setting out in a scientific way the religious and ethical content of the canonical writings of the New Testament, or reconstructing scientifically the religious and ethical world of thought which can be known from them.[34] Against this, I would say that the discipline has to lay out the history of early Christian religion and theology. That might sound virtually identical,[35] apart from the question whether one may go beyond the limits of the New Testament. In fact, there is a much bigger difference, in that one approach looks closely at the content of *writings* whereas the other simply considers the *subject-matter*. If we take them to mean the same thing, this only shows how heavily our interest in the history of literature outweighs our interest in history.[36]

What are we really looking for? In the last resort, we at least want to know *what was believed, thought, taught, hoped, required and striven for* in the earliest period of Christianity; not what certain writings say about faith, doctrine, hope, etc. The two would be identical only if spelling out the content of writings or the views of writers were the only (or at least the best) way of making plain the history of faith and doctrine itself. Although that seems clearly to be the case, the case is certainly not so clear. Who will say that the task of a history of doctrine or one of its sections is to lay out 'the content of the relevant literature'?

A section of the history of philosophy can be treated by successively developing the individual systems of each philosopher one after another – though this, of course, is not the only possible way of doing it. The reason is that the emergence of independent thinkers and the formation of complete systems can, in fact, be seen as the main content of this history. A history of early Christian faith and theology cannot proceed in this way, for the following reason. Here, with a few exceptions, *the writers' personalities and the writings as such are not important, but very subsidiary matters.*

When does an individual writer's point of view justify inclusion in an account of the early Christian development? Clearly, when he and his ideas have had an epoch-making influence on the church. Then secondly, when he proves to have been a spiritually and intellectually outstanding personality capable of producing an overwhelmingly characteristic and independent view of faith, even though not so influential. Or, perhaps, also if without being really significant, he nevertheless had a very distinct character, one that is sufficiently distinctive to be grasped historically not simply through individual features but as a whole. This is the least that is necessary.

Now let us look at some early Christian literature.

Take I Peter, the Lucan writings, Mark and Matthew so far as they do not merely codify the tradition, I Clement, James, the Didache, the Pastoral Epistles, II Peter and Jude, the Epistle of Polycarp and the Shepherd of Hermas. We know nothing, or virtually nothing, about the authors of these writings. There may and will have been amongst them personalities of some significance in their own narrow circles, as well as perhaps others about whom one cannot even say that. None of these writings shows signs of an individual mind that, even though we could not put a name to it, we could clearly regard as epoch-making or even moderately outstanding in the history of religions. None of them advances with one-sided power so much as a single conception that was significant for the whole development in a way that makes us say: the idea has become normative or established through this writing, or has even been created by it. In fact all these documents, though containing definite differences in content and situation, are so lacking in distinctiveness that what characteristic features they do have are submerged under the views that are held more widely or by the whole church. However valuable they may be for edification, and though they may be treasured as sources, a historical judgment must say that they contain simply average Christianity.

This means that these writings and their authors are of no interest to New Testament theology, just as the history of doctrine is not obliged to evaluate every episcopal writing that contains nothing except other people's ideas or the general view. Setting out the intellectual content of the Pastoral Epistles, etc., is therefore *only preliminary work for New Testament theology.* It is the *gathering of raw material,* not in itself the real historical fashioning of it.

Ephesians, which I cannot regard as Pauline, contains more characteristic features than the writings already mentioned. It contains more speculation, but basically it still belongs with them. It does not represent an independent and individual conception in any higher sense.

The Apocalypse, Hebrews and Barnabas look rather different.

It is true that the Apocalypse is a unique case within the New Testament. However, on a historical valuation, it is only one specimen of a widespread literary type. Further, this type does not so much create as draw upon the tradition and develop it in particulars.[37] But quite apart from this, and ignoring the fact that the book can hardly be considered a literary unity, one cannot see in it a total religious conception of its own. The Apocalypse is only concerned with one side of the Christian outlook, although a very important one. Its material will be significant for the chapter on the future expectation, but the author with his personal characteristics is not really of interest to New Testament theology.

The author of Hebrews was without any doubt a very well educated Christian. One can even call him a theologian. The average Christian could not have written an epistle like this. It required artistry, the higher artistry of scriptural interpretation and application. There is something quite deliberate and systematic about the way he can parallel the old covenant with the new. There are also other theological elements. Yet despite all this, one cannot demand for this epistle, either, that its contents be treated separately and systematically. Its proper theme – the glory of the new covenant in contrast to the old – is a very limited one, being confined to *one* single theme. This theme, moreover, is more a matter of scholarship and theory than of the real life of religion. Although from quite early on the epistle was treated with great respect just because of its artistry and gnosis, the subject-matter itself made it impossible for these reflections to exercise any great influence upon the general theological and religious tone of the period. Besides, despite interesting details, it is not possible to get from it a really characteristic view of the whole of Christianity as a religion and doctrine. Its value for the history of religion is to be found in the significant material that it provides for early Christian judgment on Old Testament religion, the method of scriptural interpretation, the influence of Alexandrianism, and also the development of christology.

The same sort of thing has to be said about the Epistle of Barnabas, as it is called.

There are not many solid entities left. There is no question that the preaching of Jesus and also Paul's Christianity and theology require independent treatment which is as penetrating as possible. But there is some point in explicitly discussing the situation with regard to the Gospel of John, and the Johannine Epistles which on any showing belong closely with it.

The presupposition behind the undertaking to present a 'Johannine theology' is, of course, that the gospel is not a historical writing in the usual sense, but that the author's theology is put forward through his account of the history. I consider it most appropriate to call it a doctrinal writing, and in fact a polemico-apologetic doctrinal writing, in the form of a gospel. In my view we do not know who the author was, though he was without any doubt a significant personage.

There is little enough that can be said about the direct historical effect of his work. It is still very much a question whether the related ideas which are found in the Apostolic Fathers indicate the influence of the gospel or are shared traditions to which the gospel also had access. Even if they were derived from the gospel, they would not prove much. Otherwise, apart from the Montanist movement, one can assume that the gospel had some effect without being able to show what it was. But it is all the more certain that the Johannine writings are uncommonly clearly distinguished from what remains of early Christian literature as a whole by their special character, their peculiar religious language and their world-view. So there seems no doubt that there is an independent Johannine theology. In fact, however, this is only where questions begin to arise.

Just because the gospel's outlook is not found in the antecedent literature, does this mean that it is the author's own creation? Supposing the Christian atmosphere that he breathed, the area unknown to us which produced the gospel in so remarkable a way, was already full of the elements of Christian speech that it used, namely 'Johannine' images and ideas? I am here touching on a problem which must be felt, even if it cannot be solved. We come close to the problem which is ultimately decisive for the historical understanding of the gospel. This is the question of the origin and emergence of the Johannine world of thought.[38] The two particulars must, of course, be distinguished. In one case we try to determine which alien soil has produced the ideas that cannot be understood from early Christian (including Pauline) premises, but require explanation. That is, we seek the religious significance in which ideas like Logos are taken over for Christianity. The question whether the author of the gospel or other Christians before him were the first to use this material is irrelevant here. In the other case, as here, what we ask is just that: whether in material we are accustomed to call peculiarly Johannine, the evangelist already had Christian predecessors or not. It is here, of course, very important whether or not one has to assume alien soil.

It would not be difficult to show that by no means all of what is commonly taken to be an author's own work is in fact his individual creation. I am thinking, for example, of the highly characteristic usage of the concepts of light and darkness, death and life, etc. It is compatible with having a strong sense for original personalities to assert nevertheless that such a distinctive type of religious language is not created by a single individual. What is original in original minds is generally found less in the shape of the conceptual material than in what they make out of this material. What is the position with christology, the really central point of this theology? Was the evangelist the first to formulate in the way that he does, for example, the conception of Christ as the bringer of truth and the revealer of the inaccessible God, or were there others before him and contemporaneous with him who did the same? We can leave the answer undecided. It has only to be emphasized that it is no easy matter to separate what in the gospel has been inherited and what is the evangelist's own.

However, this is not to cast serious doubt upon the justification for treating Johannine theology separately. Such treatment has, indeed, to be insisted upon. Even if the author puts forward much that is not his alone, his outstanding significance is in no way destroyed. And either way his was not so rich and creative a spirit as Paul's. Nevertheless, he was the first to forge also what he took over into this impressive unity and to shape it in his own way. But even the way in which he has set down his teachings in a historical picture of Jesus, and the many stereotyped traits and the frequent mannerisms which can only be understood as coming from the individuality of the narrator, show that his own personal participation in his theology must have been considerable. So indeed does the allusion contained in the gospel itself to the newness of its ideas.[39] But even if this were not the case, the author would, as the typical representative of a group with which he shared this particular outlook, be no less certain of a special evaluation in the history.

The same treatment is due, though in another way and on other grounds, to Ignatius. Or at least, he is more deserving of this than any of the authors mentioned above. It is not that he has had an unusually strong effect or developed a coherent theological system. But he typifies, and for us in many ways especially clearly embodies, personal Christianity at the beginning of the second century. It is perhaps doubtful whether it would be any use producing a 'theology of Ignatius', exhaustive in all particulars. But something like a character-portrait of how he thought, bringing out the characteristic traits, is needed.

To return to the starting point of this survey. If it is not possible to sketch a doctrinal system for Ephesians, James, Hebrews, the Apocalypse, etc., nor to give an exhaustive account of their ideas, still they do all come into consideration simply as witnesses for ideas, moods and interests more or less generally widespread, though here and there bearing marks of individuality. Their *positive significance* for the discipline is that they provide *the material with the help of which it is possible to conceive the physiognomy and clarify the historical development of the earliest Christianity which lies behind them.*

The norms governing the presentation are therefore not the writings but the decisive ideas, problems and spiritual or intellectual phenomena.[40] The significance of the few creative or outstanding personalities must, however, be preserved by a special account of their individual conceptions. Because if these also were treated simply as 'material', that would of course be as inappropriate as taking historically unimportant authors individually.[41] History of doctrine also combines the two points of view, the personal and the material.

It is not merely the unimportance of most of the writers which compels us to give up analysing a mass of doctrinal concepts and to abandon the individualizing treatment guided by the literature. We come to the same conclusion when we proceed from the ideas and conceptions themselves, and this is even more important.

One might suppose that it is the task of New Testament theology to depict, for example, early Christian eschatology as clearly as possible. The main lines of it have to be distinguished from individual ideas, and whatever changes can be observed have to be indicated. Can this task really be done adequately by registering the general and particular eschatological statements of every document and establishing their relationship to the rest of what is in the document? The subject-matter, rather, urgently demands that all the material should be considered together. It is quite misguided to treat individually every statement about baptism, when what is wanted above all is to dig out the historically normative views about it – how it was regarded, and an account of possible developments. What is the use of being told that in one place sin is spoken of thus, and elsewhere rather differently, if we never learn what role the concept of sin as a whole played in the early Christian understanding of salvation and of Christian life? The same question could be asked of every chapter and sub-section. Our presupposition, again in opposition to the dominant method, is here, too, that the type is far more important than the variant and that the individual conceptions and interpretations are at most points quite insignificant in comparison with the general, widespread views that influence the individual cases. This presupposition is confirmed in every concrete instance. The individual's own contribution is trifling in notions like eschatology, or angels, or in the ethical field. It is generally quite irrelevant *who* introduces a particular idea. It does not follow that the only person who hands it on, himself produced it. But even if he did actually produce it, that would not be important. The scattered material belongs together by its very nature, and if what belongs together is torn asunder into little pieces, the chance of getting an adequate impression of what is being dealt with is lost.

Splitting things up in this way also makes it more difficult to understand each individual part. A single writing contains insufficient criteria for deciding what is significant and what secondary.[42] When we place it in its proper context, the whole world of related ideas, it is easy to estimate its value and show where it belongs. This is the only way that some ideas can be adequately clarified.

From the other side, even correct observations relating to an individual writing do not in themselves amount to much. They only become truly instructive when they are made to throw light on the whole and so clarify the historical development. If in studying I Peter we analyse correctly the conceptions of Christ's death, or the ideas of the community as the true Israel, and Christians as aliens and sojourners[43] on earth, in themselves these are only isolated notices. But even the sorts of observations which can be made about allegory in Hebrews and the high value set on poverty and charity in Luke can only be properly assessed when used in a wider context.

Here, as before in some of our earlier observations, the monograph literature has to be included in our deliberations. It is not by chance that when dealt with in a monograph, a writer's conceptions are often not really made historically intelligible or are even wrongly understood. Much of it remains merely dead material, a collection of correct individual observations.[44] Most dangerous of all is a monograph on simply a single concept of an individual writer.

A further argument must be levelled against separating doctrinal concepts. A New Testament theology should try to make clear so far as is possible the development and developments. There is not, generally speaking, a very lively feeling for this task at present, and that is quite comprehensible, given the usual way of treating it. But setting that aside, let us now proceed on the assumption that the task itself is more or less generally recognized.

The most important question is, of course, the order and grouping in which the different authors are to be placed. Only someone who has no interest in historical illumination at all will see this as merely a question of form. In fact, the overall impression depends upon the course the development takes. A mere succession of different doctrinal concepts could only give a very crude idea of the development. When that is sensed, one will want to discuss the total development separately to clarify it. Further, a number of individual historical threads will be traced which take us well beyond the basic pattern and at the same time make this more fully intelligible and protect it against being wrongly interpreted. In this way, too, the basic pattern will determine, or at least in large measure determine, the impression one gets from the development when the account is taken at all seriously from this point of view.

Here again, the method of doctrinal concepts fails to achieve an adequate account of the development. It is bound to fail, today at any rate. In his own way Baur in his day succeeded in treating everything in the form of doctrinal concepts, and from his standpoint this was a meaningful procedure. For in Baur's account of the history, one well-known contrast was absolutely decisive. The different writings were all seen as witnesses to this and were characterized above all by their relationship to it. This meant that the heart of the real historical development in fact coincided with his construction of how the individual writings followed one another. Of course – if in fact this order of the writings was a true reflection of the development. But Baur's edifice was an untenable construction. However, his followers and opponents do not possess this sort of total conception of the development as hinging on *one* main point. This is no longer possible. That means that a particular arrangement of the literature can give only very incomplete expression to the character and content of the development. The successive writings or groups of writings do not strictly correspond to so many characteristic moments of the development. They do not express its really significant moments exhaustively or sharply. Yet they give the impression of doing so. Or the intention of giving a historical presentation is at certain points suspended, and in the middle of a generally developmental account things are inserted which are only externally related to it.[45] The resulting impressions are therefore only partly right, and are partly wrong or unclear. Furthermore, so that the less significant writings are not just put one after another, they tend to be given historical labels which are only half appropriate.

These observations can even to some extent be applied to Holtzmann's presentation, though he takes far more account of the developmental point of view than the others. His book contains the following main divisions: I 'Jesus and the Evangelists' (Acts and the Apocalypse are also discussed here along with the evangelists); II 'Paulinism'; III 'The Deutero-Paulines' (i.e. Ephesians, and also perhaps Colossians, the Pastoral Epistles, Hebrews and the Catholic Epistles, viz. I Peter, Jude, II Peter, James); IV 'Johannine Theology'. Holtzmann himself mentions certain difficulties about his arrangement.[46] These are directly reflected in his scheme. The evangelists should come not before but after Paul, if their individual viewpoints are being considered. The same might be said of the Apocalypse. The Catholic Epistles (apart from I Peter) are considered mainly in negative terms if they are labelled as Deutero-Pauline. I Peter would follow Ephesians better than the Pastorals.[47] As regards the post-Pauline writings as a whole, Holtzmann does not mean that every writing represents a further stage or little step on the way. Otherwise he would probably have put the Pastorals, for example, nearer to John. Nevertheless, a reader involuntarily gets some picture of a development from this presentation. The general impression is that this development from Paul onwards is characterized by the after-effects of Paul, still strong at first, but then significantly diminishing, and that it comes to an end in Johannine theology. No doubt this gives a recognizable historical line. But one can still ask: Is it enough? Did Paul's heritage provide the essential nourishment for the whole of Christianity between Paul and John? Does not this straight line oversimplify the development? Is not the Johannine view presented too one-sidedly as the peak of a development? Holtzmann can, of course, point out that he has elsewhere given important supplementary information. In particular, he has characterized the change which took place after Paul much more clearly and positively. In my view, however, the characteristics of the individual writings do not make these remarks any clearer, and have prevented Holtzmann from giving us more; he could have investigated more deliberately the development of each main conception.

Different objections will be raised against the thesis advanced here. It will be stressed from the practical, ecclesiastical side that independent and exhaustive treatment of each New Testament writing corresponds to an interest which cannot be given up. I can only repeat: scientific work cannot be tied too closely to practical needs. If a scientific task or method really grows out of the subject-matter, it cannot be refused for the sake of some practical interest, however honourable, without ceasing to be science.

But is it not also a scientific concern carefully to bring out the intellectual content of each individual writing? Is not a knowledge of their world of ideas necessary for the interpretation of each particular part? Is there not a good deal in the conceptual material, in the terminology and religious language, in characteristic combinations of ideas, which history can and may have to ignore, but which is significant for the character of the piece of writing?[48] Without doubt. But it does not follow from this that our view of the task is incorrect, or that there are several equally possible and equally necessary methods of doing it. The place for surveying the content of individual documents and indicating their special features and discussing disputed questions is, apart from in monographs, simply in commentaries; partly, too, in 'Introductions to the New Testament'. Literary relationships which are important for understanding the documents will be investigated more closely here, as circumstances allow. The results of all this will be of use to New Testament theology.

Another objection to the procedure recommended here will be that it irons out the clearly visible differences and variety of types. It will only lead to an average cross-section which provides a picture that never actually existed. But why should anyone be afraid of this false levelling out? What is truly shared will have to be done justice to just as much as what is individual but historically important. Both must be placed into a right relationship with each other. Individual writings, too, will have to be carefully considered, if they are really typical in some special way. For example, when early Christian moralism is under discussion, James and I Clement will have to be talked about. Whole trains of thought, even, for example like that of Hebrews, will on occasion have to be spelled out if they happen to illustrate a particular theme. It may be that what is really characteristic about the individual writings comes out no less sharply than it did in the individualizing method.

The closer relationships existing between individual writings will also then emerge.

Or are we to abandon this method of doing New Testament theology because the task is so difficult? To work through a wide range of scattered material, make connections and bring order out of it so that a luminous picture emerges is, in fact, a task in comparison with which simply reproducing the content of writings is a very straightforward matter. Unfortunately, however, history does not ask us when it sets its tasks whether they are burdensome for us or not. But the task cannot be insoluble. Are not the materials out of which the history of doctrine gets its pictures also often widely spread out?

Just as, of course, many issues are still open, so too a number of individual problems have not yet found a solution which is generally accepted, even amongst those interested in historical work. But that cannot be a reason for postponing this necessary change of activity until a more favourable time. Questions that are unsettled today will still be largely matters of debate in fifty years' time. It will also perhaps be advantageous to take a new look at some issues from a different perspective.

IV

Giving up treating individual writings independently means laying the axe to the root of the tree, or more correctly, blocking up at least *one* main source of the other errors of the usual method. The possibility of inadequate or misguided literary comparisons is still not excluded. But when every question is considered in the light of a wide range of material, it will, just because of this material, be easier to guard oneself against overhasty and narrow conclusions. One will be far less inclined to place too much weight upon the literary relationships. It will also be possible to assess correctly what is common property and what is the author's individual contribution. In many cases what is important will automatically separate itself off from what is unimportant, and so one will be free from the curse of trying to include everything. What has gone before is sufficient to exclude the misunderstanding that all that is necessary is to examine the individual writers, and merely gather together their statements, compute them, laboriously arrange and link them up.

It has not, however, yet been said clearly enough what our procedure involves in positive terms, and what its guidelines are to be. That can only be shown exhaustively, if at all, by going more deeply than is possible here into the material itself or into individual areas. I must confine myself to a few aphorisms on what is especially important. This is partly a matter of drawing simple conclusions from what has already been said.

One of the advantages of the historical over the literary method is its fruitfulness. This results from the undreamed-of richness of large and small questions which an overall view of the related material yields. It is, of course, assumed here that our procedure is always both genetic and comparative. We are at every point interested in distances, connections and effects. Where does this come from? How did that happen? What conditioned it? These are the questions we ask. Every historical datum is only made comprehensible so far as we are able to set it in the context out of which it has grown.

So far as we can, we shall try to get beyond the weak and imprecise judgments which, unless I am mistaken, we meet all too often these days in the discussion of biblical theology, even where historical links are taken seriously. We read that a conception 'recalls' another one, is 'related' to it, contains the 'beginnings' of it, 'links' on to it, marks an 'advance' on it or an 'intensification' of it. All this gives no clear picture of how the historical relationship is to be conceived. It only evokes an indefinite impression of general similarity, and does not clarify whether the conceptions really were stages in the strict historical sense or only seem to us to be stages from some particular standpoint. There is a very big difference, and it must be strictly observed. It is easy to construct a straight line out of a number of conceptions using the logical criterion of greater or less similarity. Whether the logical arrangement reproduces the historical actuality remains a question.[49] These indefinite remarks are admittedly necessary on occasion, but we must be perfectly clear how much they are worth.

How something emerges is always to be understood as a psychological–historical question, not merely a literary one. Literary information does not generally tell us much. Equally, we try to argue not simply from individual passages, but also on a basis of the development. Every significant idea, every influential concept, every important conception is understood as a living plant out of religious history. It has grown according to the same inner laws which today and always govern the emergence of ideas, concepts and conceptions.

In a sense our procedure is always constructive; i.e., we draw conclusions which extend as well as connect what the documents say. People's reserve about doing this is exaggerated. It only appears to be more subjective and open to error than the usual method. The danger of it lies in seeing connections which do not exist and making mistakes in one's derivations. That is no worse than taking a stand on the letter and evaluating it wrongly or making mistakes in throwing historical light on it. Besides, if we were not so used to particular ways of questioning and answers by which the matter is partly concealed from us, we would probably be more aware of how much construction is involved even today in answering 'ultimate' questions. Constructions are not the same as vague suppositions. A justified and necessary construction has firm bases which can be spelled out.

In trying to explain things we do, of course, all too often run up against gaps, so that our whole endeavour can be seen as one large fragment. But spotting gaps means spotting problems, and clear recognition of a problem is always a positive gain for historical understanding. It therefore makes sense to set out to make clear the gaps in our knowledge.[50] If we do not do this, some striking and astonishing phenomenon will not be understood and evaluated as such. Consider the concept of the kingdom of God. Let us take it as proven that Jesus spoke of a present and worldly development of the kingdom and thought of it as an ethical community growing on earth.[51] The Jewish eschatological concept of the kingdom would then have been not merely slanted gently but essentially changed. Precisely for this reason, such a reconstruction could not have taken place unnoticed. It must have been conscious and it must also, without doubt, have struck the disciples as an innovation. But in that case it is a quite remarkable fact that just this, Jesus' characteristic view, is what was lost in the following period from Paul onwards. Their own concept of the kingdom stands more in line with that of late Judaism, even though it is not quite identical with it. An explanation must be given, or else the puzzle itself must be posed as sharply as possible.[52] Otherwise an important fact – for it would be not merely remarkable, but important – will not be clearly perceived.

It is erroneous 'to think one-sidedly of the ideas contained in the New Testament and the earliest Christian literature as the spontaneous production of a Christianity considered in isolation from its surroundings'.[53] We will therefore, of course, have to pay attention to the wider religious context. This is a theme of its own which can only be touched upon here. Leaving aside individual cases, one must at any rate try to make clear how much Judaism there was in primitive Christianity, the significance of the incorporation of an Alexandrian element, what sort of Hellenic and also what sort of oriental influences played a role.

I have no fear that in this kind of explanation and historical analysis the significance of *personalities* such as, for example, Paul's, is bound to be misunderstood. Why should one not be able to recognize that a person's individuality and work itself explains much that is otherwise inexplicable? I believe that in the appropriate place the explanatory method will show us the significance of personality in the clearest manner imaginable. Now, of course, we stop making an individual responsible for an idea merely because the earliest evidence happens to occur in his work. And we give up wanting to understand on a basis of personality what cannot be understood in this way. The contrasts which dominate Johannine theology – God and world, light and darkness, life and death, truth and lie[54] – are often derived from the evangelist's own ethical energy and abruptness.[55] But the psychological approach must first show how personal abruptness can lead one to think continually in terms of these contrasts. Concrete conceptions are never made intelligible by peculiarities of personality, however marked, or at least never by these alone. There must be a reason why the peculiarities found expression in these particular conceptions.

It is frequently recognized that our literary material is fragmentary.[56] Just how fragmentary, is seldom clearly estimated. How much is there just by chance! How many ideas, speculations, theories and arguments which must have been quite important, have to be thought of as lying between and behind the documents! But in any case, what matters is not just recognizing the situation, but finding a method which copes with it. That means that we can no longer pose questions simply in the light of the literary material. We must pose them as far as possible in view of the subject-matter, the historical situation. That would certainly be a quite significant advance, and at the same time, of course, a corrective against false or one-sided judgments about the literature.

The New Testament speaks only sporadically about monotheism. To judge from the documents, it is hardly necessary for us to discuss the point. Yet historical reflection compels us to accept that the material is deceptive here. It is quite clear that of all that their new religion brought to the Gentiles who came to Christianity, what they valued about it especially included belief in the one Lord and Creator of the world. This must have seemed to them the main contrast to their earlier belief and a liberation from the spectre of superstition. It would be stupid of New Testament theology to ignore this fact or minimize its significance on the grounds that discussion of monotheism is only found in the literature from about the time of Justin. Again, the tradition gives us no information whatsoever about how the Old Testament became the Christians' holy book. That took place quite unnoticed as the church itself took shape. Even the formation of the church, the emergence of a consciousness of being the human fellowship specifically chosen and protected by God, took place without anybody documenting it. Again unnoticed, the Old Testament became the religious book of the converted Gentiles. Can nothing be said about all these matters? Must not their fundamental significance be spelled out? We have no idea on the basis of the New Testament alone what miracles and miracle-stories meant for people's religious feeling and practice.[57] We know even less about how Gentiles who became Christians understood baptism and Lord's supper in their own terms, how they understood Christ as Son of God, what the title Messiah meant to them and what it did not, or their attitude to the Jewish–Christian belief in demons. Can a history of the religion simply by-pass these matters on the grounds that we do not know much about them?

Another necessary principle is that we cannot be satisfied with establishing positive facts. It is often very important to be aware of and to evaluate what one might call *negative* facts. It must be made clear which special virtues early Christianity either created or especially valued or cultivated. But it is almost equally important to know which ones it did not foster. It is impossible here, as in any other living formation, to talk of abstract uniformity. But instead of thinking merely about individual facts, we should also consider the general direction taken by a total development. Could we not, on the basis of the premises we possess, see the development quite differently, and think of other ideas and phenomena? What questions have *not* been asked? Which parts of the world of ideas have not been completed? By asking these questions we get a clearer picture of the real development with its characteristic features. We see the frame which supports an entire development, and that is more important than the individual facts within the framework.

The usual discussions of biblical theology generally give the impression that the early Christian outlook was produced purely by the power of thought, as though the world of ideas hovered above external history as a world of its own. We must break with this view. The early Christian world of ideas is very strongly conditioned by external history, and this must be made quite clear.

Paul would never have formed his characteristic doctrine of justification by faith had he not taken in hand the task of converting Gentiles. The doctrine had a practical origin and practical purpose. It was not the other way round, as though the praxis were developed from a doctrine which had been created by religious thought and experience. Paul's contrast between man's deeds and merit and God's grace could perhaps be explained by his reflection upon his experiences with the law as a Pharisee, when he tried in vain to satisfy its demands. Or it could be explained by his experience of conversion. But his making faith into the opposite of the works of the law could never be explained in this way. The explanation for this must be that it was a question of the conditions under which Gentiles could be accepted into the Christian community. Paul saw the necessity of denying that the Jewish ritual law – originally only this, and not the 'commandments of God' were at stake – was obligatory for Gentiles. One would expect[58] that in forming his theory he would have set against the works of the law not only faith but also love and other virtues, or more generally the keeping of moral laws which are not to be broken. However, he could in fact find a positive condition for justification only in what made not only Gentiles but also *equally Jews* into Christians, something absolutely new, which distinguished the convert equally from Jews and Gentiles; and that was exclusively faith in the Christ.[59]

A different example for the significance of the 'external history' is provided by the persecutions. The outbreak of persecution is an important piece of data for biblical theology, because conceptions and feelings were powerfully influenced by it. Hope flares up with passion, enthusiasm is awakened, *hypomonē* (endurance) becomes a supreme virtue. Ethical views and ideals are in general conditioned at the core by the situation. That *philoxenia* (hospitality) was at that time one of the cardinal virtues can be explained by the situation of travelling Christians and the significance which attached to travelling and foot-slogging. Love of the brethren meant more than love of one's neighbour, because it was a matter of a small exclusive fellowship or community.[60] An essential factor in the striving for *enkrateia* (self control) and *hagneia* (purity) is that the community was surrounded by a lax and licentious world. Its position in the world is also responsible for its sense of honour, which stresses that the Lord's name must not be slandered on account of the sin of Christians.

All these observations are only meant, as I have said, as illustrations to show what is involved when we insist upon a really historical procedure, at the same time both more rigorous and more free, in place of a mainly literary one. As regards the presentation itself, it is enough to stress one thing here: we must go for the dominant features. It must, for example, come over very clearly that the earliest Christianity lived from its belief that it stood in the eschatological era, and that it saw the proof of this in its possession of the Spirit.

My account is still in need of considerable expansion. It would be quite incomplete if I did not try to develop the shape of our discipline's task through a positive description based on *the actual material*. As a preliminary, I want to glance back again at an earlier theme.

Only now can we see clearly the full significance of the question whether the discipline must attend to the New Testament alone or whether it must also include literature from farther afield.

There is no doubt that the absolute necessity of going beyond the limits of the New Testament only becomes clear from our conception of the task. If I ask what was the content and state of development of Christian belief and thought at a particular point in time, it is clear that all the material from this period is relevant to resolving the task.[61] It is therefore really senseless here to propose

some external division between writings that are essentially related.[62] This is a simple consequence for anyone who approves of
my understanding of the task.

At the same time, it now becomes clear that bringing in material
from outside the New Testament contributes significantly to the
subject-matter itself. It would perhaps always make a noteworthy,
and for certain individual questions not unimportant difference,
whether or not I add some more to the total number of doctrinal
concepts in the New Testament. But in the end this difference will
not really go deep. If, on the other hand, the writings merely provide the materials which we use in constructing the history, then
it is bound to be an extremely significant question whether there
are more materials. The more plentiful they are, the better I can
compare, the more lines I can draw, the more questions I become
aware of, and the more certain I am of finding out what is essential.

The question of the real limits of the discipline can now be taken
up afresh.

No kind of limitation used by the history of early Christian
literature, commonly called 'New Testament Introduction', can be
of any importance here. Whether a piece of writing is in the strict
sense literature or not, or to which of the literary forms it belongs,
is as irrelevant for biblical theology as it is important for literary
history. That is, the question of delimitation means something
different in both cases.

But it is also immediately apparent that the answer: 'The
Apostolic Fathers belong to the material of the discipline, but the
Apologists do not',[63] is insufficient. Nor is it, of course, improved
when we add to the 'Apostolic Fathers' other items like, for
example, the *Kerygma Petrou* (The Proclamation of Peter) or the
fragments of the older apocryphal gospels. On the contrary, it is
clear that a *fixed literary boundary* cannot be given. Not only what
comes into the period of time under consideration belongs to the
subject, but also what does not. This, too, is certainly instructive,
though only indirectly. We are to welcome anything that Justin
says which clarifies the earlier history because we want to know
about that history. In some individual questions the thread of the
development would be cut at the wrong point and the natural
connection of things ignored if we were not resolved to go beyond
the Apostolic Fathers where circumstances demand it. What Justin
gives us about argument from prophecy is directly continuous with

what earlier writers say. Are we not to be allowed to consider his evidence? On the question of the condemnation of Judaism or the Old Testament, should not Marcion and the Gnostics be considered? Is Marcion irrelevant when asking what effect Paul had? When, on the other hand, one of the Apostolic Fathers touches on a theme which only has a real history later on, then it is not significant for the earlier period and does not have to be considered just because it turns up in Hermas or the like.

Furthermore, no exact date can be given as the boundary, such as AD 120, 130 or 150. These are far too detailed specifications, and can hardly be matched with a clear idea of definite differences. It can only be said that the border is where new movements in the church begin, new ideas gain momentum and the old has run its course. This moment coincides in the literature *approximately* with the transition from the Apostolic Fathers to the Apologists. We must not, of course, think that at a stroke people like Clement, the author of the Pastoral Epistles, Ignatius and Polycarp cease to exist and make room for men like Justin and Aristides. Thoughts like those of Justin and Aristides will probably have been in circulation long before. Here, too, the literature which has survived will give a misleading impression about how things really were, and that should not be underestimated. One must certainly not forget that Justin wrote not for Christians but for non-Christians. Nevertheless, the emergence of the Apologists with their Hellenistic education is the sign of a new era. Other things more or less coincide with this: the emergence of the main Gnostic schools and the corresponding struggle of the church against them; the start of the Montanist movement; the conscious distinction of the time of the apostles from every subsequent era as the classical period; the beginnings of a New Testament canon, and so on. This is where, taken as a whole, the borders are to be found.[64] On particular issues, the boundary can only be decided in the course of the work. There will always be a certain elasticity in determining it.

V

The first main theme of New Testament theology is *Jesus' preaching*. This is not the place to go into it, but two observations can be made, indicating the special difficulties of this task.

First, the preaching of Jesus cannot be presented as an actual doctrine. That is, it cannot be cut loose from Jesus' personality, and the course of his life, so far as this can be known.[65] It is sufficient to recall that neither his proclamation of the kingdom of God nor even his preaching of the true righteousness is independent of his 'plan', his understanding of his vocation and his judgment about himself. Both personality and life will always, therefore, have to form the background of the account, and almost all the most profound difficulties about grasping a personality and a life therefore attach to New Testament theology, too. On the other hand, precisely because of this interconnection, Jesus' own world of ideas must be reproduced.[66] That is, unless one considers it impossible to say anything certain about it.

This means that at this point the presentation must be critical. Not just in the sense that all historical research is of course critical, but in a more specialized sense.

We do not possess *ipsissima verba* of Jesus. We only know about Jesus from later accounts. In these accounts, which are all directed towards the Christ of faith, the picture of Jesus' personality and his preaching is overlaid and obscured by numerous later conceptions and interpretations, as can be seen somewhat from a comparison of the three synoptic gospels, and more clearly from other considerations. There are often several layers superimposed upon each other. Accordingly, the top coats must so far as possible be set aside. But this business cannot be concluded in a merely external manner, say by comparison of texts. Criticism at individual points, and one's conception of the whole, condition each other mutually. There is little agreement about what is original and what secondary, even amongst scholars whose general position is similar. On the contrary, one might well say that there is no other central issue in the New Testament where everything is so much in a state of flux and where such diametrically opposite judgments are possible on precisely the central questions. This all means that, even here, the presentation must at every decisive point first distinguish between what is original and what has come in later, and between what is one way or the other relatively clear and what is doubtful.

We turn now from Jesus to the community, the church.

In order to be able to write an adequate historical account of its faith and doctrine in the earliest period, we should have to know more than we in fact do know.

The first thing which is largely obscure is *chronology*. We may assume that there were rapid developments in people's views. In certain circumstances ten years could be enough to alter the tone considerably. We cannot even follow the development exactly within twenty or thirty years. We cannot, for example, say with any real clarity how the Christian faith in about AD 70 differed from the Christian faith about AD 110. Dating views from indications in the literature is at best very hazardous. Who is bold enough to say at what point scruples about the delay of the parousia must have begun to be allayed? Was that only possible in about AD 90?

Secondly, the *geography* of the history of ideas is thoroughly obscure to us. One must assume that the development in Corinth and in Antioch, or in Alexandria or in the Egyptian countryside, contained remarkable differences. It is also very probable that particular views and theological ideas came from individual points and provinces and conquered the rest of the church. Of all this we know virtually nothing.

Apart from fairly well illuminated chapters from the life of Paul we are, thirdly, generally in the dark about *external events,* too, and their significance for the inner life of the community. There were probably more frictions and conflicts in it after the time of Paul than we can guess. What impression did the destruction of Jerusalem make upon the church? We can only generalize about this.

Fourthly and finally, the significance of *personalities* is on the whole unclear to us. We know a series of names from the earliest period and we know *something* about these people. But we cannot say with any certainty what their historical significance was, and particularly what it was for the history of ideas. Think of Peter, Barnabas, Apollos and Timothy. A man like Apollos, for example, will probably have had no small significance in the spreading of certain ideas. What that was we cannot say. Barnabas also was probably more than just a second-rate preacher. But what was his significance? In the period from Paul to about Hadrian, Christianity grew into a force to be reckoned with. But only a very few names from this period have come down to us. Were theologically influential personalities totally absent here? The author of the Gospel of John was certainly one such, and the importance of the author, say, of Ephesians or Hebrews may have extended further than we can tell from the epistles themselves. The fragmentariness of our knowledge is evident, too, from another angle – that here again we do not know the names. I still cannot, at least at present, convince myself that the author of the Fourth Gospel is the 'presbyter' John.

Such facts must be considered in biblical theology, too. It is, however, true that no matter how many unknown quantities may and must be mentally inserted into the eternally obscure map of early Christian history, there is *one* fact which not even the most intimate knowledge would move. This is the fact that Paul is *the* epoch-making figure in the history of primitive Christianity. He is not only the most powerful religious personality. By his missionary activity he decisively changed the physiognomy of the entire church. He made Christianity independent over against Judaism.[67] He naturalized it upon Gentile soil, and so gave it a new horizon. He is – considering all this – the creator of a Christian theology.[68] One has therefore to take one's bearings on this figure who stands before us more clearly than Jesus himself.

We must next distinguish in our presentation between the faith of the *Jewish-Christian early community* and *Christianity* on *heathen* soil. We cannot always mark the borders with any certainty. That is, it is sometimes impossible to say whether something was or was not yet to be found in Jewish Christianity, did or did not grow only on Gentile Christian soil. But this uncertainty does not alter the necessity of making such distinctions.

In the period from Paul to the end of our account one cannot make a further subdivision of even approximately similar clarity and importance. Everything must be considered together here.

So the preaching of Jesus is followed by the *faith of the early community*. In my opinion we have no direct sources for this earliest period. I Peter and James certainly do not belong here. The speeches of Acts may contain older material – that cannot be investigated here; they, too, are certainly not a direct source. We are dependent[69] upon some information from Acts and the Pauline epistles, and upon inferences from the gospels and especially Paul, and upon the nature of the historical situation. The chapter will unfortunately be short.

In retrospect the question naturally arises what the transition from Jesus to the community signifies.

Next comes a special chapter on *Paul*. The characteristic teaching of the apostle will be treated in detail. An important task is to make it historically intelligible. As I see it, the question should be stated like this: how did Paul's Pharisaic Jewish theology become, through the experience of his conversion and what followed it,[70] transformed into his Christian theology? One must reconstruct, on the basis of what Paul has written, the Jewish theology he once held. That is on the whole possible. One must also analyse his conversion experience psychologically. I do not say, explain it. All that matters here is what content and significance the experience, however it is explained, had for Paul's world of thought. This is not the place to discuss what position this point should have in the structure of the whole account. All that is being stressed is that Pauline theology must not be seen as static and complete, but as something which has come into being. It must be made clear what is Jewish heritage – and that includes some Hellenistic material, what is Christian new formation, and what is Christian amalgamation of that heritage.

It must also be stressed that not all the images and ideas contained in the Pauline epistles are to come into the presentation. In whole areas, for example in the eschatological images,[71] angelology and demonology, and concrete ethics, Paul is only one among many. There is a Pauline doctrine of redemption, a Pauline doctrine of justification, but (to exaggerate somewhat) no Pauline angelology and eschatology; there is only a Jewish or early Christian one. These and other things (such as his view of scripture) should only be touched on here in so far as they are controlled by the characteristic basic ideas and serve to illuminate these; that is in fact often the case. Otherwise the material in which Paul is not original, or where his originality is not historically significant, can be put with the material from the remaining writings. The advantage of this restriction is that what is characteristic about the apostle is clearly delimited, what in his ideas really made an impact comes over far more sharply, and what he shared or even might have shared with others is not put in a false light. We should not forget that Paul is being considered here, not for his own sake but as a member of a historical sequence.[72] But I would like to repeat expressly that when the general development is being investigated, the truly 'Pauline' material also can and must be brought in again wherever it is important for understanding this.[73] There is no need to be afraid of repetition. The same material will be considered from different sides and seen in a different light. The text-book accounts also take up the same statements of the apostle in different places.

Important questions arise about the historical contexts as a whole.

Paul signifies a very wide distance from Jesus,[74] and simply cannot adequately be understood on a basis of Jesus' preaching. Nobody can write a New Testament theology as the development and continuation of Jesus' teaching. Everything in Jesus revolves around an ethical imperative born of the most exalted religious individualism. Paul's centre is faith in a system of redemptive facts that took place simultaneously in heaven and on earth (incarnation, death and resurrection of Christ).[75] The picture of the human individual personality of Jesus has virtually disappeared in the apostle. Who could even guess from the sayings of Jesus that twenty years later the Pauline doctrine of the Son of God would be proclaimed? In short, it is an absolutely essential task to investigate the historical relationship of Paul to Jesus, to measure the distance between them and, so far as one can, to explain it. Only New Testament theology can decide how much goes back to Jesus, and how much the apostle who had never seen Jesus[76] and yet became the gospel's first witness to the Gentile world – what that fact contains! – is responsible for the emergence of Christianity.

Alongside this theme stands another, which also requires special investigation: the question of Paul's relationship to the primitive community.

Other tasks are immediately pushed into the foreground. The after-effects of Paul must be indicated as exhaustively as possible.[77] A sharp distinction must be made here between merely literary influence[78] and a real continuation of his ideas, between his general influence upon the whole church in certain basic ideas (universalism, etc.) and his particular influence upon smaller groups through his more specially theological ideas – I have in mind Ephesians, I Peter, and Hebrews. It is also necessary to distinguish between the influence exercised by the real, living Paul and that of the later Paul living in his letters. With the general recognition of his letters a new and special phase of his influence begins. In this whole problem one must not think only of the doctrine of justification and what goes with it; Christology and the conception of Christ's death have also to be considered. Finally, it has to be asked why *not more* of Paul's teaching became the common possession of the earliest church, and what of his theology did *not* and could not take root. People have rightly spoken about the non-transferability of the element of Pharisaic theology in his teaching.[79]

What has been said so far raises the question of what we know about Jewish Christianity, after Paul had on the whole robbed it of its influence.[80] It also raises another: what is involved in the acceptance of the Christian faith by Gentiles with their presuppositions. How far can the concepts and views they brought with them be observed in contrast to the world of ideas grown on Jewish subsoil?

All these themes have already brought us to the large and by far the most difficult section, where *faith and theology on Gentile-Christian soil* have to be described.

There is no single brief slogan which will characterize the content of this development. To bring it all under the heading of 'watered-down Paulinism' would mean saying nothing about the positive forces of the period. We would also have to show first that 'Paulinism' really was at one time common stock and that it is justified to make it the norm of all subsequent forms of Christianity. The expression 'Paulinism continued' says too little about what happened, because in fact Paulinism was only continued in a very limited sense, and because there is a good deal for which Paulinism did not provide the basis. When this 'continuation' is qualified by Pfleiderer through the addition 'on the soil of Hellenism', then 'Hellenism', the significance of which is unmistakable, is either a very vague concept, or else it too is too narrow to account for or explain every important phenomenon. Is it really true that 'the different forms of development found in primitive Christian and in early catholic teaching can be understood without any forcing of the evidence' from the 'reciprocal relationship of penetration and separation, priority and subordination, that exists between Paul's Christian proclamation and Hellenism'?[81] Can one really point to such a neat straight-line development of Hellenistic doctrinal formation from Hebrews to the Gospel of John, seen as increasing dependence upon Alexandrian philosophy of religion?[82]

We shall have to try to abandon one-sided schematizations and give every factor in the development its due. The actual obligation to make clear the development and change which took place from Paul onwards up to the close of the period is already fully recognized. What we now need are accounts summarizing it. But as well as or before this it is necessary to investigate in the way described the individual main areas of the world of ideas. This must be done with an eye to the development, but at the same time with an eye to the relationship between the different ideas.

It can be seen here how important it is to find the 'headings', to apprehend the themes correctly and group them correctly. That means in fact being able to take control of the phenomena, and is the quintessence of historical understanding.[83]

This is not the place to give a programmatic sketch. Nor am I trying to give an exhaustive account of the tasks which come into consideration. The following intimations are only meant as further illustrations of what I have in mind.

Closely related to the problems already touched on above (the influence of Paul, etc.) is the extremely important question of what the church thinks about Judaism, both present-day and historical Judaism, and how it sees itself in relation to it. Two further themes are at once closely connected with this. I am thinking, first, of the significance of the Old Testament for the Gentile-Christian church. How is it regarded? How interpreted? What is important about it for the church? What does the Old Testament history mean to it? What has it taken over from Judaism in the way of valuation and interpretation of scripture? How far does the Old Testament become a new book when considered in a Christian way? There is plenty of material available for answering these sorts of questions. If we consider the argument from prophecy[84] in its different forms, we come at the same time to a second theme: what can we know about the church's *apologetic* in the first place vis-à-vis Judaism? This certainly did not begin with Justin. In my view, Jesus' prophecies of his death and resurrection belong here. So does the development of the story of Judas Iscariot, as it can be seen for example in the Gospel of John. The Gospel of John does in general provide a particular wealth of material for the struggle against Judaism. One must also consider, of course, Jewish polemic against the church.

Ethics is a large topic. What are the characteristic features? How closely is their morality connected with that of the Jewish or Hellenistic world? What effect does the peculiar position of the Christian community have upon the material adopted? What role does asceticism play? What is meant by sin? What vices are most hated? How firm a tradition of ethical rules is there? What is the significance of Jesus' moral sayings and his example? What is not their significance? How far is there 'moralism'? How old is it? In what relationship does enthusiasm or fanaticism stand to it? How far are they mutually exclusive? A related question is how much actual religion there is in religious belief and practice.

Gnosis – and here I do not mean the systems of Basilides or Valentinus – cannot be passed over in silence. Rather, it has to be attended to very seriously. I presuppose that gnosticism is older than Christianity and did not grow out of it. Thus far its history forms a task of its own. But it certainly does come into contact with Christianity and is amalgamated with it. There is even an ecclesiastical Christianity upon gnostic subsoil. I believe that the Gospel of John has to be understood in this way.[85] Did Christianity produce its now special gnosis? In what does it consist? How is it related to that which grew on other soil? There is plenty of scope for questions here – and puzzles.

Problems such as those posed by the history of thought about the second coming, the rest of eschatology, angelology and demonology, and the Christian mysteries of baptism and Lord's supper, have already been touched on. Other points like the question of norms and authorities in Christianity, speculation about the church, and especially the history of Christology, can only be mentioned.

One thing, however, must be stressed rather more clearly. One of the most important facts of biblical theology is that in this period (and partly in the very early period), the original picture of the life of Jesus was more and more dogmatized. This development can be demonstrated from the gospels. What critical procedures cut out as not an authentic part of Jesus' preaching is now – with other material – evaluated constructively to depict the emergence of the gospel picture of Jesus. How did it come about that whereas Jesus was first thought of as 'his own precursor',[86] i.e. that he was called Messiah as the one who was to *become* this (Paul and the synoptics never speak of a second coming, but only of a coming of the Messiah), afterwards he *is* the Messiah who has come and who will come *again*? How did the different 'saving facts' – these are not only ascension, descent into hell and supernatural birth – which were added to Christ's death and resurrection arise? Both questions lead, strictly speaking, beyond the picture of Jesus in the gospels, but are largely related to this.

In this section *Johannine theology* will form a chapter of its own, I think at the end.

We are unable with any certainty to allocate the Gospel of John to its place in the course of the development. It will always be something of an island, but when the whole development has been completed it will not be completely isolated.

Here, too, we must exclude at the outset everything which belongs to more general themes. This includes attitudes to Judaism and to the Old Testament, anti-Jewish polemic, etc., except in so far as these matters are of interest for the actual contents of the presentation – these are above all Johannine christology, its fundamental world-view and perspective on the future with its teaching about the Paraclete.[87]

When the gospel is dealt with in biblical theology, I think we have to consider something which is generally overlooked. If it really is a matter of a doctrinal writing in gospel form, then the author's own theological viewpoint is clearly projected on to the picture of Christ's life. This means that we are not directly faced with his theology; it is veiled. Had the author presented it in so to speak dogmatic form, it would certainly not confront us primarily as a view of the life of Jesus. It would not revolve around this centre. Rather, it would show the Son of God in the light of his significance for faith, which is always a contemporary significance.[88] It follows that we must distinguish within John's picture of Christ between the picture of the life, and the christological viewpoint itself which created it. If one simply analyses this picture and considers the result to be Johannine theology, false results and questions are reached.

First, an account of the life of Jesus is bound to place in the foreground matters which have only subordinate significance for the 'theology' of John – or have a different significance from what appears to be the case. For example, the *erga* (works) of Jesus which are so strongly emphasized are for the evangelist a proof by which Jesus' status is confirmed in opposition to his opponents. They are therefore quite probably important for apologetic purposes,[89] but have nothing to do with his characteristic teaching about the Son of God. They are only significant for this in so far as they are at least in part (like the raising of Lazarus) at the same time statements about Christ and images of his essence. The important thing is then not the *ergon* and *sēmeion* (sign) itself, but what it says. This all means, too, that Jesus' omnipotence and omniscience which do, of course, point to his divine status are only so prominent in the gospel because this deals with the life of Jesus. The same thing is true of the frequency with which Jesus' freedom and autonomy in making decisions is stressed.[90] That, too, is an apologetic element.

Something else must be added. The evangelist has indeed made the picture of Jesus' life entirely into a mirror of his own ideas. But he did not in the main invent it. The picture of the history which he had to use for his purpose was the one that was already there.[91] But that means that he was in many ways bound and restricted by the tradition. The picture of the history handed down was always only up to a point capable of being pressed into the service of his ideas. There was always a remainder which did not suit them and even directly contradicted them. We hear of Jesus' human utterances and human emotions, or of Jesus withdrawing from his enemies in a miraculous way that is unthinkable for material corporeality. One might think here, and it has been thought, that the author reflected thus upon the relationship of the human to the divine in Christ, or – in the other case – thought of Jesus' corporeality in a docetic way. But this has nothing to do with docetism, as I John amply proves. The human traits[92] are, so to speak, of no importance to the 'Christ of faith'. The theologian, the dogmatician, was only interested in the general idea that the Logos became *sarx* (flesh). As soon as the Logos or Son of God was really seen and shown in history, it was inevitable that all sorts of difficulties and questions would arise not only for the evangelist's but also for our logical thinking, which simply did not exist within the author's dogmatic framework.

This point of view must not be overlooked when we consider the statements about the attitude of the evangelist or his Christ to Judaism. Nobody could write a life of Jesus which entirely separated him from the national soil upon which, according to the tradition, he had stood. On the other hand, the Judaism with which Jesus was concerned was for the author identical with the Judaism which the church of his time had to combat. Whatever can be explained as resulting from this tension plays no part in the actual theology of the gospel – or at least belongs only to its periphery.

So, to understand 'Johannine theology' we must first to some extent reverse the procedure by which the ideas have been projected on to the picture of the history.[93]

If the ideas of *Ignatius* and his religious type are to be accorded a special characterization, this will best be inserted – I say this with some hesitation – where the characteristic marks of the period are being described and summarized; perhaps at the end of Johannine theology.

We must now return once again to our starting-point and consider an important task which has not yet been mentioned.

The preaching of Jesus cannot be made intelligible unless it is understood in the context of contemporary Judaism and also in contrast to this. The theology of Paul is quite incomprehensible without a knowledge of late Jewish theology. But even apart from Jesus and Paul, from where does the mass of early Christian conceptual material come if not from Judaism? There were at the beginning very few 'Christian' concepts, even though these were extremely significant. They emerge in the nature of the case only gradually from the significance gained by specifically Christian matters such as the person of Jesus and the facts of his life or the church; or rather, through the decisive modification of Jewish concepts as a result of their relationship to these. Similarly, except for the belief in Jesus as the Messiah, what is essentially Christian only gradually becomes an active principle representing a tangible and valid factor in the whole development.[94] One must reflect above all that the main presuppositions of all early Christian intellectual construction – religious individualism with the association of achievement and reward, the idea of resurrection and judgment with its separating of this world from the beyond, the world of eschatological-apocalyptic ideas in general, the concept of the Messiah, the particular evaluation and interpretation of the Old Testament and other matters – are all the result of development on Jewish soil immediately prior to Christianity. Judaism, not the Old Testament, is the basis of Christianity in the history of religion.[95]

This means not only that the connections with Judaism must be thought through again and again, but also that New Testament theology must begin with an account of the main lines of late Jewish religion and theology – in the first place the Palestinian, and secondly also the Alexandrian. This is the necessary basis on which the account of early Christian religion and theology must stand and from which it must stand out. One of the greatest merits of Holtzmann's book is that it does not merely speak of the importance of Judaism for understanding primitive Christianity, but in fact prefaces its proper content with a detailed description of Judaism at the time of Jesus. One may hope that from now on no really scientific account will be published which does not to some extent meet this requirement.

Deissmann has insisted that not only Judaism, but also the religious and ethical position of Graeco-Roman paganism must be considered in biblical theology.[96] 'The intellectual and spiritual situation of the century around the beginning of the Christian era' must be sketched as a whole, so that Christianity is shown in connection with its age but also at the same time as standing out against its background. One can then understand how it must have looked to the people of the time.[97]

This consideration deserves careful attention and indicates a necessary aim. I have already, as occasion arose, explicitly or implicitly acknowledged that biblical theology is very seriously concerned with the question what Christianity brought to the pagan when he became a Christian, what was readily intelligible to him and what was not, and again what he brought to Christianity at the points where pagan views run parallel to Christian ones. But I would like to see Deissmann's demand met in a rather different form. When we are considering the mother-soil of Christianity, paganism is in a different position from Judaism. A fairly detailed description of the pagan world of thought at the beginning of the account would be bound to go beyond the framework of the whole. On the other hand, when the entry of Christianity into the wider world is spoken of in the course of the narrative, the facts of the religious life of paganism and its world of thought which are important here must, of course, be brought up and discussed. What will matter here, however, is not the actual philosophers, but the typical outlook of the man in the street.[98]

Finally, something needs to be said about the *name* of the discipline.

The name 'biblical theology' originally meant not a theology which the Bible contained, but a theology which has biblical character, and is got from the Bible. That can be set aside as irrelevant to us.

Nevertheless, the name New Testament theology is wrong in both its terms. The New Testament is not concerned merely with theology, but is in fact far more concerned with religion. The reasons why 'New Testament' is inappropriate do not need to be repeated. One cannot speak of 'early Christian history of dogma', because dogma in the proper sense only comes into view at the end of this period. The appropriate name for the subject-matter is: early Christian history of religion, or rather: the history of early Christian religion and theology.[99] If anyone protests that this is no longer a New Testament theology, that is a strange objection. the name is obviously controlled by the subject-matter, not vice versa.

It is certainly easier to pose problems than to solve them. No one is more acutely aware than I am how much work and what a change in our traditional way of working will still be necessary really to satisfy the programme which I have tried to establish. But it is justifiable to try to formulate the problem without having oneself solved it.

One thing cannot be denied. Biblical theology today is much less developed than the history of the apostolic and sub-apostolic age. Yet it belongs with this in the same way that the history of doctrine belongs with church history. It is not yet in the true and strict sense a historical discipline at all. May it become one!

III

Adolf Schlatter

THE THEOLOGY OF THE NEW TESTAMENT AND DOGMATICS

Foreword

Discussions about the academic discipline of theology have often been rather feeble. This is because scholars have simply described the aim of their own work and suggested that that is the whole of the intellectual task with which the subject-matter confronts us. This sort of illusion was encouraged by the fashion for making elaborate constructions which the dominance of speculative aims brought into the theology of the nineteenth century. It is probably safe to say that since then we have learned that none of us can write 'the' definitive New Testament theology. But the clarification of the relationship of one's own aims to the intellectual task as a whole *is* justified when we are consciously making use of the available methods and systematizing what we observe. Anyone who has read my *Theology of the New Testament* will perhaps understand why I wish to formulate the principles which have directed my work.

1 *The Objection to a Historical Theology of the New Testament*

Anyone who claims that New Testament theology is a historical discipline, that branch of historical research which sets out the convictions expressed in the writings of the New Testament and investigates their origin, is faced with a strong objection to his project. He will be told that he is aiming for the impossible; to make New Testament theology independent of dogmatics is an illusory fiction.

This sceptical view is widespread because it can be held from utterly opposing dogmatic positions. It alternates between being used as an attack on Christianity and as a defence of it. When it is linked with a powerful Christian dogmatics it can even become an accusation that the allegedly 'historical' treatment of the Word of the New Testament is a serious misfortune for our peoples and churches. This is because it is supposed to corrupt theological work at its very roots and dangerously to injure the faith of the man in the pew.

To deal with this sceptical view, it is necessary to be clear about the difference between dogmatics and historical work. Our work has a historical purpose when it is not concerned with the interests which emerge from the course of our own life, but directs its attention quite deliberately away from ourselves and our own contemporary interests, back to the past. Our own convictions, which determine our thought and will, are held at a distance. We keep them out of the investigation so that we can see the subject-matter as it was. Its effect on us and the way in which it might tie in with our own thinking and willing is not at this point brought into the field of our observation.

As historians, therefore, we can give only a partial answer to the overall question of truth. Our judgments about what was the case are subject to its norms without reserve. However, in historical work we do not allow the question of truth to go further than this. The question about what these ideas mean for us – whether and how they may be true for us also – does not belong here. Our goal is reached when we know what was once true for others. Yet since we cannot pose the question of truth simply in this limited way, there is always bound to be a further task alongside the historical one. That is the dogmatic task, which goes on to ask questions about the truth of what is said in the unlimited sense of how it determines our own thinking and willing. We are confronted not only with the past but also with the present, not only with what once happened inside other people but also with what is happening inside ourselves. The past sets us the question of what those who were there experienced at that time. Similarly, our present experiences confront us with the question of the content of our own thinking and willing.

When the dogmatician understands the question of truth to be what determines his own thinking – when he tries to perceive and express what was not only a reality and truth for others, but is also true for himself – he does not abandon history. He does not make himself into a hermit who withdraws from the community which gives foundation and content to all our thinking. Rather, he establishes this community more effectively and completely than the historian can. It is, of course, a common misunderstanding that, since the dogmatician orders his own relationship to his subject-matter, he describes nothing but his own self-consciousness. It has been thought that he makes judgments which are valid for himself alone and proclaims his own experiences. German dogmaticians since Schleiermacher have often lent support to this misunderstanding by the remarkable way in which they have worn their convictions on their sleeves. However, dogmatic work demands of our observation and judgment the strictest objectivity. It demands this no less than historical work, because we only get any content for our own lives through bringing ourselves in our perceiving and willing into contact with what has happened.

What happens inside ourselves is dependent upon what is going on around us; our present experiences are dependent upon other people's past experiences. If our knowledge and will were applied simply to ourselves, they would perish. The direction and success of our own lives are measured by the power and fullness of the reality with which we make contact. So the dogmatician is also constantly concerned with history, not only with his own history which he cannot separate from that of others, but also with the history which has happened and is happening outside himself. If he were to abandon the material of history he would become a dreamer. This is true not only of Christian dogmatics but of every conviction. A person can only become clear about the course of his own life by seeing the past as it exercises its power upon us. And only thus can he cast any light upon what it is that creates a unity out of many individual lives. But even then, when he studies history, the dogmatician allows the question of truth its full significance – a significance which encroaches upon us, too. He continues to stand in the present situation, in which and for the sake of which he is engaged in thought. The past is important for him as an effective reality in his own experience.

It is impossible to use the term 'dogma' to mark off the two areas from each other, even though the word is used to describe one branch of theology. When we call the theological activity which describes God's relation to us as it determines us 'dogmatics', we are using the word with respect to that *shared* knowledge and faith which unites us into a church. We are saying that this reference of dogmatics to a shared knowledge and faith is an essential characteristic of it, and is what gives it its importance. The conviction of an individual is not automatically 'dogma'. It only becomes dogma when it is the common property of a group which derives its unity from it.

The result of the New Testament proclamation was the church. It is united not in the first place on the basis of its cultic or ethical action, and not simply because its members have similar feelings. Its unity is based upon shared certainties, without which those other things cannot be achieved. For this reason the formation of dogma has always been a fact of church history, and will continue to be one for as long as there is a church. It will always be an important concern of Christianity to think out and make clear what ideas have the right and the power to unite us with one another. But it is not appropriate to invoke this task of the dogmatician for distinguishing his job from New Testament theology. This is because New Testament theology also directly affects our unity as a church. Its progress strengthens this unity and its neglect threatens and weakens it. It would be wrong to say that New Testament theology is the concern of scholars, whereas dogmatics is the concern of Christianity. The church did not emerge on the basis of the thoughts of its members – not even of its dogmaticians – but through the work of Jesus and his messengers. It remains alive by preserving its connection with this history. The fact that the New Testament history and the word which witnesses to it is the ground of Christianity's existence is expressed by the fact that the New Testament is its canon. For this reason, the work of trying to understand it touches upon what is central to Christianity and gives it its unity just as directly as does dogmatics. Its results become the common possession of all members of the group just as much as do those of dogmatics. Its errors are just as damaging to our common life as are the false tacks of the dogmatician. Since Christianity is based upon the New Testament, the interpretation of the New Testament is an act which touches its foundations.

The concept of 'system' is an even less appropriate one to use to describe the difference between historical and dogmatic work. We aim at systematization because we desire unitariness and completeness in our thinking. As such, it guides historical work no less than dogmatics. Our knowledge of history is not limited to scattered and contradictory observations. Here, too, the harmonious ordering of our thoughts is an indication that our work has been successful.

If, of course, by 'system' one means the sort of thinking associated with phrases like 'pure reason' and '*a priori*', then it must be rigorously distinguished from historical work. The latter rests entirely on observation and demands wide-open eyes and the sort of whole-hearted surrender which perceives that with which it is presented. But in any case, if the notion of 'systematics' is taken to imply that our thinking is independent of observation and can lead us to produce something out of ourselves, then it is of no more use to the dogmatician than to the historian. A dogmatician who no longer observes, but only forms judgments without first perceiving, and who instead of being given his ideas by reality, procures them for himself by free construction, is at best a poet and at worst a dreamer. Again, if we are to apprehend the factors leading to our existence, receiving takes precedence over construction. We cannot create anything without reference to what is given. However we set the question of truth, whether we direct it outwards towards what has happened before us, or inwards to what is happening within us, it is always related to something that is *given,* through which we are formed. Whatever we achieve by way of thinking remains connected throughout with what is already given for our work.

If by the idea of 'system' we are considering the completeness of our knowing, it indicates a goal which far exceeds the limits of what we can do. But here, too, there is no difference between the two fields. The historian can never flatter himself that he has achieved a perfect knowledge of a matter. Rather, with his observing and understanding he is for ever standing before limits which he cannot remove, since his knowledge inevitably ends where the testimony of his sources ends. Our knowledge of what is past rests on memory. But wherever there is memory there is also forgetting. Forgetting is just as indispensable for our intellectual life as memory is. If there were no forgetting, the difference between past and present would disappear. Precisely because what is past and gone is always partly forgotten, history will never be a fully completed science.

But the goal of perfect knowledge is just as unattainable for the dogmatician as it is for the historian. We can no more penetrate our own existence with an all-embracing knowledge than we can the past. In dogmatics also, we are dependent upon what individual certainties we can attain without being able to make them up into a perfect whole. For this reason the first and most important aim of both types of work is not to be found in what is meant by the word 'system'. It is, rather, that our thinking should be true to its own norms. Our first duty as historians or dogmaticians is to shield our thinking from inappropriate assumptions. Our thinking has had an indestructible value when it has been obedient to the norm of truth, even if it has been unable to achieve systematic completion in all sorts of ways. If the will which guides our think-ing immediately strays away from obedience to the norms of thought towards the perfection of a system, then both historical and dogmatic work equally degenerate into a fabrication of con-jectures, and become an intellectual game.

What is the basis for the widespread scepticism about the correctness of this division of the theological field? It appeals to the character of the New Testament word, which confronts us with the claim that we should be affected by it in all our behaviour and without reserve. For this reason the dogmatic question may not be set aside in favour of merely historical investigation. According to the sceptical position, it is true that the historian explains; he observes the New Testament neutrally. But in reality this is to begin at once with a determined struggle against it. The word with which the New Testament confronts us intends to be believed, and so rules out once and for all any sort of neutral treatment. As soon as the historian sets aside or brackets the question of faith, he is making his concern with the New Testament and his presentation of it into a radical and total polemic against it.

The attitude of historians and the course of historical research strengthen this scepticism. It is argued that the historian has never in fact succeeded in doing what the New Testament denies to be permissible, and in its own way makes impossible. If he claims to be an observer, concerned solely with his object, then he is con-cealing what is really happening. As a matter of fact, he is always in possession of certain convictions, and these determine him not simply in the sense that his judgments derive from them, but also in that his perception and observation is moulded by them.

It is clear that without the honest attempt to lay aside all personal concerns and the opinions of one's school or party, and seriously to *see*, academic work degenerates into hypocrisy. But even this honest attempt cannot overcome the fact that an observer sees with his own eyes only what the certainties which internally determine him allow him to perceive. The argument runs as follows.

All this should be evident from the course of church history. New Testament theology as an independent subject only dates from the Enlightenment. Up to that point the church had no need of it, even though from the beginnings its desire for Christian knowledge operated in an environment characterized by strong intellectual tensions. What was looked for here was supplied by dogmatics alone, and in such a way that nothing beyond it was needed. The Enlightenment, on the other hand, fought for the distinction between the two areas because it was guided by a polemical tendency which was working for emancipation from the tradition of the church. Since this was supported and sanctified by the New Testament, it was natural for there to be a desire to remove the New Testament to a distance from the observer where it became nothing but the object of historical consideration. Then the difference between the New Testament and the church's teaching would become clear, and both could be robbed of their power by being played off against each other.

The history of the discipline of New Testament theology then confirms this in that the variations which mark its new epochs are always occasioned by outside influences. They are not brought about by its own work but by the dogmatic convictions which, independent of this, have gained power in our academic life. In the work of the rationalists, Jesus and his messengers themselves looked like rationalists. Then this type of New Testament theology disappeared, not because of historical work but because of speculative Kantianism. Here the work of New Testament theology divided into different schools, and alongside the Schleiermacherian type there appeared the Hegelian. Again a change was then stimulated by influences lying outside purely historical work; namely, as historical research was accommodated to the methods of the natural sciences, and all religious criteria were excluded from the historical approach. If the work of New Testament theology joins in all those debates evoked by argument about these convictions which are fundamental for our consciousness of ourselves and of God,[1] then its historical objectivity is illusory.

The consequence has been that those presentations of New

Testament ideas which antedate the discipline of New Testament theology, such as for example Calvin's *Institutes,* have incomparably greater scientific value even as history than much of what has been done with all the tools of modern historical technique. The reason for this is not the intellectual weakness of the historians, but lies in their methods. The older writers were most seriously attentive to the relationship between what the New Testament said and the convictions by which they themselves were determined. They were therefore resolved to clarify its contents and be certain about its truth-value. The modern historian, on the other hand, lays the ideas which determine him on one side, saying that they are his own business and not affected by his science. In fact, however, they do inevitably exercise an influence, though this is now concealed by the fiction of a merely historical purpose. They are therefore un-tested and ungrounded, and often enough even the historian him-self is unconscious of them. With the same facility with which he passes lightly over his own convictions, he now makes judgments on the apostolic statements, too. How he interprets them and evaluates them is, of course, irrelevant for his own thought. He operates merely 'historically', merely upon an object which is dead and gone.

The result of this is the present situation which we can all see. The struggle for and against Christianity no longer takes place alone or in the main through dogmatic work, but predominantly in the field of historical research, particularly in New Testament theology. Historical investigations serve as weapons for the attack and defence of religious positions. It is therefore clear that the historian's objectivity is self-deception, and that the convictions which influence him have a dominating influence upon his work. Otherwise why would there be this struggle? Polemic is not a feature of historical work, but grows out of dogmatics. So the fact that historical literature is put at the disposal of religious polemic as much as it evidently is, means that it has formally and openly contradicted the independence of historical research. So the earlier position of theology, in which history and dogmatics were inter-twined, has been re-established. A psychologically well-grounded law has operated here, one which removes the artificial distinc-tions made by the teaching work of the theological faculties. In an age when Nietzsche's *Antichrist* and Harnack's *What is Christianity?* are widely read books, it is a singular archaism to speak of historical work on the New Testament, work which is only concerned to perceive what has happened. This archaism can only be explained as a result of the isolation of academics, which is comparable to that of a painter who is decorating the walls of a house with frescoes while flames burst out of the roof.

2   *The Obligation to Historical Work*

If the allocation of New Testament theology to the realm of history implied a rupture of its connection with dogmatics, then it really would be nothing but a fiction which ought to disappear. The sceptical view as sketched out above is correct in saying that to label this task historical can never mean that the convictions which determine us no longer affect us when we are performing it. No improvement in the art of writing history could achieve this, and it should not try to, because a discipline which would make us into a lifeless mirror for the past would be an inhuman undertaking. It cannot be done, and so its results are worthless. At no point in our lives do we have the task of self-annihilation. That remains true even when the demand for this self-annihilation is qualified by its being limited to the moment of doing a particular job.

All efforts at self-annihilation only result in the disturbance of our own human existence. Our being confronted by the past, and its demand to be seen as it was, does not mean that we should annihilate the present. It is true that when other people are the object of our perception and understanding we are required in some way to get free from our own selves. This leads to a genuine surrender of ourselves to other people, and indeed only a person who is prepared to give himself in this way can receive. But this conscious turning away from our own selves is never self-annihilation. Someone who wanted to deny and destroy himself in this surrender would not have given anything.

Making a man into a machine for observing is nowhere less feasible than with regard to the New Testament; because, regardless of whether a person appropriates its content or keeps it at a distance, still his will is involved at the deepest level. So in every piece of work done according to the norms of historical science, the writer and the reader should be aware that a historical sketch can only take shape in the mind of a historian, and that in this process the historian himself, with all his intellectual furniture, is involved. If this fact is lost sight of, then it is no longer science in which we are involved, but crazy illusions.

The connection between historical science and dogmatics, between the experience of others and that of oneself, between the history which happened once and the history which is happening now, cannot be set aside until historical work is complete – as though only its completed results are instructive for the dogmatician, and determine his judgments. That would be to perceive only a half of what is going on here. The relationship between the two functions is there right from the beginning of historical work, and it is a matter of inter-reaction. It does not simply come in at the end, but permeates the whole course of historical work.

The dogmatician in us supplies the historian with the capacity for making judgments through which he distinguishes between what is possible and what is not, and between what in the outline of history produces effects and what is dead. When we look at the past, our knowledge of the present enables us to clarify what happened and the forces which gave it shape. The relation between the two functions that we are discussing will never be established in terms of merely one-sided dependence, as though one had exclusive priority and so was the cause and giver, whereas the other was exclusively secondary, on the receiving end and getting its shape from the first. In fact, in the unity of human existence there is always a two-way connection between them both. Both are involved in giving and receiving.

The relation between historical research and dogmatics leaves no room for the question which is in control and which is derivative. Neither is simply independent; neither is merely the basis of the other. And neither is merely derivative or conditioned. Historical research has its independent foundation in the completeness of the past. Similarly, the certainty of dogmatics is something *primary* which influences all our looking back to what has happened, because it arises out of the present and apprehends what is creative of our own human existence.

The historian's neutrality becomes a fiction when it leads to insistence on a complete separation between these two distinct functions. At the present time, the historical literature on the New Testament is overladen with conjectures which are offered to us as history. The reasons for this are partly our failure to *observe*, and the appearance of imagination in place of observation. But also there is the failure of historians to give some account of the motives which determine them. They assume that their 'presuppositionless history' gives them the power to overlook and not subject to criticism the presuppositions which do in fact determine them. However, we shall in fact only get free of and rise above our presuppositions by paying conscious and rigorous attention to them.

All this does not mean that the separate development of our two functions is contradicted or shown to be impossible. We are not talking here about a carving up of the self into two centres of thought which exist in isolation. We are talking rather of two *functions*. They do possess in the unity of human existence something which always holds them together. But a certain independence is also called for, corresponding to the variety of responses which enrich our existence.

What has happened in the past demands of us, by the very fact that it *has* happened, that we grasp it in its *givenness*. The question here is whether we are all wrapped up in ourselves, or whether we are able to be genuinely open to the past so as to be able to see things other than ourselves. I believe that we are given a capacity for seeing. But this cannot be proved to someone who denies it. The rule 'Do and you will know' applies here. As is the case with all fundamental convictions, *action* is the potency which shapes our consciousness.

Now if our viewing is to cut loose from ourselves and be free to grasp what is there to see, then the process will have to be neat and complete, and this is assisted by a distinction between historical work and the dogmatic question. If we turn our attention straight away to the connections which exist between our object and our own ideas and will, then there is always a danger that we will break off our observation at the point where our own interest in the object ends. Our perception might be directed exclusively towards what we can at once make our own.

Church history gives an urgent reminder of our duty to use our eyes steadfastly and with no other motive than to perceive the object. When the Enlightenment, polemically motivated as it was, demanded a biblical dogmatics in place of the church's tradition, and so brought about the birth of New Testament theology, it had a very good case. This was because the church's capacity for observation had in fact been seriously damaged by a confusion of the two tasks. The church's judgments about the relationship between scripture and church doctrine and action, between the faith of the New Testament and its own piety, were often very confused. Different lines which sometimes even crossed each other were often bundled together, and this lack of clarity had equally damaging effects upon the historical and the dogmatic sides. However, clarity about the relationship of the church's action to the word of scripture is advanced when in the first place the question of the content of the New Testament statements is resolutely put for its own sake, and when we have an intellectual discipline whose only concern is to know and to understand what is *there* in the New Testament.

The justification for a New Testament theology conceived as history is that the independent development of historical science gives a measure of protection, admittedly not infallible, against arbitrary reconstructions of its object. It secures us against producing a mixture of what scripture says and what the church teaches, or a mixture of the Bible and our own religious opinions, in which neither the one factor nor the other is correctly grasped and fruitfully applied. The historian's good conscience consists in his being clear about what he believes and why. Conversely, the good conscience of the Christian dogmatician, and his ability to mediate effectively what the New Testament presents us with both to himself and the church, is partly dependent upon the faithfulness and success with which we do our historical work on the New Testament.

If the objector says that this historical work is no longer opportune today, the history of modern thought can be used to contradict him. It is clear from the literature on New Testament theology as well as from other fields how modern thinking is opposed to the older logical ideal. Formerly the dominant concerns of thought were taken from 'reason' and its concepts, and the intention was to form ideas that were universally valid. Now, however, people are concerned even in their thinking to do justice to the personal life of the individual. The justification for an idea is no longer based on its origin in and contribution to a common stock of ideas, but rather on its derivation from personal experience and expression of that in all its concrete particularity.

So if a person brings his own individual concerns and his own personal experience to the New Testament history in order to confirm the legitimacy of his relationship to it, his observation in this particular direction will be considerably sharpened. But at the same time, this association of the past with the particular act of one's will which guides one's observation in the present, is very dangerous. In the modern period, when our thinking is more individualistic than formerly, it is particularly important that we cultivate those historical concerns which require of us the selfless act of genuine seeing. Through this act, our heightened individual life is augmented by coming into a full, effective relationship with the reality outside and above itself. Our thinking and willing thus become a part of the wider human community.

Reflections based on the laws which govern our thinking activity do not conflict with the claim that the apostolic word makes upon us. They are, rather, confirmed by it, since the demand for faith requires the clarity of an observation which is selfless and complete. No doubt this claim does contain the summons to a union which submits us to it complete with all that we are. That does not mean, however, that we can tailor it according to our requirements. It does not stand there like a beggar asking for a gift – the gift of understanding, acknowledgment and practical application. Since its purpose is to provide a foundation for our faith, it stands above us and forbids us to mix it up with the substance of our own mind. We are not to cut it down to the size of our own thinking and willing. The demand for faith contains within itself a claim to sovereignty. This claim comes from God's goodness and so does not aim to humiliate and impoverish us, but to grant us life and gifts. However, for the same reason, it never ceases to demand a resolute and complete subordination of ourselves to it. The New Testament makes this claim because of what it is in itself. It can only be allowed this claim if it can give grounds for it by its own contents. For this reason it must be perceived as it actually is.

It is, of course, true that the historian's position of neutrality *vis-à-vis* the word of Jesus cannot be his last act, nor can it regulate his relationship to that word. The word does not let hovering on the fence go on indefinitely. What the end-result of a historian's work means for the historian depends upon the history which takes place inside him. This is given him by a kind of dogma which shapes his own experience.

3   *The Limits of New Testament Theology*

Doubts about the correct purpose to be assigned to New Testament theology can also take the form of wanting to make it into the theologian's sole and final task. It is said that the sequence of ideas with which the New Testament confronts us does demand to be examined historically, but that when this is done the work of theology is finished. There is no room for a second discipline alongside this one, which would exist as a strange sort of parallel to it. When New Testament theology has done its job successfully, according to this view, Christianity is understood and a judgment on it achieved.

This line of argument is also to be found linked with opposing religious standpoints. It may take the following form. When the New Testament is fitted into the course of the history which produced it, its claim upon us is done for and the Christ sinks into the past. Or it may be argued that when a New Testament statement is given to our understanding, what is given is the ground of our faith. The only other processes of mediation which are necessary for us, if the New Testament witness is to stir us, belong simply to the sphere of the will. It is now a matter of obedience. Therefore anything beyond New Testament theology is the concern of life, not of academic work.

Both these standpoints might concede that there may be intellectual obstacles which get in the way of a correct attitude to the New Testament. These can be investigated by the science which is concerned with pathological processes. One side will call in Enlightenment man to remove religious prejudices. The other side will call in the religious apologist who is concerned with those conditions of the consciousness which are responsible for the denial of God and the repudiation of Christ, and will try to overcome such disturbances. But dogmatics has always been definitely distinct from apologetics, because its work is not in the first place directed towards cases of degeneration or confusion in the consciousness; rather, it strives to achieve the sort of knowledge which gives a positive basis to the faith of the community and the individual. It is being said here, however, that this goal is reached with New Testament theology.

These are some of the reasons why in pre-Reformation and

Reformation theology there was never any distinction between the theology of the New Testament and that of the church. A unitary system of doctrine, like for example Calvin's *Institutes*, was the only legitimate form of doctrine. It seemed to be a consequence of the basic idea of the gospel that once established, a scriptural statement should get itself across into our thinking and willing under its own power. There should be no further need of mediation.

Nevertheless, the church has never limited its intellectual activity simply to hearing the New Testament. Its thought has always travelled in different directions, beyond what is given us in the New Testament. This should not be judged a fault nor considered as degeneration. It arises directly out of the relationship in which the New Testament stands to us. So it crops up, though in a variety of modifications and individual forms, whenever and wherever the New Testament is operating.

Since the attitude to which the New Testament calls us and leads us is faith, our agreeing with it follows through our own personal act. This, however, means that the New Testament statement and the content of our own consciousness should enter into discussion and mutually come to terms. Only this can ensure that our acknowledgment of the apostolic word takes place without an inner break: not by violence or coercion, but with a willing and whole-hearted openness of ourselves for it. Only this can plant it in our personal existence.

To elevate the New Testament theology in itself to the status of dogmatics would be to work with an un-Christian conception of obedience and to try to subject ourselves to it in such a way that we no longer remain in possession of what we are. This is a self-contradiction which always fails. It leads to the well-known hybrid, disobedient obedience, which we have seen often enough in the history of the church.

If the presentation of the New Testament statements needed nothing more than an order to us to conserve what was already known, then our going along with it would become an achievement of our will. That, however, is something different from the sort of faith the New Testament asks of us. The New Testament calls for certainty. It is also a matter of choice – but not a choice which lacks any basis. This choice knows what it is choosing and why it is choosing it. Its grounds cannot be established without thought. So Christianity has always recognized that the New

Testament confronts it with a double question. There is not only
the question of what the New Testament itself presents to be
heard and understood by us, but also the question directed towards
us: how that message is related to the content of our own intellectual being.

These far-reaching tasks do not arise only as a result of intellectual degeneration, though this may unfortunately gain ground
as much in the intellectual climate of nations as in the consciousness of individuals. But our task is not simply that of bringing
health by the removal of illusions and the clearing away of such
forms of the will as have to be rejected. It is also the case that we
bring to the New Testament something of value, and the relation
of this to the New Testament has to be determined.

In the first place we bring those thoughts which stem from
human nature. But that is not all – as though our sole task were to
unite our natural consciousness with the consciousness of God
given us by Jesus. We also bring religious values. This is partly
because our communion with God does not come to us only as
something extra and from outside, but gives us our existence and
essence. It is also because the church, through which the content of the intellect is given us, and the course of our lives, which
shapes us inwardly, are both themselves tools which serve God's
sovereignty and his grace. They do not simply obstruct and
obscure our thinking and willing. They also fill them with God's
good gifts. Our relationship to the New Testament is one of subordination. It is not described correctly when an absolute contrast
is made between the present as utterly deserted by God and un-
touched by his rule, and a past which was filled with the revelation
of God. This not only contradicts our experience which is for ever
mediated to us by our own life and that of our church, but also
contradicts what the apostles say. They do not see the conclusion
of Jesus' work being followed by the night of total abandonment
by God. There remains an indestructible reconciliation which summons the world to God. There remains Christ's rule which spans
the aeons, and there remains the presence of the Spirit which
leads the believer's knowing and willing from God to God. This is
the indestructible basis of the fact that the word of scripture stands
over the church, and a clear indication of that fact. It also makes it
impossible for the church ever to be content to be nothing but a
receptacle for the word of scripture, and merely a repetition or

imitation of the first disciples. It has its own independent life, and that life is something of value.

New Testament theology itself sharpens our eyes for this independent life of the church by showing how primitive Christianity's expression of its faith was rooted in its own historical situation, and is therefore something individual and unrepeatable. By confronting us with the peculiar life of the apostolic community and clarifying it for us, New Testament theology makes it impossible for us to transform the New Testament into a series of abstract statements and models which hover around suspended over and above reality. It also strengthens our awareness of the need for dogmatic work, because when we are thus aware that what was once the case can only become real in a particular moment of the past course of history, then the question cannot be avoided: how is what once happened in the past made new in the present? How can we verify that something is the cause of our own being alive when it came into existence in a life that has in part become foreign to us?

For this reason the religious question is never settled by simply handing on what scripture says. The question is always: what does scripture mean *for us*? This 'us', with all it involves, takes us into the realm of dogmatics, and the dogmatician does not fulfil his task simply by becoming a New Testament theologian. He has to give concrete and tangible content to the picture of that humanity to which he himself belongs and for which he does his work. It is for this generation of humanity that he works at a form of dogma which is not simply imposed on us from outside, but arises naturally from within, and so can become a bond uniting the community.

The same considerations apply to those who tell us that once they have a historical account of the New Testament they can get free of its claim upon them. They, too, can only by-pass the act of thinking because they have already made up their minds about the question of God and the will. If they cannot give good grounds for their decision, then as well as showing the fettered dependence of those religious people who will not think, they also evidence that self-glorying arbitrariness which undertakes to determine our relationship to the world by its own power. Both these ways of destroying our will are similar, and are causally related to each other. If, on the other hand, their will knows what it is denying and why it is repudiating the Word of Jesus, then they, too, are basing their relationship to the New Testament on dogmatic work. Their dogma is different from the one the Christian dogmatician gets from the New Testament and has as his conviction only in its result. Its object and purpose are the same.

The uncertainty which is obvious in current work on New Testament theology is partly connected with the question of the relation between historical work and dogmatics. If we are controlled by the idea that what we perceive in the New Testament is meant to become our own personal possession, then there is always the danger that historical work will be destroyed because the concrete individuality of what happened is replaced by ideal pictures – pictures which are supposed to show the meaning of assurance of God, communion with Christ, love, faith and repentance, to the piety of every age. This tendency is strengthened by the seductive glitter that our intellectual activity gives to abstractions. It can often appear as though abstractions are the surest means of getting the New Testament statements to take effect in our own thinking, because of the way they float indefinitely in the air. Does not the general embrace all particulars? Will not, therefore, 'the permanent element in Christianity' consist in the ideal element? When Jesus is made into an 'ideal man', and New Testament faith and love into an indefinite ideal picture of some sort of confidence and goodness, then their value seems secured for everyone. The concrete individualized character of a real event, on the other hand, makes it unrepeatable, and to some extent even incomprehensible.

However, when we no longer see in the New Testament what the piety of the early period was, but only what ought to be the Christianity of every age, the historian is no longer giving the dogmatician what he ought to be giving him, because the historical task is obscured. The dogmatician also needs realities. He cannot be satisfied with the supposed nature of faith, but must know how God created faith. An idea of what the church ought to be is not enough. He needs to perceive *that* a community emerged whose peculiar characteristic was its relation to God, and *how* this community emerged. The relevant factor for him is not an image of Christ which merely gives expression to our own wishes, but a knowledge of what the Christ was like. Abstractions cut loose from realities are just as useless in practice as they are vacuous in theory.

Our task is to attach our concrete, historically-conditioned lives to God. We get the necessary assurances for this not by logical fictions and ideas, but through facts. These facts do not come from ideal men, but from men like ourselves, and that means historically-localized men who lived their lives with God as their source and their goal. Dogmaticians do not need a general conception of faith and love. What they need is a definite perception of what is meant by good will and confidence in God in the concrete situations of a human life.

This means that New Testament theology is not giving the dogmatician the material which he needs when it removes the temporal and spatial colouring from the New Testament events. It gives him what he needs by making the New Testament as accessible as our capacity for seeing allows. The task this gives to the dogmatician is then a large one, because he has to tie up the completed realities of the New Testament with the equally concrete and definite reality of his own life. But since this task is posed by the very fact of our human existence, it must not be broken off uncompleted.

In order to oppose the idealizing tendency which turns the New Testament statements into pallid abstractions, the current literature often shows a taste for giving the New Testament conceptions a touch of antiquity by fanciful turns of phrase. Since the texts themselves give no occasion for this, people bring in the supposed background to the material for the purpose. Jesus' words about God's royal sovereignty are thought to be the product of fiery apocalyptic dreams, and Paul's worship of Jesus is thought to be based on gnostic speculation about a pre-existent primal man. Paul's distinction between the spirit and the flesh in himself and everyone else is supposed to derive from his view of everything being penetrated by an ethereal fluid which he called the Holy Spirit, and so on. The scent of antiquity on the apostolic word, which shows it to belong to the past, is made clear by a characteristic which is still incomprehensible to us. But the effort to shield the New Testament word from being accommodated to our own spiritual life goes wrong when it distracts historical work from the given material of the apostolic word itself. If we surround it with pieces of background which contradict its clear statements, we are making historical research into a work of fiction. In my view, New Testament theology only fulfils its obligations by observation, not by free creation.

4 *Statistics and Aetiology*

The first task of New Testament theology consists in perceiving the given facts of the case, and it would be childish to worry that there is no more work left for us to do since countless scholars have been observing the New Testament for a long time now. That would show how little we were aware of the size of the task posed by the formula 'observation'. What has happened in the past far exceeds in its fullness and depth our capacity for seeing, and there is no question of an end being reached even of the first and most simple function of New Testament study; namely, seeing what is there.

But the task cannot be limited simply to this. It also embraces the observation of those processes through which the New Testament convictions emerged. We have to grasp as best we can how this happened. This research on the causes will also stimulate, broaden and verify the primary work of observation.

It is admittedly conceivable to set up New Testament theology as consisting simply of a statistical account of the ideas in the New Testament.[2] The teaching activity of the church has always done this statistical work, even before New Testament theology existed as an independent discipline. The vast literature of commentary material on the New Testament serves this task. A New Testament theology sketched out as statistics only differs from a commentary in form. What a commentary establishes according to the given structure of the texts, this sort of New Testament theology sets out by subject-matter. It is structured by the similarities and differences to be found in the doctrinal content of the statements, thus removing the form given by the documents.

But the significance of New Testament theology today rests on the fact that it is not content simply to gather material like a statistician. It sees its main task in raising the question how the convictions found here in the New Testament arose. It is concerned not only to perceive but to explain, and it really grasps what is related by showing the conditions through which the latter emerged. These sorts of questions neither damage the historical purpose of the investigation nor trespass upon the dogmaticians' territory. The enquiry concerns what gave rise to the ideas of the New Testament, and that is not a part of our own existence, but took place in the consciousness of early Christianity, or at least affected it.

Statistical work itself always leads to aetiological considerations about how the history arose, considerations which touch on the processes which gave rise to the content of the New Testament. That is because what we have here is not a number of separate statements which lie there unrelated. The New Testament relates them with a living bond as ground and consequence, as what conditions and what is conditioned. The idea of causation does not have to be brought into the New Testament from outside. It is already powerfully present, because the New Testament itself grounds and develops its results before our eyes. This would not be the case if its contents consisted of abstractions, 'concepts' cut loose from history, or if it contained a doctrinal norm with fixed formulae that exercised authoritative control without reference to their basis, or if what we had were mysteries where no account of their basis and meaning is either wanted or able to be given. None of these possibilities describes what was the case with the founding of the church. The men who were responsible for assembling the church showed remarkable power in forging links. They let their thought be controlled by a will which would convince other people and so established their dogma. Since what we have in the New Testament is not something beyond time and history, but rather living and evolving processes, purely statistical work which does not show this aspect of New Testament thought remains incomplete and incorrect.

The first task here is to note the connections which link up the individual statements of the apostles and show how one comes out of another. The conditions of any thought are, first of all, those processes which accompany it in consciousness. The apostles' statements reveal an internal life, surprising alike in its firm, all-controlling unitariness and in its richness. It thus confronts us with a claim to be 'understood' and makes this possible. An account of Paul is inadequate if it tells us what he thought about flesh, how he understood the death of Jesus, what he counts as faith and how he values it, but fails to show how these judgments are related. One depends on another. It is not there for its own sake, but on account of its proximity to something else. Its distinctive content comes from its proper place in the unity of the apostle's total consciousness. By clarifying these connections we 'understand' Paul. In this way we 'explain' how he came to say, 'I am crucified with Jesus' and why he evaluates nobody 'according to the flesh', and why he sees faith as his righteousness.

Someone who tells us that John contains teaching about the Logos and that he has a negative view of the world, that his ethics are concentrated in the idea of love, and that you can see how for him faith in Jesus means a person's entry into eternal life, is still not fulfilling the historical task that is set us. In history one thing is as it is because of something else. John's statements are understood by perceiving how one produces another and how all reveal the same unitary will.

In all these directions the historical task is inexhaustible. It is posed in the same way by the word of Jesus. His sovereign will, his divine sonship, his witness to God's sovereignty, his call to repentance, his willing the cross, his fellowship with the disciples – in short the whole sequence of his acts – are not just one item after another. We fail to do them justice if we simply note each one separately. His knowledge of himself as Lord of the community is grounded in his filial relationship to God, in his knowing himself empowered to call sinners and in his authority to bear his cross. Jesus will be comprehensible to us in proportion as these connections are perceived. It is thus that we grasp why he spoke with Nicodemus in one way and not another, why his command to his disciples was as the Sermon on the Mount tells us, and why he used the name 'king' as is witnessed by the report of the crucifixion.

But it is also the case that our inner life is causally connected with our external situation. It therefore becomes 'understandable' to us when we spell that out, too. All observations which draw out the connection of the New Testament statements with the history of Christianity belong here. So does the relationship of the apostolic preaching to the ideas of its surrounding world. The New Testament itself confronts us with this aim because it keeps before our eyes the firm connections between its history and its teaching. It tells us that its ideas took shape not in isolation from the surrounding world nor simply in a struggle against it, but under the control of a will to win it, and to correspond to the spiritual need of the time in such a way that its word might be understood and appropriated. In this work of seeking acceptance, Christian preaching was motivated by a strong love, and expressly used and fostered connections with what mankind already possessed.

We would therefore miss an important aspect of New Testament teaching if we repudiated the question whether and how far Christian convictions can be seen to connect causally with the intellectual background of the age. If agreement in sequences of thought can be shown here, this tells us something about their derivation. They cannot have sprung to birth each time as something completely new. Rather, they are causally connected and represent a coherent and unitary process.

The border between observation and supposition fluctuates here. So a flood of hypotheses, and with them rationalism and controversy, ensues. This obliges us to tread carefully, but at the same time compels us not to neglect this part of the work. We have to show so far as possible what sober observation directed to the facts can understand about the processes in which the ideas of the New Testament emerged.

Different constructions of New Testament theology emerge, depending on what methods are used to explain what we have. As early as the eighteenth century, attention to the special character of each New Testament writer caused it to be noticed that they all expressed their own individual ideas. We therefore have the job of making clear the particular type of piety shown by each of these 'types of teaching'. This method has lasting validity because the history which is our concern here is very largely the product of community leaders; these men had the power to make the rich life they led visible, and to insert it into the whole subsequent course of history as effective potency.

This procedure brings out an essential characteristic of the early history of Christianity. This is that it is based upon those processes which constitute the personal existence of the individual, and succeeds by using nothing except what regulates the inner attitude of a man towards God. The individual is placed in a communion with God which is appropriate to him. The community's leaders thus possessed in their thinking and willing something granted them, and show their independence with striking power.

An account of Jesus should not depict a mass movement in Palestinian Jewry, but *him*. Similarly, the Christian mission in the Greek-speaking world was not sustained by a group of Paul's disciples, but by Paul, complete with the firm convictions his own history had given him. For this reason biographical investigation of Paul is indispensable.

Again, carving up John into a Johannine school was a wrong-headed conjecture. Here, too, world-historical influence attaches to the unique content of a strong individual life. Part of the task of New Testament theology is, therefore, to show the community leaders' intellectual and volitional links with their history and the differences between them. Because of this, New Testament theology must be divided into as many theologies as there are New Testament authors.

However, if only these methods are used, the field of vision is narrowed and an essential part of the history is lost. The eighteenth century, which created these methods, had forgotten the meaning of community and the power of social life to set history in motion. Early Christianity did not consist simply in a few apostles each producing a store of religious ideas and powerfully combining them into the unity of a personal life. What emerged at that time was the community, and this united the individuals in the harmony of a shared faith and action.

We have in the New Testament the phenomenon of the construction of dogmas. But it is not a matter of the imposition of a doctrinal norm from outside; rather, certainties evolve and take root in everyone, producing fellowship. The authenticity of this construction of dogmas is proved by the way in which it created a common will that united the community's action. Given this, New Testament theology cannot simply pass on to the differences, where the personal gifts and characteristics of individuals can be seen. Even these do not arise in isolation from the community, but in working for it. The apostle is, of course, older than the community, since it was assembled by him. But for that very reason, all his thinking and willing is directed towards the community, and it is a misunderstanding to see him as a solitary thinker in isolation from his vocation and activity. This theology is aimed at the community and takes its shape from it. Church and New Testament belong to the same evolutionary process. New Testament theology, therefore, is faced simultaneously with two tasks. Each individual formation is worthy of special attention. At the same time, one must take care to observe that all these perfectly free and personally believing men still constituted a unity. Their fitting into a complete organism and sharing a common task led to the evolution of the community.

A further essential difference in the total historical picture depends on whether we see in the New Testament views which grew up together, or whether we put them in sequence, with each one evolving from another. New Testament theologies sketched out on the basis of Hegelian dogma owe part of their strong influence to the unitary way in which they regarded the whole of the New Testament material in the light of the idea of development. The thought of Jesus was allowed only the role of the first impulse, introducing the whole movement. The conclusion of the movement was supposed to be found in John, who was considered the highest manifestation to emerge from early Christian history – though only when his Jewishness had been removed. The transition was supposed to have been caused by Paul and the reshaping of Christian convictions which he brought about. This schematization made a strong impression upon many people's imagination, and is widely thought to be the result of scientific investigation.

With the Hegelian starting-point came a concentration of interest in the particularities and oppositions in the New Testament doctrinal constructions. Here in the movement of ideas, diverging into oppositions and continuing through struggle, were sought the moving forces of all history and those which produced Christianity. Since metaphysical presuppositions are here directly woven into the historical picture and give it a dogmatizing tendency, historical work inevitably began to lurch. The ideas which were imported to explain the New Testament history stood in sharp opposition to the way in which the men of the New Testament themselves thought. For them God was not an idea nor simply the giver of ideas. Nor did they see struggle as the basis of their action. It was inevitable that history should be given a new shape in the form demanded by the dogma of the narrator. It can now be taken as generally agreed that the question of development in New Testament history must be kept free of all pressure from metaphysical laws.

The work of Jesus is clearly distinct from that of his community. It is the most important causal factor leading to doctrinal formulation in the New Testament. How far what followed from him was a genuine development uniting what the community achieved, with its source in what Jesus gave it, is at present a hotly disputed question. Motives which are not only foreign to Jesus but which would destroy his thought are frequently read into the New

Testament. He did not seek to bring men into contact with God through magic. The community, however, is supposed to have gone in for this sort of magical means of producing salvation. He himself did not understand his sonship in a gnostic way, nor the effect of the divine spirit in a fanatical way. The community is said immediately to have joined gnostic theories to the divine sonship and fanatical tendencies to the idea of the spirit. It is therefore a dominant question in New Testament theology today whether the religious history of the community can be understood as a development of what was created through Jesus, or whether we have here to draw upon outside forces to make the movement of history comprehensible.

The question has its own form with regard to each of the disciples known to us. There is a considerable distance separating I Peter from the Peter of the synoptic gospels. The same is true of the Johannine literature and John in the synoptic gospels. Is this a matter of development, or of constructions which cannot be harmonized and do not belong within the development of a single life-span? This question is also posed with alluring depth in Paul, on the one hand by the way in which Colossians describes the community's fellowship with Christ, and on the other by the Pastoral Epistles. These epistles make capable leadership, proving itself in activity, into the characteristic mark of anyone who wants to work in the community. Are such remarks the final, maturest conclusion to the thought and will found in the earlier epistles, or do we have here extraneous elements even in these documents authenticated by the name of Paul?

Within the church an epoch is clearly marked by the transition of Christianity to the Greeks and the emergence of Greek communities. How was the new form different from the older form of the church, and in what way was it united with it? How are we to conceive the relation of the Palestinian teachers, Matthew, James, John and Peter, to each other and to Paul? All these questions demand precise observation, and so resistance to the attractions of fixed metaphysical theories. Such theories give food for the imagination, but not genuine knowledge. There are two opposing conceptions here. One sees the New Testament types as independent forms which grew up simultaneously and which derive their unity from the fact that they belong to the same community, and exercise the same gift of Jesus. The other view tries to derive one type from the other through direct dependence, as between master and pupil.

The fellow-workers of the apostles are also worthy of careful attention from the historical point of view. Mark, Luke's anonymous informant, Luke himself and the author of the Epistle to the Hebrews should be attended to, both for the sake of finding out what we can know about what was established and generally assumed in the community, and also for their own sake. How the convictions of the community's leaders were felt in the wider circles that shared in their work is itself not without historical significance.

People who want to carve up the New Testament into a series of emergent forms will look for help from the chronology of the individual documents. This is thought to guarantee the possibility of marking off the various stages in the gradual formation of Christian ideas. If what we possessed from the teachers of Palestine was literary compositions which antedated the foundation of the Gentile church, then the chronology of the documents would really be of fundamental importance for the structure of New Testament theology. In fact, however, our documents are all contemporary with each other in the sense that they all come from the period following the establishment of the Greek church. This fact must be taken account of. The statements we possess from the Palestinians should not be evaluated without Paul being borne in mind. Beyond this it is scarcely permissible to draw conclusions about the history of doctrine from the date of the epistles. That would be to confuse statistics with history. The date of an epistle does not automatically tell us the age of its contents. It does not even tell us the period when an epistle became influential in the church. A man is older than his book, and the Johannine theology was present in the church for a long time before the gospel was written. Similarly, Paul's doctrine of justification was normative for the Greek church for a long time before Paul wrote his Epistle to the Romans. The fact that limitations are set to our observation by the meagre extent of our sources, and that these cannot be overcome, must not lead us to fill in the gaps with romancing constructions. The glory of academic work is not that it knows everything, but that it sees what the witnesses make visible and is silent when they are silent.

Another question which might lead to widely differing groundplans of New Testament theology concerns the limits of the area of research. Are there any limits at all, once one includes the task of observing the processes through which the New Testament convictions arose? Are we to think of the Palestinian or the Greek background of the Christian community? Both areas embrace not only a vast wealth of contemporary forms both of thinking and acting; in addition they are parts of a history which reaches back into a measureless past. Further, these areas which even themselves cannot be limited, are also merely parts of the total movement of human history.

As a result of the application of scientific methods to history, there has arisen a tendency to abstract all historical particularities from religious data, and to see them as a unitary thing, as 'religion', which operates according to the same psychological laws everywhere, among animists as among Christians. This intellectual procedure nurtures an inclination for further leaps into the distance because the causal process which occupies the mind of the researcher becomes all the more interesting the further it stretches, and the development stands out all the more clearly, the more forms which are different in other respects can be tied up with each other through a causal line. However, we would be well-advised to distinguish sharply here between what is for the time being nothing more than a construction of the imagination, and what is really the result of insight into the data. The necessary task of New Testament theology remains undone so long as it lurches up and down the wide front of the statistics and history of all religions in an attempt to establish how far back anticipations of and analogies to the ideas of the New Testament can be found. In view of the importance of New Testament theology for the church, it would be a serious loss if instead of penetrating its clearly defined area of research, it got lost in combinations which use material from all areas of the history of religions.

Scientific interests also counsel against this view of the task, because sharpness and correctness of observation are bound to suffer when they abandon the temporal and spatial unity of their object, and do not stay within the orbit of what influenced the emergence and effect of the New Testament convictions in the Christian community. For example, if the products of Babylonian or Indian religious history are brought in to explain New Testament statements, the explanation will inevitably contain a touch of imagination in it. Appeal to an alleged similarity takes the place of showing the process by which these parallels came into the Christian community. One should at least indicate some possible way in which a Christian belief of such a clearly recognizable and firmly evidenced character was able to use oriental models. It may be true that the forces which operated upon early Christianity stretch back through a long history into various areas. But the reason for their influence on the New Testament is not that they were once Babylonian, but that they had at that time become Jewish, or perhaps Greek. So the question of 'the synagogue and Babylon' is a part of our area of research, whereas 'Paul and Babylon' or 'John and India' are games for fertile imaginations.

If we disregard historical processes which belong wholly to the past as far as the New Testament is concerned, and are separated from it by an impenetrable wall, there still remains the question whether we should not describe the neighbouring religious areas at least in so far as they give us religious material which is contemporary with the New Testament. This might be valuable in making judgments about the causal processes. So far as I know, Lutterbeck was the first to include an account of Palestinian and Hellenistic Judaism and the religion of the areas of Greek civilization in his outline of New Testament theology. But these areas are themselves in need of historical investigation – especially the Palestinian synagogue contemporary with the work of Jesus and his messengers. This task is a field of its own and requires independent attention. The further we proceed beyond the present-day beginnings of the work,[3] the clearer the connections become which lead from the surroundings of Christianity to their own new formations.

If we are going to go beyond the limits of the New Testament period, then it is above all the contents of the Old Testament canon which should be considered. Otherwise the historical picture will be seriously distorted; since of all the factors reaching back into the past, none is so important as this.

If we possessed an Old Testament theology written from the standpoint of the first century and clarifying what was for the Jewish and Christian communities the content of the canon, this would give New Testament theology a valuable piece of clarification and confirmation. The possibility of such a presentation is admittedly seriously limited by the situation with regard to sources, but not even the information in the sources we have has yet been collected and worked through. However, the independence of New Testament theology remains unchallenged, even over against the pre-history which directly determines it, namely, the religious history of Israel. This is because the New Testament community is a formation complete in itself with its own central point. It grew out of a new impulse which is more than simply a repetition of old material.

We must also consider the delimitation of the field over against the later history of the church. It is true that the fact of the collection of the New Testament writings into the church's canon gives their study a practical importance which does not apply to later literature. By virtue of the fact that they are canonical, these writings have had an influence upon all generations and members of the church and have determined their communion with God. But this consideration seems to make the decision about methodology depend on our present situation rather than on the actual historical position. Is it not controlled by a dogmatic idea here? The word 'canon' gives expression to a dogmatic judgment which relates the New Testament to our own religious practice. The historian, on the other hand, should be guided purely by observation of what comes from the course of history itself. The ecclesiastical literature closest to the New Testament in time seems to join on to it in a straight development. Our use of it can be further justified by the fact that the only documents preserved for us from the time between the apostles and the apologists are ones which were for some time brought into a certain connection with the New Testament. Their help seems all the more valuable in that the New Testament gives us so little source material. The fruit of the apostles' labour is the church, as it exists in the following generations and is made present for us through its literature. It would seem that only by laying this out *in toto* can we get a complete account of the apostles' work and sufficient basis for a historical judgment about it.

But the distinction between the New Testament writings and the later literature is not based upon an arbitrary fiat. It has historical reasons. By canonizing these writings, the generations following the apostles expressed where they found that word through which the church emerged and receives for all time its connection with the Christ. They found it not in the utterances of contemporary teachers and leaders, but in the writings of these men who speak to us in the New Testament. If we obscure this fact, we come into serious conflict not with a dogma but with history. The account of a martyr's death, say that of Polycarp, was never co-ordinated with the account of Jesus' crucifixion, nor was a theological treatise, like for example that to Diognetus, ever valued on a par with an apostolic letter. The exhortation of a bishop never possessed the same weight as that of an apostle. We are confronted with the fact that in the consciousness of the church the work of Jesus' disciples was kept distinct from what church members with their religious gifts were able to achieve. And this judgment sprang directly from the basic article of Christian conviction, their evaluation of Jesus as the Christ. For this conception of the Christ did not spread the revelation of God equally over the whole course of history; it localized it at a particular point. That gave the disciples of Jesus an importance which the intellectual or ethical achievements of those who came later could never replace. The apostolic office only existed in the church once, and this has resulted in the distinction between their writings and everything that the churches produced thereafter.

The judgment of the church did not approve the close conjunction with the New Testament writings even of the documents we possess. Since later literature is determined by new motives which distinguish it from the aims of the apostolic word, this judgment is sound. The later literature is concerned partly with the development of church order and partly with theology. Here it is influenced by Greek ideas which are not found in the earlier period. I cannot see how presentations of New Testament theology in which quotations from the epistles of James and Ignatius, the Didache and the Pastoral Epistles, are all mixed up together, can give us genuine knowledge. This does justice neither to the New Testament documents nor to the work of the second generation. But the decisive factor in shaping New Testament theology is not where the stronger spiritual force or the loftier ethics are to be found. These differences in value recede in the first place behind concern for the facts. The reason for rejecting this mixing up of ecclesiastical and apostolic writings is that it corrects the historical facts of the matter by reference to the historian's own dogmatic judgment. If he cannot understand why a gospel should be distinguished from other narratives, or a word of Paul from the reflections of another theologian, this is because the notion of the

Christ is without significance for him. But that view should not be read into the early church. That would be to misunderstand what the church was and how it arose. Its foundation was faith in Christ. For this reason it always stood under the word of his messengers. This is recognized by the fact that New Testament theology has as its subject-matter the New Testament, and nothing else.

Here, too, of course, knowledge of the borderland is indispensable for the historian, both as regards what fits well with the apostolic community and what is new and contrasts with it. The former shows how the apostolic word continued to take effect, and the latter how it stands out against the cultural currents of its time. But from a historical as from a dogmatic point of view, understanding the New Testament is a task of its own.

One might again consider limiting the field in New Testament study by reference to the concept of 'theology'. Is the whole span of New Testament thought part of its theology? We have theology when an idea is effectively related to God-consciousness. So far as our picture of the world or nature exists independently alongside consciousness of God, this knowledge can be considered irrelevant or simply natural and fortuitous for religion and theology. So the total inventory of our consciousness would contain far more than belongs to our theology, and comprise statements which not only a third person, but even we ourselves would find ineffective as regards religion. Is not the same thing true of the New Testament? We cannot avoid the question by saying that its revelatory intention makes all its statements theologically important, because revelation does not take place independently of men. It happens through men. The apostles' humanity is not concealed or extinguished so as to make God visible without men, over and above them. Rather, when God is witnessed to, revelation makes the humanity of his messengers visible and effective. Nor can the task be limited by rules set by a dogmatician: this or that is indifferent for religion – e.g. the picture of nature in the New Testament writings, or their statements about the spirit world, and so on. These sorts of rulings may indeed tell us what is or is not part of the dogmatician's religion. But this is no guarantee that the men of the New Testament have been objectively and faithfully grasped. How far the work has to be taken in this respect cannot be laid down before it is done. In the first place, the whole content of the New Testament is to be observed. How far then the structuring shows certain groups of statements to be only loosely connected with the theological centre, or quite distinct from it, is not a preliminary question of a methodological sort. It is in fact a result of the work itself.

5   *Objections to the Explanatory Intention of Historical Work*

When the task of explanation is included in the purpose of New Testament theology, doubts about the legitimacy of the enterprise get stronger. Is not this thinking bound to deteriorate into rationalism? says the opponent. When historians explain what has happened, and that means, of course, try to give a complete explanation of it, they bring in a pile of conjectures which not only conceal the facts of the matter, but directly attack them and brush them aside for the sake of the explanation. And so the New Testament collapses under the weight of the literature on New Testament theology, just as once in the synagogue the Old Testament was buried under the Talmud and Midrash. Claiming to be alone competent to make the New Testament comprehensible, this discipline sets itself up above it, and suppresses the authority of the New Testament in favour of that of the historian.

There is admittedly plenty of evidence to show that academic work is always tempted towards rationalism, towards a pride of judgment which expects to get the whole of reality into its own intellectual grasp and so reduces it to its own field of vision. But these cheap thrills are not overcome by ignoring and despising the task of obtaining a coherent understanding. That would only produce the appearance that the unwholesome roots of the conflict lie in the very fact of a relationship between the New Testament and academic work. In fact, however, a construction that has cut loose from observation is the enemy not only of the New Testament, but also of the aims and rules of academic work. It may be that a tendency towards rationalistic conjectures which are far away from the facts clings to all academic work. But we must be continually aware that this conflicts with science as well as with the New Testament; it is irrational as well as impious. When our object is driven out by a theory which denies the real and puts our imaginings in its place, we oppose not only the past, but at the same time the ground and law of our own thinking activity, and so our own existence. In opposing the object we are also opposing the subject. The borders between dreaming and thinking, between scientific and rationalistic explanation, are established by the laws which govern our thinking. These demand evidence in support of judgments, which means that we are here dependent upon sight and hearing that give material and basis for such judgment.

Where judgment cuts loose from the perception which is indispensable to it, where the intellect's productive power tries to be in command and play the creator so that what we produce is no longer connected with a prior receiving, where thought circles around one's own self, as though this could create from itself the material from which knowledge comes and the rules by which it is to be judged, there we have rationalism. It stands in irreconcilable hostility to the very basis of the New Testament, because acknowledging God is the direct opposite of rationalism. But this rationalism is at the same time the road to dreamland and the death of intellectual integrity.

The danger is frequently increased by unclear theories about thought-processes which demand of academic work unlimited reliance on what thought can achieve and assert that everything that happens can be fully understood. Where this kind of postulate influences even concrete individual chains of thought, it produces apparent values in which a self finds only itself in what has happened and fixes its will in theories instead of enabling it to see. Not even the theologian, of course, will admit that there is any such thing as an absolute mystery, a 'thing in itself' which existed unknown, without being preceded by thought and shaped by it. But he dare not confuse his own thought with God's, and so must not offend against the limits which are set, as though it were intolerable that we should also have to acknowledge what is incomprehensible. This is his protection against thinking *a priori* and against rationalistic construction. But every dogmatic position is tempted to this. It is found where God is acknowledged and where he is denied, in religious and irreligious colours, as orthodoxy and as heterodoxy. In all our concepts and general rules the same thing recurs, that good or bad they are only powerful when they enter real life and direct our behaviour towards definite objects. This means that the dogmatician alone cannot protect the historian from rationalistic perversion of what has happened. The most important factor making a New Testament theology scientifically respectable or worthless is whether a scholar possesses the veracity of the genuine observer in concrete cases, or whether in his work he makes bold to determine the course of history to suit himself. He must protect himself against this in the course of his work by not proceeding to make a judgment before carefully and modestly perceiving, surrendering himself to the data, and never once allowing himself to judge, but first making himself feel the whole range of the conditions which produce the knowledge.

This gives the basis for answering the last and sharpest argument against New Testament theology. This objection says that undertaking to explain the word of the New Testament historically is fundamentally irreligious, whether it is then rejected or joyfully welcomed as an act which frees us from religion. As soon as we begin to discuss the origin of the New Testament convictions we have inevitably and utterly denied an essential characteristic of the New Testament, namely its property of being God's revelation. The New Testament calls God its author because Jesus speaks as Son of God and his messengers as God's messengers, no matter what the historian's own convictions may be; from this comes the interest he brings to the material. Here he investigates statements which claim to be God's revelation and derive their historical power from the fact that they have worked and continue to work as such. But concepts like 'being historically conditioned', 'development', 'belonging in a context', with which New Testament theology deals, seem to many people to destroy the statements the New Testament makes about itself. An act of God transcends all other causality, leaving only one dependence, namely on God. If causal connections with what went before are recognized, then a concept of the world is brought in from which the idea of God is excluded. This objection is especially lively when the evolution with its extended web of conditions reaches beyond biblical history and successfully involves its background also. The New Testament is then thought to have been made dependent upon the tarnished products of human work, Pharisaism and Hellenism, rabbinate and gnosticism, instead of on God's activity alone. It is therefore widely thought from a great variety of religious points of view that divine origin and historical mediation are mutually exclusive.

This antithesis between the idea of God and history can be proved to be false from the course of our own life and from the

New Testament. Taken seriously, it tears apart the relation of our own life to God; our own consciousness is cut loose from God as radically as the New Testament is. We have in our consciousness nothing which is not conditioned by history, whether our individual history or that of the large communities in which we live and on which we depend. If history is excluded from God's influence on the grounds that it is merely transitory and human, there exists no conscious relationship to God granted us in our personal life.

As well as conflicting with our own experience of religion, this train of thought also conflicts with the fundamental statement of the New Testament. Though it often claims to be the necessary and correct sign of faith, grounded in the New Testament, in fact it attacks it at the kernel. This witnesses to God's giving which is seriously meant and efficacious; it makes man someone who receives it, and it shapes him. God's creating and giving penetrate man's existence and consciousness in their concrete, historically determined form. It establishes him and becomes visible in and through him. God does his work of grace and judgment not outside man and so, too, not beyond history, but in it and through it. So the New Testament utterly repudiates the thesis that revelation and history cannot be united, and this at the same time destroys the view that historical research is a denial of revelation.

The argument is, of course, concentrated in our view of Jesus. As soon as Jesus is made the object of historical investigation, it appears to many people that the undertaking itself, quite apart from its particular results, involves denying Jesus the name of Christ and divine sonship. Yet precisely here, and especially clearly, God is the maker of history, not its destroyer. The sending of Jesus makes us certain that God is the maker of the man who has a relationship with him. Through him comes the history which is rooted in God's will and fulfils it. The first part of this history is achieved in the inner life of Jesus himself.

Finally, behind a negative judgment about history there stands the awareness of an unresolved opposition between man and God, and so a pre-Christian idea of God. People are afraid of God's act, as though it threatened the reality of human life. So they try to protect this reality by denying the act of God. They think that when God acts, he annihilates everything that exists besides himself. This all-absorbing God, who will tolerate no world beside himself, and who must be denied for the sake of the world's existence, is not the God of scripture. This is how man, oppressed by the sense of God's having left him, conceives him. In fact, the relation of God to us constitutes also our relation to the world. We do not get lost from his sight by being strongly affected by what happens all around us. Nor does he get lost from our sight. In this and no other way we are his work: as members of this common life. We emerge from it in the different relationships of dependence which form us. For he gives us active life, not as isolated essences, but in the togetherness produced by historical processes.

What agencies have served to create the factors which, as the revelation of truth and grace connect us with God, cannot be established by a dogmatic certainty that the historian possessed before observing anything. The question can only be answered on the basis of insight gained in the process itself. Because we receive God's revelation through history and become what we are through it, there can be no knowledge about it which is independent of historical perception. How God works cannot be known apart from this. It is the essential characteristic of revelation that we see the frontiers between truth and illusion, good and evil, holy and unholy, with unmistakable clarity. If these frontiers are removed, the consciousness of God is destroyed and the revelatory value of the event is denied. But that does not remove man as a developing being, with the complexity of his consciousness and the corruptness of his will, from fellowship with God. The holy, which man is given as his own, comes by his being made holy in thought, will and nature. But how God's sanctification of him works, how far down it reaches into the profane and corrupted sphere of human history and here finds the medium for revealing God's grace and fulfilling his will, can only be learned from the facts. The incomprehensible character of a divine dispensation which sanctifies humanity arises not only in individual historical cases, but exists equally in the very fact of there being a divine ruling, calling and sanctifying. This brings man with all the marks of his humanity into a relationship with God; it makes him capable of receiving God's revelation and bearing witness to him.

Because of the close connections between historical work and the convictions by which we live, it is inevitable that New Testament theology will be drawn into the intellectual and ethical struggle about God and Christ. Every conviction has the right to try to prove itself from history and to overcome its opponents on this basis. For example, a historian may reject the idea of God, whether altogether or in the area of scientific thought, on the grounds that the latter permits only this-worldly language, and sees the world as a closed system containing within itself all the conditions for its unfolding processes. But then his presentation of the New Testament annuls its central statement, and he is being quite logical when his judgment contradicts the causal links of the New Testament presentation at every step. One cannot deny from the outset the legitimacy of this account of New Testament theology any more than one can an account which proceeds on the assumption that Jesus' messianic idea is a proof of mental illness, that the messianic idea is one of many vacuous concepts in the history of religion which for a time exercise great power but then burst, and that the fact that this idea was able to take possession of Jesus' will and so achieve reality was caused by mental disturbance on his part. This sort of account makes the explanatory part of the task a resolute battle against the New Testament. It is unlikely to escape the danger of totally reshaping what happened according to the demands of the scholar's own standpoint. Every consciousness has the right to test its account by the reality we are given, and so to verify its dogmatic statement by being portrayed as the law which shapes the course of history. All the concept 'science' demands is that no matter what intellectual furniture leads someone to make a judgment, he is clear about what factors are influencing him, and so ensures that his perception can distinguish between the part of his judgment which comes from observation of past events, and that which rests on his own immanent certainties.

Admittedly, difficulties are caused by the sharply opposing views we find in the interpretation of the New Testament and, above all, in the picture of Christ. It is widely thought that the uncertainty of historical research counts against Jesus, or at least shows the defective nature of the reports which witness to him. Since there are as many pictures of Christ as there are viewers of Jesus, and as many interpretations of the New Testament as there are exegetes, it is thought to be hopeless to seek any well-grounded judgment here. One form of this view goes as follows: one can only affirm with certainty about the New Testament history what is doubted by none of the participators in scientific research, or is at least not contested by the majority. But complaints about scientific disagreement miss the point that this is a sign not that

Jesus and his word are weak, but that they are powerful. The disagreement comes from the impact of the word of the New Testament on the whole content of our ego with an energy that both
gives the determination of faith to join him and evokes rejection
to the point of hatred. It grasps our thinking and willing at their
nodal points; the image of God with which it confronts us keeps
our entire intellectual position in motion. Our contact with the
word, therefore, provokes an extraordinary variety of points of
attraction and repulse.

Thus it is not incorrect to say that New Testament theology,
like dogmatics, stands on the boundary of science, and is perhaps
even over the boundary, if by 'science' one means agreement and
fixed tradition and successful co-operation by many researchers
leading to a unitary result. To reach agreement about the New
Testament we must be united in the basic direction of our thinking
and willing. That is asking a lot. It will always involve our view of
nature, the will's norms, the concept of guilt, the whole content
of our God-consciousness. It touches on the greatest enterprises
of human discovery.

The inner peace which both scientific work and religious life
need in the face of scientific argument is supported by insight into
the conditions of historical work and their relationship to the job
of dogmatics. We have to be clear that historical criticism is never
based on historical fact alone, but always has roots in the critic's
dogma, too. Also, that dogmatic or faith judgments never rest on
historical work alone, because our convictions never come simply
from the history which lies behind us but from the effects of that
history in our experience. If we recognize the connection between
the two aspects, we shall no longer use the disagreement which
burdens historical research as justification for historical or dogmatic scepticism. It must be clear that as dogmatics gets from history
content and justification for its statements, so too the emergence
and growth of dogmatic knowledge has a verifying and purifying
effect on historical judgments. Then the possibility and even
relative necessity of a variety of historical efforts can be understood. They will no longer simply be accounted as the confusion
of what is past or the uncertainty of its documentation. Nor will
hopes be entertained of settling historical disputes by developing
historical methods or gaining further results. What is needed is
clarification and broadening of our dogmatic knowledge so that

we can really do history which is not a useless war between an inflated self and what happened, but makes judgments that grasp the real course of events.

Precisely when historical knowledge is being directly used in a stimulating way for polemical purposes, those who share responsibility for the public state of knowledge must take care to do justice to the historical aim of New Testament theology in its simple integrity. They will not bring an end to the fight, but will see that it is fought with honourable and clean weapons.

6   *New Testament Theology and New Testament History*

If the subject-matter of New Testament theology consists in the convictions found in the New Testament writings, then it differs from the historical work which clarifies the events through which Christianity came into being. Even though from the side of both New Testament history and New Testament theology, it is perfectly clear that they can only prosper in continuing relationship to each other, still there is intrinsic justification for a division of labour, though no separation, at this point.

Both sides must remain connected, because the New Testament contains no abstract, timeless ideas. History here becomes the basis of religion and of its doctrine. So the question of its meaning and origin cannot be answered without observing the events of which it speaks and from which it stems. An account of the history of Jesus, his messengers and his community therefore precedes a New Testament theology and serves as its basis. At the same time, this is the indispensable tool for those whose New Testament research constructs the events it presupposes. The convictions of those working here have had a great effect upon their versions of the events. This history does not consist of deliberate changes in the situation of the community or the important individuals in it. It consists of acts which stem from their will and so are based on the convictions of those who performed them. Paul's missionary work, for example, is conditioned throughout by his faith. If an author conceals the apostle's faith by blurred ideas, he will achieve no clear picture or certain judgment about what happened through him and what made him provoke such changes in human history. Finally, no division between history and doctrine does justice to Jesus' work and death. The events of his life do not simply get a particular colour from the ideas he wove with them. Their entire source and origin is to be found in his convictions. He acted on the basis of his mission in the certainty of being the Son and the Christ. So discussions of what happened through him which ignore his inner life are worthless. It would be equally worthless to list his ideas as his doctrines, independently of his experiences. Whatever of his sayings do not originate in his own experience and action come from his background in the community of his time. They are not what made him the source of a new history. To list what Jesus taught as general statements would simply add up to his Judaism, even if it included a concept of the Messiah. This shows that ahistorical constructions of the 'teaching of Jesus' conceal the real course of history.

Both these branches need each other and move on lines which constantly make contact. But we are justified in distinguishing them because, like all other events, those in the New Testament also have a natural side which inevitably demands historical work. Even if the nodal points of this history are acts in which the actors' reason and spirit shows its power, still their action belongs in the web of natural conditions which is constructed out of a host of alternating and corresponding threads. That makes the question of what happened an intricate one, and the question of the conditions which shaped it even more so. This is why the knowledge granted to the apostles is more important than the events. It is the permanent result of the history, whereas the history itself is largely forgotten and lost without trace. Their word, on the other hand, cuts loose from the turn of events and becomes a permanent power. It is this intellectual result of the course of history with which we are in the first place engaged, because this is responsible for the continuing effect of the New Testament. The dogmatician needs to know it. For the means whereby the New Testament history grasps and moves our own history is through the word which has come from it.

This judgment was already the guiding principle of the New Testament authors. They do make the connection of their doctrine with their history quite clear, but at the same time they consciously give precedence to doctrine over knowledge of events. In the texts which aim to show us the will of the Christ, his history in the sense of the chain of events can only be imperfectly obtained. Whereas the apostolic doctrine is richly documented, large parts of the career of the apostles and the early church have sunk fully into oblivion. The Johannine word, for example, is preserved in the threefold form of gospel, exhortation and prophecy. The historical events on the other hand which brought about the separation of John from Jerusalem and his entry into Asian Christianity, are totally obscure, although from the historical point of view considerable importance attaches to them. The word by which Paul called Timothy to him in Rome is preserved for us; the events which preceded and followed it are lacking, although they would have contained the report of the apostle's death. The church has preserved Paul's instruction to man to be justified before God; we do have a reminiscence of his own conversion, but it gives us no complete picture of those events. This evaluation of doctrine by the first Christian generation determines also the historical work of all subsequent ones, because the latter derives its purpose and criterion from the condition of its sources. The two branches of our historical research are unequally served by these. The history of the earliest church has to be satisfied with few facts. Its main task is to clarify the holes in our view of the history which cannot be filled. We can, on the other hand, get a New Testament theology. What once was the case stands here quite clearly, even today.

Jesus can only be understood when we contemplate his history, because with him most clearly of all, thought and will, word and deed are united. Yet even here the aim of the work looks very different when it is thought to be a matter of illuminating external events, rather than of discovering the inner motivation which Jesus himself had and which he communicated to his disciples. Taking one's guidelines from the intellectual side of his history relativizes the importance of many issues that cannot be avoided in an external history.

Of the special sub-divisions in the discipline of New Testament history, one has particular significance for New Testament theology, namely the history of the literature, or critical introduction. Judgments made about the literary history of the documents determines directly our notions about the course of the inner processes in earliest Christianity. An objection can be launched against New Testament theology from this side, to the effect that it remains a provisional and unsuccessful undertaking so long as important matters concerning the history of the literature remain in doubt, that is, for as long as there is dispute about the history of the con-

struction of the synoptic texts; the origin of the Johannine literature in John, the disciple of Jesus; and of the Lucan writings in
Luke, the companion of Paul. But it would be a quite inappropriate
procedure to postpone the work of New Testament theology until
the problems of critical introduction are settled. For New Testament theology is for its part an indispensable tool which critical
introduction constantly uses in its own work, because a good many
of its difficulties come from the inner religious history of the
community. It is true that their observations which are empirical
in the narrower sense, those which linguistic statistics, topography
and background, and the history of the transmission of the documents provide, are especially cogent precisely because they confront us with perceptible factuality and do not stretch down into
the depths of theological work. But none of the currently disputed questions of New Testament introduction can be resolved by
this sort of data. In every case considerations from New Testament
theology obviously play an important role.

The relationship of New Testament theology to a discipline which
has scarcely begun, namely the history of language, is similar. Earlier
discussion of this was concerned only with the relationship of New
Testament Greek to literary Greek; this is without significance for
New Testament theology.[4] However, exact observation of the
process by which language was constructed has some significance
for it. This took place in the Christian community because a set of
ideas which was foreign to the Greeks had to find expression in
Greek. That does not mean that completely new constructions
were formed or attempted. This would have contradicted the
nature of language, which can only be understood when it uses
materials already available, even in expressing new ideas. It would
also have contradicted the aim of Jesus' messengers, which was not
to invent a secret language, but to let their word be understood and
done. New forms of language, however, come into existence when
the Greek available has been used in the formation of new thought.
This process was made easier and guided by the fact that the community thought in Aramaic as well as in Greek from the start, so
that Christian construction of language in the Greek area followed
the model of semitic constructions.[5] The transition from the language of Palestinian Judaism to Christian preaching was straightforward. Although insight into the relation of the New Testament
word to non-Christian linguistic usage, both in the Palestinian and

the purely Greek area, will be of considerable help to New Testament theology, the latter is nevertheless independent of this field, because the apostolic documents are sufficiently clear to be self-explanatory. The meaning of their words is governed in the first place by their own usage. History of language for its part needs a knowledge of New Testament theology to see correctly the processes which belong to its sphere. What has changed is not in the first place, or mainly, the natural element of the language, but the thought and will of those speaking. This is what has led to a new use of language. If theology cannot get a clear picture of the over-arching events, then much of what is characteristic for the development of the language remains obscure.

The close connection between the external history and the development of Christian convictions leaves room for the borders of New Testament theology to be drawn in different ways. The most complete exclusion of the historical material was effected by 'biblical dogmatics'. When historical and dogmatic work began to be separated, New Testament theology took its questions from dogmatics, but thought that theological questions could only be answered by means of historical work, the aim of which was historical understanding. That led to the works of biblical dogmatics which aim to develop Christian teaching in the earliest period in a systematic way, by setting biblical statements alongside every statement in the church's system, and discussing their relationship to the ideas anchored in the church.

The interest which was satisfied by this way of working is not without some permanent justification, because the reason why historians are concerned with the statements of the New Testament is that they determine the conviction of Christianity and have produced its present theology. This methodical, deliberate and complete comparison with what the later dogma of the church contains, provides results which are valuable for the historical picture. This is not only because in this way the influences affecting the church's dogma emerge, but also because our eyes are thus sharpened so that we can perceive the original Christian convictions more clearly. Books of biblical dogmatics are helpful to the dogmatician, too, because by this method comparison of the two trains of thought remains the firmly maintained purpose of the work, and so the evaluation of historical results by dogmatics is made easier.

The disadvantage of the procedure is that it carries over the results of dogmatic work into the New Testament and so can easily short-circuit the historical aim. The questions here are not obtained from the historical event itself, but are brought to it from the train of thought of a dogmatics which has been established at a different time. The guiding interest is directed to the church's doctrinal task, not to understanding the New Testament word. It is difficult to avoid bending this in the direction of intellectualism here. The apostles begin to look like gnostics who have an opinion about every mystery with which contemplation of the world presents us. This procedure can therefore only be applied with safety where we can presuppose that the two trains of thought are, or at least ought to be, essentially identical. When one considers that the purpose of dogmatic work is to gain knowledge, whereas the purpose of the New Testament word is beyond this to call men through God to God, and when one recognizes that dogmatic work has been and must be influenced by later situations and knowledge, it becomes advisable not to take the questions which guide the investigation from the dogmatic tradition, but to get them from the New Testament material itself.

The danger that the New Testament may be fitted to a model which is alien to it will be warded off more easily if we use as basis for our investigation not a dogmatic system, but a simplified model of the religious phenomenon. The New Testament statements relating to those phenomena which are essential for every stage of piety and every feature of believing existence will then be gathered up. Monographs on the central Christian concepts serve this purpose. The sovereignty of God, Christ, sin, justification, love and faith establish the content of the New Testament word. New Testament theology will always proceed in this direction because the characteristic feature of the New Testament word is that it awakens and regulates these phenomena. By applying this sort of model, the excellence of the work can be tested to see how far it is able to express the New Testament statements in their concrete, historically conditioned form.

Sharp opposition to biblical dogmatics is expressed in the judgment that New Testament theology is a misguided undertaking because the New Testament does not contain theology but religion. But this judgment only applies to people who are still unclear about the inner difference between that form of knowledge which we call science and the word directed to us by the New Testament. Whereas scientific thought is not aimed beyond the intellect but seeks to construct ideas, the proclamation performed by the New Testament allows no separation of thought from the other functions which together with it constitute our existence. This is not because it occupies a lowly stage of culture and so has not yet reached the heights of scientific aims, but because it rejects and judges as monstrous a consciousness of God which remains mere consciousness and establishes nothing other than intellectual activity. It sees in God's relationship to us something which moves us totally, and so it gives us certainty of God, that we should believe him, serve him, live through him and for him. Because through God's relationship with us, knowledge of God comes to relate us to him, the New Testament is consciously and irreconcileably opposed to every form of thought which is only meant to produce a religious concept. Complete reserve towards intellectualism is an essential characteristic of Jesus' work, and it is carried on right through the apostles and in the organization of the earliest community in a perfectly classical manner. A New Testament 'theology' which obscured this difference and described the men of the New Testament, say, on the model of the Greek thinkers or like modern academics, really would be radically perverting its material.

But there is no need to associate the concept 'theology' with an artificial separation of thought from existence. The linguistic usage of the whole church does not require this. It does not in the least connect 'theology' with the character of abstraction from the real purpose of life and abandoning central functions in favour of the mere construction of concepts. Thus when someone wants for the moment to set aside the more far-reaching purposes of theological work and indicate a restriction to the intellectual aspect, it is customary to speak not of 'theology' but of 'academic' or 'scientific' theology. It has remained an element in the public consciousness that 'theology' is not always or necessarily associated with a renunciation of the goals which reach down into our existence. It is worth emphasizing the strong link which theology has with the New Testament for the sake of avoiding its atrophy into an abstract scholasticism. This link does not make the concept 'theology' vacuous or curtail it. The New Testament confronts us with intellectual activity and conceptual construction which, though not directed to intellectual goals alone, still by their energy and fruitfulness on any showing represent a high point in the movement of human thought.

The work of those by whom Christianity came into existence, from Jesus right through the apostles, was never concerned just to obtain ideas about God's government. But it is equally certain that a characteristic of their participation in God is that it was something known. It emerged through the participation of thought in God's word and will, receiving through him a rich and definite content. When we take from the New Testament the knowledge which is associated as cause and effect with Christian experience, we obtain its 'theology'.

Theology will for a long time yet have to resist the Greek tradition as this is continued in Protestant orthodoxy, and then in rationalism and still today in speculative forms. It resulted in the fact that the whole of New Testament history was considered as merely the history of thought. This meant that New Testament theology had fulfilled its task when it had defined the concepts which the apostles attained and explained how they arose. It is a considerable scientific advance that through the reaction against speculative Kantianism, even German academic work has now become aware of the relationship between our willing and our imagination. This has resulted in a new way of enquiring about New Testament theology. But even this new current has its dangers, and needs to be protected against exaggerations. We are told that New Testament history is misunderstood when the events which determine it are taken to be achievements of thought; that the forces at work here and the great results effected belong to the sphere of the will; that it is more important to observe Jesus' feelings and apprehend his character than to ask how he conceived of the kingly sovereignty of God; that in considering Paul's assault upon the Greek world, the impulses which drove him are far more important than the formulae which he invented about the purpose of the law, the death of Christ and the justification of believers. This shift in the direction of work is an advance, in that it frees us from the domination of an ideal of thought that was constructed outside the New Testament and was forced upon it from outside. It is true that the power of the men of the New Testament did not consist solely in their thoughts. They were able to will and act, and the way in which they were able to do this was very significant for the course of history that they brought about.

The content of their thought determined the way in which they lived and showed itself to be genuine conviction by giving them their will. How it did that forms an important object for our observation.

But working like this can easily lead to the replacement of observation by free constructions of the imagination. We cannot perceive other people's will directly, but only through the ideas through which they establish their will, make it conscious and translate it into activity. If this is not understood, imagination is given free rein to shape the historical picture out of its own conjectures which go beyond all observation, under the pretence of discovering hidden motives.

There is a science of New Testament history for as long as those engaged in it are talking about the will that moves it. This is done by clarifying through thought its grounds and goals. The object of a New Testament theology which wants to remain a science is the New Testament word. This is something given; it keeps it away from dreamland and in touch with reality. We must, however, be constantly watchful that it does not consist of abstractions, or of thought-constructions arising outside the will and real life. They must come from these and be created for them.

It is therefore not advisable for New Testament theology to imitate the modern separation between dogmatics and ethics in theology. It can, of course, be clearly recognized from the New Testament writings that the considerations which suggest this division of labour for us today were already partly operative for the founders of the church. They give their ethical admonitions a measure of independence alongside the parts which bear witness to the divine action for the world. The disciples recalled two clearly separable actions of Jesus: he instructed them about good and evil, and he showed them how God's sovereign revelation was taking place in what they saw. So, too, it is no coincidence that the ethical portions of Paul's epistles are a rounded whole at the end of the epistle; nor that alongside his gospel, powerfully written simply to establish faith, John should have written the epistles, whose entire interest is equally concentrated upon love. There was a sense for the difference that enters our thinking through its being sometimes directed upwards to perceive the divine activity, and sometimes turned inwards to the form of our own will, to construct the rules which put this on the right lines.

But both kinds of thinking, one giving a person certainty of God, the other giving him the certainties which determine his action, are consciously and resolutely united in the apostles' thought. Thus both mutually establish and strengthen each other, and are only complete when they are united. To divide up the apostles' theology into 'dogmatics' and 'ethics' would be a perversion of their actual material and would obscure one of its essential characteristics. The New Testament knows of no concern with the divine which does not produce ethics, because it determines our will and action. Nor does it know of a directing of our will which we have to find for ourselves without reference to God. An apostolic dogmatics without any ethics would mean a falsification of it, because without an account of the action granted us by him, its statements about God and Christ would not only be incomplete; they would have lost sight of the purpose which controlled them. The behaviour to which the knowledge of God calls us is not in the apostles' opinion hitched externally on to it as an addition which could be dispensed with, or as something different or new that is not essentially connected with it. Rather, this is included in God's work for the world and is indispensable for the creation and maintenance of our communion with God. Similarly, anyone who writes an ethics of the New Testament, whether it be what is called 'the morality of Jesus', or what may be called Pauline or Johannine ethics, comes into conflict with the reality if he gives the impression that morality is here independent of religion and exclusively a matter of the human consciousness and human will. The New Testament accounts of our obligations include the reasons for them, and this leads us not simply to individual self-contained sections of New Testament dogmatics, but to the totality of it. For example, if we produce a morality out of Jesus' words, our historical purpose goes astray if we do not bear in mind that Jesus' words on moral issues are all calls to repentance, not reflections on ethical themes. They are challenges appealing for repentance, showing its necessity and indicating its goal. Conversion to God comes about when one has the will to reach God's sovereignty and escape his judgment. Its fulfilment rests upon God confirming his sovereignty over man and acting towards him in his sovereign grace. We are therefore continually confronted by the claims of Jesus upon the community's behaviour, with his dogmatic convictions. Without these, his statements about morality cannot be understood. Pauline ethics cannot be described without making clear what the Christ meant for Paul, and this requires a complete account of Paulinism. Since the consideration of ethical statements always needs observation of the dogmatic reasons for them, and since, too, understanding dogmatic statements makes us pay attention to their ethical goals, New Testament dogmatics and New Testament ethics inevitably develop as a pair. It is therefore not advisable to divide the work at this point.

BIBLIOGRAPHICAL NOTE

In addition to the literature mentioned on pp. 169–80, the following works should be noted.

A useful list of earlier literature (divided into beginnings, critical and radical side, apologetic and conservative side, systematizing and dogmatic works, individual doctrinal concepts) is provided by Holtzmann, Vol.I, pp.1–5. R. Schnackenburg, *New Testament Theology Today*, Geoffrey Chapman 1963, also contains substantial bibliographies. Amongst Wrede's contemporaries, C. A. Bernoulli, *Die wissenschaftliche und die kirchliche Methode*, Freiburg 1897, reviewed by Troeltsch (*Göttinger Gelehrter Anzeige*, 1898, pp. 425–35), posed the problems sharply. W. Bousset reviewed Krüger and Wrede in his 'Zur Methodologie der Wissenschaft vom neuen Testament', *ThR* 2, 1899, pp.1–15, and M. Reischle, 'Historische und dogmatische Methode der Theologie', *ThR* 4, 1901, pp.261–75, 305–24, wrote on Troeltsch. These viewpoints are still integral to present-day discussion of what New Testament theology is, or should be. Further back, and on the other side of the fence, M. Kähler's review of B. Weiss in *Theologische Studien*, 1870, pp.576–607, is still worth reading. Much of F. C. Baur's work has recently been reprinted in Germany. The English translation by Peter C. Hodgson of the introduction to *Lectures on the History of Christian Dogma* in *F. C. Baur on the Writing of Christian History*, Library of Protestant Thought, Oxford University Press 1968, is particularly to be welcomed.

From recent systematic theology see K. Rahner, *Theological Investigations*, Vol.5, Darton, Longman and Todd 1966 (also Rahner and Schlier in *LThK* II, cols.444–51); W. Pannenberg, *Basic Questions in Theology*, vol.1, SCM Press and Fortress Press, Philadelphia 1970; E. Jüngel, *Unterwegs zur Sache*, Munich 1972; K. Reinhardt, *Der dogmatische Schriftgebrauch in der katholischen und protestantischen Christologie von der Aufklärung bis zur Gegenwart*, Munich 1970. The literature on the theme of scripture and tradition and on the canon is enormous, and most of what is written about hermeneutics in theology involves views about New Testament theology. E. Dinkler, 'Principles of Biblical Interpretation', *The Journal of Religious Thought* 13, 1955–56, pp.20–30, is helpful. See also his article 'Bibelkritik (NT)' in *RGG*³ I, cols.1188–90.

From the historical and exegetical side the essay by C. K. Barrett and chs. 13–17 of Vol.1 and the essay by G. W. H. Lampe in Vol.2 of the *Cambridge History of the Bible*, Cambridge University Press 1970, 1968, are relevant. W. Bauer, *Orthodoxy and Heresy in Earliest Christianity*, Fortress Press, Philadelphia 1971 and SCM Press 1972, raises important questions for New Testament theology.

Of the many survey articles, E. F. Scott, 'The Present Position of New Testament Theology', *HTR* 6, 1913, pp.60–75 concentrates upon Weinel and Feine; M. Brückner, 'Die neuen Darstellungen der neutestamentlichen Theologie', *ThR* 16, 1913, pp.363ff., 415ff. discusses Feine, Weinel, Schlatter and Holtzmann. See also C. T. Craig, 'Biblical Theology and the Rise of Historicism', *JBL* 62, 1943, pp.281–94. K. Stendahl's article 'Biblical Theology' in *The Interpreter's Dictionary of the Bible*, Abingdon Press, Nashville 1962, I, pp. 418–32 is important. See also O. Betz, 'History of Biblical Theology', ibid., I, pp. 432–7. On the question of structure see B. Reicke, 'Einheitlichkeit oder verschiedene "Lehrbegriffe" in der neutestamentlichen Theologie?', *ThZ* IX, 1953, pp. 401–15.

The first modern Roman Catholic New Testament theology was that of M. Meinertz (1950). See also his 'Sinn und Bedeutung der neutestamentlichen Theologie', *Münchener Theologische Zeitschrift* 5, pp.159–70. The next was that of J. Bonsirven (1951). Also from the Roman Catholic side see D. M. Stanley, *Towards a Biblical Theology of the New Testament*, West Hartford 1959, and W. Harrington, *The Path of Biblical Theology*, Gill and Martin 1972.

Works on New Testament christology often raise wider questions about New Testament theology. This is certainly true of E. Güttgemanns' work on Pauline christology, *Der leidende Apostel und sein Herr*, Göttingen 1966. See also P. Vielhauer's review of F. Hahn, *The Titles of Jesus in Christology*, Lutterworth Press 1970, 'Ein Weg zur neutestamentlichen Christologie?' in *Aufsätze zum neuen Testament*, Munich 1965, and Hahn's reply in *Verkündigung und Forschung* 2/1970. The latter's essay 'Probleme historischer Kritik', *ZNW* LXIII, 1972, pp.1–17, is also helpful. E. Jüngel, *Paulus und Jesus*, Tübingen ²1964, is rich in implications for the discipline. From a more conservative position see H. R. Balz, *Methodische Probleme der neutestamentlichen Christologie*, Neukirchen 1967.

NOTES TO INTRODUCTION

1. From a very different standpoint, F.-M. Braun begins his article, 'La théologie biblique', *Revue Thomiste* 61, 1953, pp.221–53, as follows: 'Les expressions *théologie biblique* et 'théologie du Nouveau Testament' sont devenues courantes, mais ceux qui en usent les emploient en des sens si divers qu'elles risquent d'entrentenir de lourdes confusions.'

2. Quoted from W. G. Kümmel, *The New Testament. The History of the Investigation of its Problems*, Abingdon Press, Nashville 1972 and SCM Press 1973, p.98. This very important essay is being reprinted in the forthcoming volume on New Testament theology edited by G. Strecker in the 'Wege der Forschung' series of the Wissenschaftliche Buchgesellschaft, Darmstadt.

3. See especially E. Käsemann (ed.), *Das Neue Testament als Kanon*, Göttingen 1970, and I. Lönning, *'Kanon in Kanon'*, Oslo and Munich 1972, which present a wide variety of viewpoints. See also below, pp.64ff.

4. See below p.71. Most illuminating here is G. Ebeling's essay ' "Sola Scriptura" and Tradition' in *The Word of God and Tradition*, ET Fortress Press, Philadelphia, and Collins 1964, pp.102–47, unfortunately marred by poor translation.

5. See below pp.184f. C. F. Evans, *Is 'Holy Scripture' Christian?*, SCM Press 1971, pp.25ff., has some pertinent comments about the 'fantasy' of apostolicity. But it would be incorrect to suppose that because the traditional pseudo-historical defence of the notion of canonical scriptures has crumbled, the notion itself is therefore worthless.

6. B. Weiss, *Biblische Theologie des neuen Testaments*, 1868. Quotations are from the ET of the third edition, 1879, T. & T. Clark 1888–9.

7. Ibid. For Schlatter, see below p.136.

8. So H. J. Holtzmann, *Lehrbuch der neutestamentlichen Theologie*, Tübingen 1896–7, pp.12f. References to second revised ed., 1911.

9. Weiss, op. cit., p.11 n. This stands in some tension with the quotations given above from pp.17 and 18.

10. See W. Klatt, *Hermann Gunkel*, Göttingen 1969, p.21.

11. See his article, 'The Dogmatics of the "religionsgeschichtliche Schule" ', *The American Journal of Theology* XVII, 1913, pp.1–21. Troeltsch summarized his views in an essay first published in 1898, 'Historische und dogmatische Methode in der Theologie', *Gesammelte Schriften* II, pp.729–53, an ET of which, ed. J. L. Adams, is forthcoming from Beacon Press.

12. Harnack (b. 1851; professor in Leipzig, 1876; Giessen, 1879; Marburg, 1886; then going to Berlin in 1888) was personally known to some of the group. Wellhausen (1844–1918) marks an epoch in Old Testament studies, and since the appearance of *Die synoptische Evangelien* in 1863, which established the two-source hypothesis, Holtzmann (1832–1910) had been a leading

figure in New Testament criticism. P. de Lagarde (1827–1891) of Göttingen was also considered by Harnack to have influenced the group. This relationship did not prevent Harnack and Wellhausen from being sharply critical of the new programme. For their attacks on Gunkel, see Klatt, op. cit., pp. 36ff.

13. See my forthcoming *Introducing Gospel Parallels*, Duckworth 1973.

14. A similar history of religions corrective to Harnack's *History of Dogma* was attempted by Troeltsch, *The Social Teachings of the Christian Churches*, 1908–12, ET Allen and Unwin and Macmillan, New York 1931.

15. The first edition of *Die Religion in Geschichte and Gegenwart* (*RGG*), 1909–13, was edited mainly by Gunkel; *RGG*², 1927–31, was edited by Gunkel and Zscharnack; the journal *Theologische Rundschau* was founded by Bousset & Heitmüller; the Vandenhoeck and Ruprecht (Göttingen) series *Forschungen zur Religion und Literatur des Alten und Neuen Testament* (FRLANT) was edited by Bousset and Gunkel (1903–19), and then by Gunkel and Bultmann. Very few of the major works of the group were translated into English. Harnack was the last German scholar to have a large impact in England during the first part of the present century. The history of religions school may be seen as the point where English and German critical scholarship moved in different directions. The *theological* parting of the ways came later, after the First World War.

16. The classic example is B. H. Streeter, *The Four Gospels*, Macmillan 1924, which ignores the new history of traditions approach to the synoptic gospels. Form criticism was inadequately understood in this country because of a failure to assimilate its roots in the history of religions. Cf. R. Bultmann, *Existence and Faith*, Fontana Books 1964, p. 59.

17. This has only begun to be overcome in the past twenty years. The recent translations of Wrede's *Messianic Secret*, James Clarke 1972, and Bousset's *Kyrios Christos*, Abingdon Press, Nashville 1970, are indications that this bridge-building will involve renewed attention to the work of the history of religions school.

18. *Die Anfänge unserer Religion*, 1901, 1904.² ET published by Williams and Norgate 1903–4.

19. 1913; second revised ed. published posthumously, 1921. See n. 17 above.

20. *Das Urchristentum*, incomplete and posthumously published, 1917. ET *History of Primitive Christianity*, Macmillan 1937, reprinted as *Earliest Christianity*, Harper Torchbooks, New York 1959.

21. *Die Theologie des neuen Testaments*, 1948–51, ET published by SCM Press and Scribners, New York 1952 and 1955.

22. F. C. Baur, *Vorlesungen über neutestamentlichen Theologie*, ed. F. F. Baur, Leipzig 1864. Reprint forthcoming from the Wissenschaftliche Buchgesellschaft, Darmstadt.

23. A gloomy picture is given by E. Käsemann, 'The Problem of a New Testament Theology', *NTS* 19, April 1973.

24. *Paulus*, 1904, reprinted in *Das Paulusbild in der neueren Deutschen Forschung*, ed. K. H. Rengstorf, Darmstadt 1964. ET 1907, reprinted by the American Theological Library Association 1962.

25. See below, pp. 103ff. P. Wernle's account (see n. 18) of 'the development

of the church's theology' after Paul contains very little on individual books. In his *Biblische Theologie des Neuen Testaments*, 1910, H. Weinel structures Part II ('Early Christianity'), Book III ('The Christianity of the Developing Church'), pp.429–641 in the second, 1913, edition, entirely according to the subject-matter, with references to the doctrinal concepts in individual books confined to an appendix. In Bousset's *Kyrios Christos*, only Paul and the Johannine writings have independent chapters. Chapter 7 on 'The Christ Cult in the Post-Apostolic Age' is followed by ch.8 on 'The Structuring of Christianity on the Basis of the Christ Cult and its Various Types', which contains sections on the Christianity of Ignatius (as Wrede proposed), of certain epistles and of I Clement. Bultmann's Part IV, 'The Development Toward the Ancient Church' is also structured according to subject-matter, as is Conzelmann's 'Development after Paul' (*An Outline of the Theology of the New Testament*, ET SCM Press and Harper and Row, New York 1969) which, in opposition to Bultmann and more akin to Wrede's historical structure, is placed between Paul and John.

26. Wrede is unclear, for example, about the period prior to Paul. Credit for recognizing the importance of pre-Pauline *Gentile* Christianity is due to W. Heitmüller, 'Zum Problem Paulus und Jesus', *ZNW* 13, 1912, pp.320–37, reprinted in *Das Paulusbild in der neueren Deutschen Forschung*. Heitmüller was followed by Bousset (ch.3), and especially by his pupil and successor Bultmann (*Theology of the New Testament*, I, pp.63–183).

27. *Die Chronologie der altchristlichen Literatur bis Eusebius*, Vol.1, Berlin 1897, p.viii. This was not the last case of a theologian considered radical in his day having very conservative views about the New Testament.

28. It says a great deal for the soundness of Schlatter's 'observation' and his flexibility that his conservative judgments about authorship do not destroy the value of his New Testament theology. He lets the apostle Matthew write late enough to react to Paul's Gentile mission; and he can recognize that James 2.14–26 was probably directed against a misunderstood Paulinism, whereas Weiss and Beyschlag deny this.

29. E.g. J. D. Michaelis. See W. G. Kümmel, op. cit., p.84.

30. See e.g. his article 'Historiography' in James Hastings, *Encyclopedia of Religion and Ethics*, reprinted in John Macquarrie (ed.), *Contemporary Religious Thinkers*, SCM Press and Harper and Row, New York 1969. See also above n.11.

31. This is emphasized by G. Strecker in his helpful article, 'William Wrede', *ZThK* 57, 1960, pp.67–91.

32. See the concluding dissertation 'On the Dogmatic Import of the Life of Jesus', *The Life of Jesus Critically Examined*, Fortress Press, Philadelphia 1972 and SCM Press 1973, pp.757–84.

33. *Das Christenthum und die Christliche Kirche der drei ersten Jahrhunderte*, Tübingen 1853, ²1860; reprinted Stuttgart – Bad Cannstatt 1966. ET published by the Theological Translation Fund, 1878.

34. This issue is sensitively discussed in his essay 'Was heisst "Wesen des Christentums"?', *Gesammelte Schriften* II, pp.386–451.

35. I have argued that this is the case in M. Pye and R. Morgan (eds.), *The Cardinal Meaning*, The Hague 1973.

36. An excellent account of this discussion is provided by J. M. Robinson,

'Hermeneutic since Barth', in J. M. Robinson and J. B. Cobb Jr (eds.), *The New Hermeneutic*, Harper and Row, New York 1964.

37. See G. Ebeling, 'What does the Phrase "Biblical Theology" Mean?', *Word and Faith*, Fortress Press, Philadelphia and SCM Press 1963, pp. 79–97.

38. His epoch-making *RGG*[2] article on Paul (1930) was preceded by 'Zur Geschichte der Paulus-Forschung', *ThR*, NF 1, 1929. See also the Epilogue to *Theology of the New Testament*, II, pp. 237–51.

39. 'Paulus-Forschung', pp. 52f.; *Theology of the New Testament* II, pp. 248ff.

40. Cf. Bousset's *Jesus* (1904, ET London 1906), and Bousset's response to Wrede's *Messianic Secret* in *ThR* 1902, pp. 307–16, 347–62.

41. See especially Bultmann's essay 'Die Frage nach dem messianischen Bewusstsein Jesu und das Petrus-Bekenntnis', *ZNW* 19, 1919–20, pp. 165–174, reprinted in *Exegetica*, Tübingen 1967, pp. 1–9. See also *Existence and Faith*, pp. 41ff.

42. *The Messianic Secret*, pp. 281ff.

43. His chair was established by the king of Prussia in 1892 to counter-balance Harnack's influence, following the controversy which arose when Harnack told students that he wished the church would give up using the Apostles' Creed.

44. *Das Christliche Dogma*, 1911; *Die Christliche Ethik*, 1914, 1961; *Der Dienst des Christen in der älteren Dogmatik*, 1897, reprinted Munich 1969.

45. See especially 'Atheistische Methoden in der Theologie', 1905, re-printed in *Zur Theologie des Neuen Testaments und zur Dogmatik*, Munich 1969, pp. 134–50.

46. This neglect is deplored by Käsemann in a eulogy on Schlatter, *New Testament Questions of Today*, SCM Press and Fortress Press, Philadelphia 1969, pp. 4f.

47. Vol. I, *Das Wort Jesu*; Vol. II, *Die Lehre der Apostel*.

48. See T. Schlatter (ed.), *Adolf Schlatters Rückblick auf seine Lebensarbeit*, Gütersloh 1952, p. 233.

49. Op. cit., pp. 232f.

50. In his introduction to a new edition of F. C. Baur's selected works, Käsemann comments that 'a generation which has undeniably run into a general crisis of historical understanding must go back to the beginnings of historical criticism and think over afresh its necessity and its problematic, in order to win for itself the way to freedom and to be able to do its work better and more clearly' (*Historisch–Kritische Untersuchungen zum Neuen Testament*, Stuttgart–Bad Cannstatt 1963, p. viii).

51. See especially those of H. Conzelmann, 1967; K. H. Schelkle, 1968–; W. G. Kümmel, 1969; J. Jeremias, Vol. I, 1971.

52. See n. 39.

53. *NTS* 19, April 1973.

54. See *New Testament Questions of Today*, pp. 168–82, where Schlatter is not mentioned by name.

55. See below pp. 131f., which reads almost like a polemic against crude forms of Barthianism.

56. *Der Evangelist Matthäus*, Stuttgart 1929, [6]1963.

57. E.g. H. Gunkel, *Die Wirkungen des heiligen Geistes nach der populären*

Anschauung der apostolischen Zeit und der Lehre des Apostels Paulus, 1888, ³1909; J. Weiss, *Jesus' Proclamation of the Kingdom of God*, 1892. ET, Fortress Press, Philadelphia and SCM Press 1971; W. Bousset, *Jesu Predigt in ihrem Gegensatz zum Judentum. Ein religionsgeschichtlicher Vergleich*, 1892; id., *Die Jüdische Apokalyptik in ihrer religionsgeschichtlichen Herkunft und ihrer Bedeutung für das Neue Testament*, 1903, etc.

58. See M. Hengel, *Jews and Greeks*, SCM Press 1973; P. Stuhlmacher, 'Neues Testament und Hermeneutik – Versuch einer Bestandsaufnahme', *ZThK* 68, 1971, pp. 121–61. See pp. 153f.

59. E.g. *Wie sprach Josephus von Gott?*, 1910; *Jochanan Ben Zakkai, der Zeitgenosse der Apostel*, 1899; *Die Theologie des Judentums nach dem Bericht des Josefs*, 1932, etc.

60. See below, pp. 143, 156ff., F. C. Baur was also aware of this and spoke of Jesus' religion rather than his theology. *Das Christenthum und die Christliche Kirche*, pp. 73f.

61. For an extreme example, see Renan's *Life of Jesus*, 1863: 'We attach ourselves in religion to the grand intellectual and moral line at the head of which shines the name of Jesus. In this sense we are Christians, even when we separate ourselves on almost all points from the Christian tradition which has preceded us' (Everyman edition, p. 236).

62. The abrasive correspondence between Barth and Harnack gives a sharply profiled account of their different ways of considering the New Testament. See J. Moltmann (ed.), *Anfänge der dialektischen Theologie* I, Munich 1966, pp. 323–47. ET J. M. Robinson (ed.), *The Beginnings of Dialectical Theology* I, John Knox Press, Virginia 1968. Now reproduced with commentary: H. M. Rumscheidt, *Revelation and Theology: An Analysis of the Barth-Harnack Correspondence of 1923*, Cambridge University Press 1972.

63. The close association of theology and proclamation is clear in the essays 'The Need and Promise of Christian Preaching' (1922); 'Church and Theology' (1926). Cf. 'The task of theology is at one with the task of preaching' (*Beginnings*, pp. 167, 177; Rumscheidt, op. cit., pp. 32, 42).

64. Karl Barth, *The Epistle to the Romans*, Oxford University Press 1933. pp. x, ix.

65. The successive prefaces to his *Romans* give a clear account of his aims. He mentions the 'positive theology' of Schlatter as that 'to which I feel myself most nearly related' (p. 16).

66. Cf. the often-quoted grim prophecy of Schlatter's pupil P. Althaus: 'The association of a radicalism which despairs of historical knowledge of the history of Jesus with an ahistorical theology for which revelation consists only in the destruction of history will become a popular theological method' (*ZSTh*, 1922, p. 765 n. 3).

67. See R. Bultmann, 'Liberal Theology and the Latest Theological Movement' (1924), in *Faith and Understanding* I, SCM Press and Harper and Row, New York 1969, pp. 28–52.

68. The phrase is used to cover all Bultmann's work in this field, and not simply his *Theology of the New Testament*. That and the *Commentary on John* are the important works, but several essays, and *Jesus and the Word*, should be included.

69. *The Epistle to the Romans*, pp. 10, 8.

70. 'The Problem of a Theological Exegesis of the New Testament' (1925), reprinted in *The Beginnings of Dialectical Theology*, pp. 236–56, esp. p. 252. Cf. *Theology of the New Testament*, II, p. 237: 'It is of decisive importance that *the theological thoughts be conceived and explicated as thoughts of faith*, that is: *as thoughts in which faith's understanding of God, the world, and man is unfolding itself.*'

71. *Theology of the New Testament*, II, pp. 239, 240.

72. But notice Schlatter's qualifications. Below, p. 155.

73. *Beginnings*, p. 253.

74. *Existence and Faith*, p. 347.

75. Whether Christian theology should be rooted in the rigorous historical study of the New Testament (as both Wrede and Schlatter thought) may be disputed, and is in practice very often denied.

76. Quotations in this paragraph are taken from *Existence and Faith*, pp. 107ff., 114.

77. The short essay 'What Does it Mean to Speak of God?' (1925), in *Faith and Understanding*, I, pp. 53–65, is therefore fundamental for understanding all his theological work, including the demythologizing proposal.

78. *Beginnings*, p. 253.

79. *Existence and Faith*, p. 348.

80. *Beginnings*, pp. 253, 256.

81. *Beginnings*, p. 256, modifying the translation.

82. For Bultmann's reception of Dilthey see especially 'The Problem of Hermeneutics' (1950), in *Essays Philosophical and Theological*, SCM Press 1955, pp. 234–61, and *History and Eschatology*, Edinburgh University Press 1957.

83. *Essays*, p. 253.

84. *Essays*, p. 254. Cf. the introduction to *Jesus and the Word* (1926), ET 1934, reprinted Fontana Books 1958, p. 13: 'Thus I would lead the reader not to any "view" of history, but to a highly personal *encounter* with history. . . .'

85. *Existence and Faith*, p. 348.

86. *Essays*, p. 261.

87. *Jesus Christ and Mythology*, Scribners, New York and SCM Press 1960, pp. 32–4.

88. Käsemann stressed this in 'Probleme neutestamentlicher Arbeit in Deutschland', *Die Freiheit des Evangeliums und die Ordnung der Gesellschaft*, Beiheft zur *EvTh* XV, 1952, pp. 144–7. Bultmann alluded to it rather cryptically when he claimed that 'demythologizing is the radical application of the doctrine of justification by faith to the sphere of knowledge and thought' (*Jesus Christ and Mythology*, p. 84; cf. *Kerygma and Myth*, SPCK 1953, p. 211).

89. *Existence and Faith*, p. 347.

90. *Existence and Faith*, pp. 342–51; *Essays*, pp. 252–8, etc.

91. See E. Käsemann, *Perspectives on Paul*, p. 11.

92. N. A. Dahl, 'Die Theologie des Neuen Testament', *ThR* 1955, pp. 21–49. See p. 25. This essay is the most illuminating account of Bultmann's work which I have read, and I am greatly indebted to it. An English translation is forthcoming in a collection of Dahl's essays entitled *Anamnesis*, Oslo and Yale

University Press 1973. See also M. Barth, 'Die Methode von Bultmanns *Theologie des Neuen Testaments*', *ThZ* XI, 1955, pp. 1–27, esp. p. 25.

93. British theology has been better than German in this respect, and W. Pannenberg scores highly over his existentialist opponents.

94. *Faith and Understanding*, pp. 28–52, 280 (see n. 108 below): *Kerygma and Myth*, p. 12.

95. *Kerygma and Myth*, p. 12.

96. *Essays*, pp. 253f.

97. This does not mean that *Sachkritik* was unknown in the nineteenth century. I. A. Dorner, *History of Protestant Theology*, ET 1871, Vol. II, p. 186, calls 'theological criticism . . . the self-criticism of the canon through the instrumentality of believing enquirers'. Like Bultmann, Dorner echoes Luther's canon criticism in this connection.

98. 'The fault of the earlier research is not that its proponents practised (theological) criticism, but that they did so in unquestioning dependence on a modern world-view, taking this rather than the central intentions of the text itself as their criterion' (*Faith and Understanding*, p. 280, correcting the translation). See below n. 108.

99. Marcion's methodological crime, like that of orthodox book burners, was (in all good faith) to have destroyed some of the tradition, and thus to have reduced the raw material available for future theological debate. In the introduction to *Jesus and the Word*, p. 13, Bultmann says that the book gives 'information about my encounter with history'.

100. See n. 108. *Beginnings*, p. 241.

101. Other spirits than that of Christ may lead a theologian to reject a piece of tradition. This danger must be guarded against just as the arbitrary misuse of allegorical interpretation to read one's own view into the tradition was guarded against. Aquinas, for example, insisted that one should not find a meaning in a scriptural text by allegorical interpretation which was not found elsewhere in scripture as the literal meaning (*Summa Theologiae* I. 1.9). A similar means of controlling the modern form of critical interpretation would be to look for 'constants' in the tradition and argue that no interpretation of the tradition is Christian if it lacks these. They can be written into one's definition of Christianity, as in Schleiermacher's 'monotheistic faith belonging to the teleological type of religion, essentially distinguished from other such faiths by the fact that in it everything is related to the redemption accomplished by Jesus of Nazareth' (*The Christian Faith* § 11, p. 52), which contains two or three such constants: the man from Nazareth, the assumption that he is decisive for human existence, and something about the positive way in which he is decisive. Any interpretation of the tradition so critical that it surrendered these features could hardly be called Christian. Of course, one's definition of the 'essence' of Christianity is itself a matter of historical and theological study of the tradition (cf. Schleiermacher's *Brief Outline*).

102. As Wrede and Schlatter recognized. See below pp. 92ff., 159.

103. Bultmann echoes this dictum from Schleiermacher's *Hermeneutik* in *Faith and Understanding*, p. 93.

104. *Faith and Understanding*, pp. 83f. 'For what Paul says in I Cor. 15.20–22 of the death and resurrection of Christ cannot be said of an objective historical

fact', whereas vv. 3ff. are 'an attempt to make the resurrection of Christ credible as an objective fact'. This whole essay on Barth's interpretation of I Cor. is important. Cf. pp. 72, 86, 92f.

105. Op. cit., p. 72.

106. *Beginnings*, p. 240.

107. *Beginnings*, p. 239.

108. *Faith and Understanding*, p. 280. What is merely an ambiguity in the original (*Glauben und Verstehen*, I, p. 262) becomes total obscurity in the ET. Bultmann's point is surely that the liberals were not wrong to reject part of the tradition by practising theological criticism: i.e. criticism in the light of their own apprehension of Christianity (unhelpfully translated 'used critical methods'). Their mistake was to make their world-view normative for their view of Christianity and so criticize the tradition in the light of that instead of in the light of the 'central intentions of the text'. By omitting 'central intentions of', the translator renders Bultmann unintelligible.

109. Review of Barth's *Romans*, in *Beginnings*, p. 119.

110. *Theology of the New Testament*, II, p. 238. Bultmann's own theological outlook is evident here in his assumptions that 'speaking of God's dealing and of the relation between God and man in juristic terms' or 'speaking of God's relation to the world in mythological or cosmological terms' or 'expressing God's transcendence in the terminology of mysticism or of idealistic thinking' are 'inappropriate to faith's (whose?) understanding of God's transcendence'. The same is true of what he says about Pauline christology in *Faith and Understanding*, p. 280. See below, n. 131.

111. Especially in his review of Barth's *Romans*, his discussion of Barth's *The Resurrection of the Dead*, and his essay on 'The Problem of a Theological Exegesis of the New Testament'. It does not arise in the important essays on historical method, 'The Problem of Hermeneutics' and 'Is Exegesis without Presuppositions Possible?'

112. E.g. *Faith and Understanding*, pp. 86, 93, 280f.

113. *Faith and Understanding*, p. 86, modifying the translation to include 'at first sight'.

114. 'Bultmann the exegete sees himself compelled, on the presuppositions of his own systematic theology, to interpret the Pauline eschatology on the basis of the Johannine. . . . The question of the reasons for this state of affairs and of whether such a procedure is justifiable should determine the continuing dialogue with him' (Käsemann, *New Testament Questions of Today*, p. 17).

115. Dahl, op. cit., pp. 47f.

116. *Beginnings*, p. 120.

117. See n. 131. Italics mine.

118. *Beginnings*, p. 120.

119. See Dahl, op. cit., pp. 38–49.

120. Thus Conzelmann, *An Outline of the Theology of the New Testament*, p. 160.

121. Dahl, op. cit., p. 45.

122. *Perspectives on Paul*, p. 59.

123. Op. cit., cf. pp. 54 and 39.

124. '"The Righteousness of God" in Paul', *New Testament Questions of Today*, pp. 168, 171f.

125. Op. cit., pp. 181f., 173.

126. *Faith and Understanding*, p. 279. This essay is extremely important.

127. In the same passage Bultmann quotes (and repeats on p. 285) Melanchthon's 'to know Christ is to know his benefits', and continues: 'The teaching of justification demonstrates forcibly that christology does not consist in speculation on the nature of Christ; that christology is the proclamation of the event of Christ's coming, and that an understanding of the event requires not speculation but self-examination, *radical consideration of the nature of one's own new existence*' (italics mine).

128. Käsemann objects that Bultmann does not follow up the 'and vice versa' of his own claim (*Theology of the New Testament*, I, p. 191) that 'every assertion about Christ is also an assertion about man and vice versa', (op. cit., p. 112). See also pp. 12, 56, 78, 126, 165f. and passim. These essays are largely concerned with the relation of christology, soteriology, anthropology and ecclesiology, which is a matter of 'perspective'. Käsemann's perspective on Paul is guided by his own theology of the cross, but is defended exegetically.

129. Käsemann agrees with Bultmann about the existential implications of historical study: 'Methodologically, the historical is not simply that which can be shown to be what actually happened, but the field on which the self-understanding of the interpreter is either confirmed or shattered, or else triumphs by violence. We ourselves are at risk here' (*New Testament Questions of Today*, p. 173, n. 4). Bultmann explains his interest in history in a letter (31 December 1922) to Barth which illuminates the difference between them, see B. Jaspert, *Karl Barth – Rudolf Bultmann Briefwechsel 1922–1966*, Zurich 1971, p. 9.

130. *Essays*, p. 280.

131. Bultmann, on the other hand, makes anthropology the criterion of everything else in Paul: 'If we have rightly understood Paul's fundamental purpose, then the standard for the criticism of his anthropological, cosmological and christological statements is the recognition that the teaching is proclamation of the Christ event as a summons and that the explanation of it is the presentation of the Christian's understanding of his existence. Concepts and presentations which are not rooted in the proclamation collapse under criticism, even though they could once have been for Paul a genuine expression of what he intended to say. The mythological picture of Christ as a pre-existent heavenly being served Paul as a way of saying that in the Christ event we are not confronted by a person of this world nor by the fate of a man of this world; but in that event *God's act* confronts us. We no longer need that particular image; yet we do still hold the christological belief of Paul' (*Faith and Understanding*, p. 280).

132. On the medical metaphor for what 'contradicts or dissolves the essence of Christianity' instead of 'containing the germ for development of some new divisions', see Schleiermacher, *Brief Outline*, § 54–62. This document is fundamental for the discussion of theological method in a historically conscious age.

133. Military language is appropriate. Both protagonists insist upon the

critical and polemical character of theology, e.g. *Faith and Understanding*, pp. 218, 279. See also below, p. 124.

134. E.g. *Perspectives on Paul*, pp. 22, 55, 75, 81. The emphasis upon Paul's apocalypticism is relevant here.

135. Op. cit., pp. 18–23.

136. Op. cit., pp. 12f.

137. Dissatisfaction with Bultmann as a theological guide in the late twentieth century, coupled with full appreciation of his epoch-making importance, is echoed in Käsemann's comment that 'contemporary theology . . . could have learnt as much from Marxism as it did from Kierkegaard' (op. cit., p. 11). See also Dorothee Sölle, *Politische Theologie. Auseinandersetzung mit Rudolf Bultmann*, Stuttgart 1971.

138. See above n. 91; also *New Testament Questions of Today*, p. 110 n.

139. Cf. Albert Schweitzer on *The Quest of the Historical Jesus*, A. and C. Black [3]1953: 'Their hate sharpened their historical insight' (p. 4).

140. Cf. E. Troeltsch, *Gesammelte Schriften* II, p. 427 and n. 139 above.

141. We can ignore Renan's slanging of 'the ugly little Jew'. Note 61 above shows that he cannot be seriously considered a Christian theologian.

142. *Paul*, ET 1907, p. 76.

143. Op. cit., p. 123.

144. This link was further broken in the history of religions school by W. Heitmüller, who declared that 'in some ways Paul is not so much the father of the Reformation as of the early and medieval church' (*Luthers Stellung in der Religionsgeschichte des Christentums*, 1917). Schlatter also contributed to this in *Luthers Deutung des Römerbriefs*, 1917, but Schlatter, unlike the history of religions school, considered 'the righteousness of God' to be central to Paul.

145. 'It is monstrous that men of any historical training should attach any importance whatever to this Paul . . .' (*Deutsche Schriften*, 1886, p. 71).

146. Op. cit., ch. 4.

147. See especially 'Jesus and Paul' (1936), in *Existence and Faith*, pp. 217–39.

148. Cf. 'Urchristentum und Religionsgeschichte', *ThR*, NF 4, 1932, pp. 1–21; *Primitive Christianity*, ET Fontana Books 1960, pp. 71, 175.

149. See II Peter 3.15f.

150. Harnack, *History of Dogma*, I, p. 89; cf. p. 136. He calls 'the history of Pauline theology in the church, a history first of silence, then of artificial interpretation' (p. 283).

151. This is especially clear in *De Spiritu et Littera*.

152. The critical role of Paulinism within the Christian tradition is clearly recognized by Harnack, op. cit., pp. 135f. Käsemann sees radical Protestant theology in this light (*New Testament Questions of Today*, p. ix). Is this not the role of 'Protestantism' within the 'catholic church'?

153. See especially his *Salvation in History*, ET SCM Press and Harper and Row, New York 1967, and especially Bultmann's review of *Christ and Time* in *Existence and Faith*, pp. 268–84.

154. *Perspectives on Paul*, pp. 63ff.

155. Op. cit., p. 14. It is unnecessary to add to the comments made on this book by Leander E. Keck, 'Problems of New Testament Theology', *Novum Testamentum* VII, 1964–65, pp. 217–41.

156. Dodd's work is continued in B. Lindars, *New Testament Apologetic*, SCM Press 1961. Both books deal with some of the materials and methods of early Christian theology, not its finished product. See also C. F. D. Moule, *The Birth of the New Testament*, A. and C. Black 1962, for the context of its development.

157. Op. cit., p. xiv. See below, p. 83.

158. Op. cit., pp. xv, xx, xvif.

159. He speaks of the 'thoroughly misplaced modesty' of exegetes who 'suppose that they merely do this historical donkey work for the systematic theologian' (*New Testament Questions of Today*, p. 7). And, 'My work is intended to have doctrinal implications' (p. *x*).

160. E.g. Käsemann, *Jesus Means Freedom*, SCM Press and Fortress Press, Philadelphia 1969.

161. See *Das Neue Testament als Kanon*; also I. Lönning, '*Kanon im Kanon*'.

162. This is reflected in the structure of the work. The *theology* of John follows the *theology* of Paul, and precedes 'the development towards the ancient church'. See Conzelmann, *Outline*, p. 8.

163. W. Pannenberg, on the other hand, develops the notion of 'universal history' and is therefore able to allow theological statements to relate to reality as a whole and also to assert the historical character of reality.

164. E.g. *Faith and Understanding*, pp. 286–331; *Existence and Faith*, pp. 67–107, and passim.

165. See especially 'Kerygma and Sophia – Zur neutestamentlichen Grundlegung des Dogmas' (1948), in *Die Zeit der Kirche*, Freiburg 1972, pp. 206–32; 'The Meaning and Function of a Theology of the New Testament', in *The Relevance of the New Testament*, New York 1968.

166. *An Outline of the Theology of the New Testament*, p. xv.

167. See Käsemann, 'Konsequente Traditionsgeschichte?', *ZThK* 62, 1965, pp. 137–52, esp. p. 150.

168. It is too soon to say whether Pannenberg's work will prove fruitful for New Testament theology. The New Testament exegetical support he received from U. Wilckens in 1961 (*Revelation as History*, ET Macmillan, New York 1969, pp. 55–121) was rather weak.

169. G. van der Leeuw, *Religion in Essence and Manifestation*, referred to Bultmann's interest and help (p. *v*). W. B. Kristensen, *The Meaning of Religion*, The Hague 1960, is a good guide to the subject.

170. This may be partly because the work is mostly done by Christians, within Christian faculties, for Christians, in which case the secularization of religious studies should prove healthy for the discipline. Sometimes another factor comes in. Some (liberal) Christian scholars have theological motives for emphasizing the historical distance. The more mythological the New Testament can be made to appear, the stronger the case for re-interpretation becomes. If the 'myth' were approached more sympathetically, its interpretation might not have to be so drastic.

171. How often is the phenomenology of worship considered when eucharistic doctrine is framed – or even in the courses on worship in clerical training?

172. This has implications for theological syllabuses. The history of

biblical interpretation is an important area in which exegetical and systematic study converges. Where it is neglected, these two disciplines often fail to fertilize each other.

173. Cf. *Beginnings*, p.252. Read 'is' for 'in'.

174. Ibid. The translation 'see the text with the eyes of faith' is misleading.

175. Ibid. I have paraphrased, because the translation is not quite clear.

176. Cf. R. L. Hart's phrase 'revelation fundament' in *Unfinished Man and the Imagination*, Herder, New York 1968.

177. Bultmann comments that 'the concept of the canon is intended to guard the contingent character of revelation and avoid the misunderstanding that revelation has to do with generally discernible truths or with the faith of individuals who are especially strong in piety . . .' (*Beginnings*, p.255). Barth also allows extra-canonical material to bear Christian testimony, in principle (*Beginnings*, p.179; Rumscheidt, op. cit., p.44).

178. So G. Ebeling's Habilitationsvorlesung in Tubingen 1946. ET in *The Word of God and Tradition*, pp.11–31.

179. See H. Oberman, '*Quo Vadis?*', *SJT* 1963, p. 250.

180. This corresponds to Ninian Smart's 'principle of the conservation of richness', in *Prospect for Theology*, Nisbet 1967, pp.93–116.

181. Ebeling's observations (op. cit., pp.143f., 148–59) are important. The English translation contains errors. The point is not that Käsemann has misunderstood the Reformation (!) but that his thesis about the canon does not affect the Reformers, if they are correctly (i.e. critically) understood.

182. Perhaps the best work being done in this area is by H. Gese. See especially 'Erwägungen zur Einheit der biblischen Theologie', *ZThK* 67, 1970, pp.417–36; also 'Natus ex virgine', H. W. Wolff (ed.), *Probleme Biblischer Theologie*, Munich 1971, pp.73–89; 'Psalm 22 und das Neue Testament', *ZThK* 65, 1968, pp.1–22. H. J. Kraus, *Die Biblische Theologie. Ihre Geschichte und Problematik*, Neukirchen 1970, presents a variety of viewpoints, but thinks in terms of the two Testaments rather than the one tradition.

183. Wrede praises Holtzmann for this. See below p.115. Eduard Meyer, *Ursprung und Anfänge des Christentums* (3 vols., 1917–23) reaches Jesus at the end of Vol. 2, and devotes only Vol. 3 to primitive Christianity.

184. See Käsemann's severe criticism of Bultmann, *New Testament Questions of Today*, pp.35–65, esp. pp.42, 55f.

185. Barth said that the historical Jesus was a construction having no authority and theologically irrelevant (*Zwischen den Zeiten*, 1929, p.447). Bultmann took up positively this aspect of Barth's Romans (see *Beginnings*, pp.110–3). This can be understood in the polemical situation *vis-à-vis* liberal Protestantism.

186. This has become a problem since the rise of historical consciousness destroyed the old argument from prophecy (see, for example, H. S. Reimarus, *Fragments*, Fortress Press, Philadelphia and SCM Press 1971). Any suggestions will have to meet the conditions imposed by historical research. See C. Westermann (ed.), *Essays on Old Testament Interpretation*, SCM Press 1963 (especially the essay by Zimmerli), and B. W. Anderson (ed.), *The Old Testament and Christian Faith*, SCM Press 1964.

187. Cf. Käsemann's question 'whether the earthly Jesus is to be taken as

the criterion of the kerygma and, if so, to what extent . . . Does the New Testament kerygma count the historical Jesus among the criteria of its own validity?' He answers 'roundly in the affirmative', even though for Paul and John 'the principal criterion of the Christian message is the spirit'. Paul was experiencing difficulties with the appeal to the spirit since his opponents in Corinth also appealed to it. He therefore reasserts its connection with the earthly Jesus through his 'word of the cross'. Jesus is the criterion of everything Christian, and the historical quest helps us to distinguish between what is truly Christian and what are falsifications. 'This criterion was not ill-chosen. It has become binding for Christianity, and I think it will always be indispensable. For it makes possible . . . that continuity of direction and that solidarity of faith which I feel bound to make the central object of my concern' (*New Testament Questions of Today*, pp. 47f, 50). See also Schleiermacher's definition, n. 101.

NOTES TO WREDE

1. The original German text of this study began with the following preface:

On 21–23 April 1897 the theological faculty in Breslau held a vacation course for clergy. The following pages contain the lectures which I gave on that occasion. Some of my remarks have been filled out or modified, but on the whole, form and content follow what was said then. The footnotes have been added.

This background should not be ignored in judging the work. It still bears traces of its origin. The large number of footnotes, for example, though not, I hope, more than are required by the subject-matter – more likely there are too few for it – are nevertheless to my taste a defect of form. But to insert their content into the text itself would have required a complete reconstruction, and that seemed to me undesirable.

The fact that my account is sketched out here by way of opposition to the latest textbook of New Testament theology is justified by the prestige of its author and also by the similarity of my critical position to his. Nevertheless, my remarks should not be understood as a formal review of Holtzmann's book. Even on the issues which are relevant here I have not tried to be complete.

I have had to say a plain 'No' to the textbooks of B. Weiss and Beyschlag. It is, of course, clear that this is not meant to minimize in any way the merit these men have earned in other fields, but I do want to emphasize the fact.

In this work I have often thought with special gratitude of my friend A. Eichhorn in Halle. Though the occasion may seem to some too trivial to say it, I am still obliged to indicate that with regard to historical method I have learned most from discussion with him. Even though the particular question how to write a New Testament theology has not been one of our topics, I am nevertheless quite clear that without his influence some of what stands here would not have been written, and some of it would have been said differently. At particular points I have remembered some stimulating remark or another of his.

Finally, I may be permitted to insert some of the introductory remarks with which, as the first lecturer, I opened the vacation course:

No one will expect vacation courses to remove the far-reaching tension between clergy and university theology which is characteristic of the present time. This tension cannot simply be accounted for in terms of people's vices – party passions and ambition on the one side, human conceit and unbelief on the other. It comes, rather, from a more deep-seated historical necessity, namely an inner difficulty in the relationship between the Protestant church and science, and cannot be removed or even greatly relieved by vacation courses. But when within this tense situation, direct and living contact between the representatives of both sides takes place, as happens in a vacation course, it is something to be welcomed warmly by all those on both sides who think highly of the clergy's task and do not despise science, and who regret the present sharpness of the tension.

2. As Deissmann thinks: 'Zur Methode der biblischen Theologie des Neuen Testaments', *ZThK*, 1893, p.126.

3. Cf., for example, B. Weiss, *Lehrbuch der biblischen Theologie des Neuen Testaments*[5] (ET of 3rd ed, *Biblical Theology of the New Testament*, Edinburgh 1888, p.2; here, as elsewhere, page references to the ET only are given). Beyschlag, *Neutestamentliche Theologie* (ET *New Testament Theology*, Edinburgh 1894, [2]1896, I, p.4) speaks of an 'essentially historical discipline'. What does '*essentially* historical' mean?

4. According to Beyschlag, 'the conviction of the revelatory character of the biblical religion' (I, pp.4f.) comprises the presupposition of biblical theology, but 'the way of treating it does not depend upon accepting this' (p.5). A simpler way of stating that would be to say that it does not comprise the presupposition of the discipline. B. Weiss writes (p.3): 'New Testament theology must presuppose that this normative character of the New Testament writings has been demonstrated by dogmatics [which one?], unless it wants to surrender the right of being an independent discipline alongside the history of doctrine.' Unfortunately that is to make the point in question itself into the basis of the proof. Weiss does not, of course, want to deny the possibility of ignoring the presupposition and treating biblical theology as the pre-history or, as I would say, the first period of the history of doctrine, separated in only a formal way from the rest. To say in any other sense that it *must* be treated as an 'independent discipline' is already to presuppose the normative character of these writings – which is what we were supposed to be trying to establish. Anyone who, like Weiss and Beyschlag, gives up the doctrine of inspiration, i.e. the *a priori* concept of revelation, can only logically determine the relationship of biblical theology to the idea of revelation in the following way. Biblical theology investigates the New Testament writings first of all without presuppositions, to find out the content of the biblical religion. Then afterwards a judgment is made about what is discovered: it is revelation in such and such a sense – i.e. the judgment is demonstrated. For before I can call something revelation, I have to know what this 'something' is. But then it is clear that the question of revelation is one for dogmatics, and no concern of biblical theology. The same applies, of course, in an analogous way, to theologians (like Ritschl's pupils) who see the revelation not in the religious ideas contained in writings, but in the historical person of Jesus.

5. Read Lagarde, *Deutsche Schriften*, latest full edition 1886, p.55.

6. This is true also of their religious value. It takes some doing to put II Peter or the Pastorals above the Didache or I Clement in this respect. If, however, we are interested in 'what preaches Christ' (Luther), then it is not only James to which Ignatius is superior.

7. I must be allowed to presuppose these matters here. It is impossible to deal with our theme at all without making certain assumptions about the New

Testament. In general I only presuppose judgments of literary criticism about which there is a large measure of agreement.

8. Harnack, *History of Doctrine*[3], p. 135; cf. p. 48, says: 'The view that the New Testament in its totality embraces a special type of literature is strictly speaking untenable. But it is correct that there is a great gulf fixed between its most important parts and the literature of the period immediately following.' In view of John, I cannot consider this right. An important element in Harnack's judgment is the notion that Paul, the author of Hebrews and John stood on a level not reached by anyone else, in that they understood Judaism (or rather the religion of the Old Testament) as religion, but as spiritually superseded; they subordinated it to the gospel as a *new religion* (p. 135). Harnack also believes that John's conception of Christ and the gospel had so little influence upon the subsequent development partly because of its 'criticism of the Old Testament as religion . . . or rather the independence which is here bestowed upon the Christian religion on the ground (?) of its exact knowledge of the Old Testament which results in its developing the "concealed impulses of the Old Testament"' (p. 96. See also pp. 82f., 90, 91).

This conception, and the singling out and putting together of those three men under this point of view seems to me misleading. I cannot, of course, give adequate reasons here, since the position in Paul is very different from the other two, as is that in Hebrews from John; and in any case, Barnabas, Justin, Marcion and others would have to be brought in. I can only allow myself the following observations. The 'concealed impulses of the Old Testament' which John is said to have developed will be hard to indicate, and when Harnack elsewhere (p. 98) specifically connects John with the 'ancient faith of the prophets and psalmists', his characterization does not seem to me to be a happy one. John's contrast between Christianity and Judaism does not itself prove that he understood Christianity more profoundly or had a better grasp of its independence and newness as religion than, say, Ignatius. It only proves that he was one of those educated Christians whose view extended beyond the inner relationship of Christian faith and life, who was able to reflect upon Christianity as a whole and its relationship to Judaism; and also especially that he, like other Christians of his time, took a lively interest in this relationship to Judaism because he had to enter into debate with the hostile synagogue. John 1.17 must be interpreted neither in a Lutheran nor a Pauline way but in an 'early catholic' one. Moses simply gave the mere *nomos* (law) with the compulsion of its external decrees, which have nothing to do with higher truth; Christ brought knowledge of the inaccessible and invisible God, and so truth and with it grace, since truth means life. This point is correctly spelled out by Holtzmann, *Lehrbuch der neutestamentlichen Theologie*, Vol. I, p. 491.

9. Where does the apostolic age end? When the last apostle died is quite unimportant for this question. It is rather a matter of the point in time at which people began to feel that they belonged to the second generation. Even if this point can perhaps be fixed approximately, we are still hardly in a position to say what, after the death of Paul, formed the content of the period. Even if we can do that, the consciousness of living in the second generation would not in itself be a clear dividing line. For this consciousness does not

yet mean an end to belief in the imminent parousia nor the marking off of a special apostolic epoch, absolutely normative for a long future development.

10. *Das Dogma vom Neuen Testament*, Giessen 1896, especially pp. 11ff. Krüger's observations on the illegitimate influence of this dogma can be multiplied. To give just one example: a lexicon of the New Testament which at most occasionally considers late Jewish and extra-canonical early Christian Greek, does not correspond to the demands of the subject-matter, because the New Testament is not a linguistic island. Such an approach does material damage to the understanding of even the vocabulary of the New Testament, because it ignores material which is important for this understanding. I am also in agreement with Krüger that textbooks on the history of doctrine make the same mistake as textbooks on biblical theology, only in reverse, when they use the later New Testament material only rarely or not at all in their descriptions of faith in the post-apostolic age (cf. Krüger, pp. 17f.). The most striking case of this in Harnack's *History of Dogma* is that he is not prepared to use the Gospel of John in his presentation.

11. Schleiermacher's *Brief Outline of the Study of Theology* still remains an admirable book. But what it teaches about, for example, 'exegetical theology' has no real basis.

12. Holtzmann, I, pp. 24f., nevertheless makes that evaluation determine the limits of the discipline. Of course, in principle he wholly acknowledges the alternative conception and looks to research in the future which will go beyond the New Testament framework. But what are we waiting for? According to Holtzmann's Foreword (p. viii), where he is already arguing with Krüger, we are waiting until the historical viewpoint has won a decisive victory over the unhistorical one on the real battleground, the New Testament. But one may as well ask when this victory will be won as whether it has not already been won. Again, can this shifting of the limits not in itself contribute something to the struggle? Certainly the most important thing is that the fighter himself is able to 'look beyond . . . the traditional confines' and so see the New Testament in its historical context. But it will also be very important for this whether or not the boundary of the disciplines forces him to look beyond in this way.

13. On this cf. pp. 101ff.

14. Raising to some extent the objections that I reject here, Harnack, *ThLZ* 16, 1886, col. 413, says: 'The undertaking of "doctrinal concepts" uses the methods appropriate to the utilization of legal texts as sources of law.'

15. So, for example, B. Weiss, p. 165.

16. Not even Holtzmann, II, pp. 310ff., makes this clear. He speaks quite abstractly about 'hope as the central idea'. He contrasts this 'brancing off into a future direction' with the Pauline material in the epistle (?). Beyschlag, I, p. 406, finds a primitive semi-Old Testament form of doctrinal speech in the fact that the concept of faith is 'still frequently' (!) represented by hope or obedience. Holtzmann, II, p. 305, also speaks of Hebrews' confession of hope and *hypomonē* (endurance) without considering the situation presupposed by the epistle (10.32ff.).

17. Stade, 'Über die Aufgaben der biblischen Theologie des Alten Testaments', *ZThK* III, 1893, p. 37.

18. The New Testament does not contain merely 'pure religion'; so Beyschlag, I, p.2.

19. Alongside 'New Testament theology', a special 'history of New Testament or early Christian concepts' would be a valuable and desirable supplement. This would investigate the historical origin of the most important concepts of the New Testament; it would discover the changes they have undergone and the historical reasons for them, and also illuminate their influence. The task has many points of contact with New Testament theology, but is quite different from it.

20. For example, all psychological definitions of faith (act of will or of obedience, receptivity, relationship to hope, believing to be true, etc.) can at once be said to be unimportant. It is also wrong that trust is the essence of *pistis* according to Paul, even though *pistis* in Paul does include the meaning 'trust'. This interpretation is simply a reflection of the Reformation conception of faith. For Luther faith *is* essentially *fiducia* and even *fiducia specialissima*, *personal* certainty of salvation. In his doctrine of justification Luther was concerned with men in the church. For them, the important thing was that what they believed in general was valid for themselves. Paul is more concerned with faith and becoming a believer in contrast to the unbelieving world, and so with the affirmation of a definite content of faith. It is no coincidence that Paul has no interest in the psychological concept of faith. It is also without historical significance whether among the post-Pauline writers one describes faith more in opposition to *dipsychia* (doubt), another more as believing to be true, yet another more as standing fast or as approaching hope. Even James 2.19 needs only to be noted in so far as we are dealing with the meaning of the passage with regard to justification. James has no special concept of faith, and despite everything, *pistis* is also a cardinal virtue for him. Very little is important for the post-Pauline concept of faith, except e.g. that *pistis* becomes *fides quae creditur*.

21. I am only repeating here what Eichhorn has expounded in exemplary fashion for another area: *Die Rechtfertigungslehre der Apologie*, Studien und Kritiken, 1887, pp.416f.

22. See pp.259ff. Similar examples could easily be added.

23. I must be forgiven for again touching on a theme about which I wrote only recently in a review of Jülicher's *Einleitung* (*Göttinger Gelehrte Anzeigen*, 1896, pp.517f.) and Gunkel's *Schöpfung und Chaos* (*ThLZ*, 1896, col. 629). But it is relevant here, and meanwhile one can hardly indicate the transgressions of literary criticism often enough. Gunkel's contribution on this subject must again be emphatically noted.

24. A few examples are noted below, n.31.

25. This is naturally not true of all textbooks.

26. The tendency to emphasize differences and contradictions, even where they are not important, is partly a reaction against harmonization in the interests of dogmatics. This is quite natural, but is none the less itself a kind of dogmatizing.

27. Though I am not thinking of him in what I have written about literary criticism.

28. Deissmann has certain reservations about it.

29. Compare Holtzmann's judgment on the work, I, pp. 11ff. On the whole I am in full agreement with him, though I do not find the book so 'exemplary' in form as Holtzmann does.

30. In his Introduction, pp. 17f., Beyschlag replies to this objection. He says that it is his aim to translate the language of the New Testament out of its ancient and hence now unfamiliar form into contemporary forms of thought and language. He contrasts this translating with working on the temporal shell. It almost seems as if kernel and shell could not be separated without 'translating'.

31. Do Acts 14.16f.; 17.26ff. necessarily contain 'recollections of the natural revelation in Rom. 1.19f.' (I, p. 459)? When Acts 13.32 has Christ's sonship beginning with his exaltation, is this the effect of Rom. 1.4 (ibid.)? How far is it necessary to acknowledge a Pauline background for the picture of Abraham in Heb. 6.13–18; 11.8–19 (II, p. 306)? Was not, for example, Abraham the prototype of faith in Jewish theology, long before Paul? (Cf. my *Untersuchungen zum I Klemensbriefe*, 1891, p. 69, n. 2; 71, n. 4. Passages like I Macc. 2.52: 'Was not Abraham found faithful in temptation, and it was reckoned unto him for righteousness?' would undoubtedly be considered Pauline by Holtzmann if they stood in the New Testament. So would those which he himself has cited in II, p. 340, n. 4; p. 342, n. 1.) The Johannine *doxa* (glory) is said to be partly explained by II Cor. 3.7ff. (II, p. 452); the synoptic narrative of the transfiguration 'would not be there without this Midrash on the shining face of Moses as he came down the mountain' (I, p. 424; the *Handkommentar on Mark* 9.2ff. derives the Old Testament colouring of the transfiguration narrative from this). The Johannine term *monogenes* (only-begotten) is said to go with the *idios huios* (only Son) of Rom. 8.32 and even with the use of the word at Luke 7.12 (II, pp. 433, 426ff.). When the Johannine Christ pronounces a 'confession of his own sinlessness' at 7.18 and 8.46, this happens 'following' II Cor. 5.21 (II, p. 445). When Jesus was credited with sinlessness by the apostolic church in the first place, 'the occasion for this could be found in sayings where he warned against judging other people (Matt. 7.1f. = Luke 6.37), whereas he knew himself to be qualified to participate in the future judgment (Mark 8.38; 13.27; etc.)' (I, p. 269). I think that accounting for an idea like Jesus' sinlessness by a kind of deduction from individual sayings was an unfortunate notion. And we must make a clean break with the conception that Paul is the actual source of whatever afterwards is reminiscent of him, and that those who came later always had Pauline passages in their head and had meditated on them.

More instances of this nature could be cited. But the individual errors are not very prominent in the work as a whole. What has to be emphasized here again is the way in which they bring literary comparison as such, and the method associated with it, into the foreground. Consider, for example, a part like the section on Ephesians. The numerous minute comparisons between Ephesians and Colossians and other Pauline epistles might be justified in the treatment of a problem of critical introduction. But what are they doing in a biblical theology? Similarly, to show that Pauline conceptions are echoed in the Gospel of Luke is really of little more interest to a history of early Christian belief than evidence of Schleiermacher's influence upon some third-rate theologian would be in a history of nineteenth-century theology. These literary comparisons are not produced simply at points of some importance for a particular writing. They are continually cropping up.

As well as literary criticism, we find a whole host of unimportant matters discussed in Holtzmann's work, whereas important questions are either missing or receive insufficient attention.

32. To give just one example here. In what follows I shall try to give more as the occasion demands. The idea found in Ephesians that by his death Christ removes the wall of partition between Jews and Gentiles is said by Holtzmann (II, pp. 228ff.) to be the 'most far-reaching and original of all (the author's) ideas'. Like other writings, Ephesians takes a theoretical interest in the question of the relation of Jews and Gentiles to salvation. It was originally the law which separated them. However, since the law is removed by Christ's death – a Pauline idea – the contrast between them ceases to exist and the one stands as close to salvation as the other. By an easily-understood process of reflection, therefore, Christ's death is taken to establish peace between Gentiles and Jews. Never mind the fact that Holtzmann might have shown more sharply how the conception emerged. His analysis of it is certainly correct, and he is right about its Pauline basis. But his discussion does not make clear what its historical significance is. I think one must make clear that, pregnant though it is, this conception of Christ's death cannot have been historically influential. It is only valid inside theoretical reflection on the relation between Gentiles and Jews. It simply did not exist for someone who was not much bothered about that. It is, moreover, very questionable what it meant for the author of Ephesians himself. It is certain that he was able to express the saving effect of the death of Christ in quite different ways; he knew about that without any reflection. It is at least quite possible that this is an interpretation occasioned by the special theme, rather than an idea that is equally important to the author at all times.

33. However, see below n. 40.

34. I, p. 22.

35. Holtzmann, too (when considering the removal of the New Testament limits to the discipline), occasionally speaks of 'the history of early Christian religion' (I, p. 25).

36. This is partly (but only partly) explicable from the way in which modern New Testament study arose. Harnack's recent remark, though made in another context, is warmly to be welcomed: 'The problems of the future lie not in the realm of literary criticism but in that of history' (*Die Chronologie der altchristlichen Literatur bis Eusebius*, I, p. xii).

37. See the work of Gunkel already mentioned.

38. Reference to Paul explains very little here, though it is certain that Paulinism is one of the presuppositions of Johannine theology. I think, too, that Harnack (p. 93) is right in observing that to refer to Philo and Hellenism is by no means sufficient.

39. John 16.12ff. See Weizsäcker, *Apostolische Zeitalter*, pp. 537f. (ET *The Apostolic Age*, II, pp. 213f.).

40. I welcome especially the fact that Holtzmann has also made a start towards the method of treatment I have in mind, in that after the proclama-

tion of Jesus he devotes a separate chapter to the 'theological problems of early Christianity'. True, he deals here first only with the faith of the earliest Jewish Christian community, and even there sticks far too closely to the literary point of view (cf. the characteristic transition in I, p.349: 'We first turn to a second work of the author who wrote to Theophilus (Acts), and at the same time to the synoptic gospels so far as they . . . come into consideration as books of prayer and teaching'; also the special sections on Mark, Matthew, Luke-Acts and the Apocalypse, I, pp.419–76). But in many ways he goes beyond the earliest community and deals with a whole series of themes in a historical manner, drawing in a good deal of material. There is systematic consideration of the doctrinal narrative in the gospel, and of theological concepts like pre-existence, supernatural birth (why not also Jesus' receiving the spirit at his baptism, which is closely related to this?), ascension, descent into hell; also baptism and Lord's supper, gnosticism in the New Testament, the 'new law' and so forth. These parts are perhaps the most valuable in Holtzmann's book. No one will read them without profit and enjoyment. But he has not made much more than a start. Many other themes should be dealt with in this way. Often it is only the necessary historical observations that are given, and these only sketchily, and they are still too much influenced by literary perspectives, as already noted. The corresponding first sections of Harnack's *History of Dogma* may also be recalled here. They are perhaps not the most successful parts of the great work, but more stimulus and real 'biblical-theological' understanding can be got from them than from complete textbooks of New Testament theology.

41. Cf., however, in addition, below p.107.

42. Cf. above n.32.

43. Holtzmann, II, p.317, calls them 'doctrinal specialities' of the epistle.

44. The first part of von der Goltz's monograph on Ignatius (Texte und Untersuchungen, xii, 1894) confirms this in some respects.

45. Beyschlag, I, p.22, argues for a 'certain accommodation between a chronological arrangement and one by subject matter'.

46. Holtzmann, I, p.27. Deissmann (p.136) recommends putting the contents of the smaller New Testament writings as appendices after each of the three main formations; synoptic (?), Pauline and Johannine Christianity. Thus James should follow the synoptic material. This shows that he is at a loss to know what to do.

47. Lest a literary label (pseudo-Paulinism, Catholic Epistles) which says nothing about the actual content of the epistles should become normative. Cf. Holtzmann himself, II, p.316.

48. Consider the Paulinism of the Gospel of Luke, and so on.

49. A trifling (though in fact slightly questionable) observation of Holtzmann, II, pp.233f., seems to me typical. The formula of Eph. 6.23, 'peace and love with faith', is said to be half way between Gal. 5.6, 'faith working through love', and I Tim. 1.14, 'with faith and love'. This is logically correct, if one thinks about the Pauline *pistis*. But it is not historical. The development onwards from Paul cannot be imagined as though faith had first to lose a part of its specially Pauline significance before love could come in as a formal equivalent to it.

50. Making clear what we do not know is also important for a correct evaluation of our positive information.

51. Holtzmann, I, pp. 207f., 339; see also pp. 222 and 347.

52. In fact, of course, this 'puzzle' is rather an argument against the supposition that Jesus thought of a present kingdom in the modern sense. It may be added that although he must have felt his spiritual conception of the kingdom to be something new, he never, so far as the sources (including Luke 17.21) show us, indicated that he understood the concept of the kingdom any differently from his contemporaries. That is still significant, even if what it means is only that the evangelists were no longer conscious that Jesus was the sort of innovator they show him to have been. Holtzmann has failed to make us aware of this difficulty. He has not really fitted Jesus' concept of the kingdom into the development from Judaism to the early Christian community at all.

53. Harnack, *Die Chronologie der altchristlichen Literatur*, I, p.xi.

54. See above, p. 88.

55. See also von der Goltz, p. 171. Holtzmann has some relevant comments against this, II, pp. 382, 384.

56. For example Beyschlag, I, pp. 4, 17f., is also correct here.

57. Holtzmann touches on the theme, I, pp. 399ff. Cf. Deissmann, pp. 135f.

58. That is, in fact, easier to imagine in Paul than in Luther and his followers. Paul can write at I Cor. 7.19: circumcision is nothing, and uncircumcision is nothing; but (what matters is) keeping the commandments of God. In I Cor. 13 he can place love above faith and hope. In *Galatians* he can oppose the significance of circumcision and foreskin with faith working by love. He can also make statements like that at II Cor. 5.10. These are all things which a fastidious protagonist of the Protestant doctrine of justification could never have said on his own and which must worry him a lot. One might add in parenthesis that had these passages come in Ephesians or I Timothy, they would have been seen as clear signs of a deutero-Pauline or even un-Pauline attitude.

59. How the extensive formulae of Romans are to be explained from this point of view does not belong here. What I have said concides fully with what has most recently been spelled out by P. Wernle, *Der Christ und die Sünde bei Paulus*, 1897, about Paul's doctrine of justification. Cf. especially pp. 54, 79ff., 92ff., 100, 121. Wernle says that the doctrine of justification was 'mission theology' (p. 79). So far as I can see, Holtzmann has at no point put sufficiently sharply the question how the formula of justification by faith arose. Yet this is a question of the first order for Pauline theology.

60. In a large church where the concepts of brother and neighbour overlap, or at any rate cannot be clearly distinguished, love of the brethren will in the nature of the case always be a 'half-forgotten bit of Christianity' (cf. Rade in *Die Christliche Welt*, 1892, no. 5ff.). It can only be otherwise in sects, conventicles or fraternities which are in some way exclusive. Love of the brethren cannot be artificially concocted. Although Holtzmann talks a number of times about the relationship of love of the brethren and love of one's neighbour, I can find no historically satisfactory account of it. Compare, for example, II, pp 221f. Holtzmann can here say about Paul that the peaceableness

and compassion, etc., recommended allow 'no more doctrinaire distinguishing between persons to whom this love should be directed. Otherwise even Pauline morality would fall under the judgment of the Sermon on the Mount: "Do not even tax-collectors and sinners do as much?" ' The word 'doctrinaire' here contains some misunderstanding, and the saying quoted is somewhat inappropriate. All that is said about the commandment to love in John is (cf. II, pp. 388f.): 'However, that is meant rather differently from the morals of the Sermon on the Mount. . . .' It is misleading and distorted to see 'the middle link between Jesus' all-embracing command and John's definite restriction' in Paul.

61. In the section on the theological problems of early Christianity, Holtzmann automatically brings in extra-canonical material at several points.

62. In this sense I have called the separation of the New Testament writings from those related to them just tolerable in critical introduction to the New Testament, but downright mistaken in biblical theology (*Göttinger Gelehrte Anzeige*, 1896, p. 529). Cf. on this Holtzmann, I, p. vii.

63. See above p. 73.

64. I have not brought up the question whether one should take it further, say up to AD 200, and do not need to if it is admitted that the early Christian epoch excites particular interest in an extra-special treatment. But ideally a New Testament scholar should certainly be able to look a little further than Justin.

65. This is well said by Holtzmann, I, pp. 124ff., 127, 343f.

66. Holtzmann, I, p. 126: 'The contents of consciousness exist as ideas. These begin where a person is aware of something, unite at the point of what is being thought of and then press on to achieve the resulting aims of the will.'

67. See, however, Harnack, *History of Dogma*, I, p. 89.

68. Weizsäcker, *The Apostolic Age*, p. 123.

69. A similar view is held by Holtzmann, I, p. 350.

70. Consider what was spelled out on p. 100.

71. This gives me an opportunity to return briefly to my sharp criticism of Kabisch, *Paulinische Eschatologie* (*ThLZ* XIX, 1894, no. 5). I cannot withdraw my objections to the book. But in retrospect I wish that I had recognized more clearly that the strong emphasis upon eschatology in Paul and his connection with Judaism was a corrective to the usual view and performed a useful service.

72. I have in mind approximately the same demarcation as Weizsäcker has made (*The Apostolic Age*) in meeting the conditions of a truly historical presentation, in his extremely sensitive sketch of Pauline theology.

73. The same applies to John.

74. Cf. also Holtzmann, II, pp. 4, 217. Wendt has rightly drawn attention to this theme recently (*ZThK* IV, 1894), though I cannot agree with his method and results.

75. The opening words of E. Hatch's posthumous work, *The Influence of Greek Ideas on Christianity*, 1890, may be recalled here: 'It is impossible for anyone, whether he be a student of history or no, to fail to notice a difference of both form and content between the Sermon on the Mount and the Nicene Creed. The Sermon on the Mount is the promulgation of a new law of conduct; it assumes beliefs rather than formulates them; the theological conceptions which underlie it belong to the ethical rather than the speculative

side of theology; metaphysics are wholly absent. The Nicene Creed is a statement partly of historical facts and partly of dogmatic inferences . . . The contrast is patent. If anyone thinks that it is sufficiently explained by saying that the one is a sermon and the other a creed, it must be pointed out in reply that the question why an ethical sermon stood in the forefront of the teaching of Jesus Christ, and a metaphysical creed in the forefront of the Christianity of the fourth century is a problem which claims investigation.' It is a long way from Paul to the Nicene Creed. But if one asks on which side of this contrast he mostly stands, who will be able to reply without hesitation: on the side of the Sermon on the Mount?

76. That means the same as a great distance in time and space from him.

77. In a section which forms one of the high points of his work ('Rückblick und Ausblick', II, pp. 203ff., and closely related to it, I., pp. 490ff.), Holtzmann has made some very valuable remarks about this, but they could be supplemented.

78. The Pastoral Epistles mean to be Pauline. If, however, the Paul they honour is not so much the real Paul as rather *their* Paul, i.e. the perfect representative of normal church orthodoxy, it is less a matter of the after-effects of Paul than of an appearance of this (but see Holtzmann, II, p. 259).

79. Harnack, op. cit., p. 89; Pfleiderer, *Das Urchristentum*, pp. 615ff. (ET *Primitive Christianity*, II, pp. 237ff.); Holtzmann, II, p. 205. Here, too, the fact that the Pauline gospel is conditioned by the individual is recognized.

80. This does not, of course, exclude the possibility that Hellenistic Jews played an important role as teachers of Gentile Christians.

81. Pfleiderer, p. v (reference to German text).

82. See pp. 696, 672: Chapter 9 of Pfleiderer's *Paulinism* (ET 1877, II, pp. 51ff.) is entitled 'Paulinism under the Influence of Alexandrine Philosophy'; see pp. 54, 77f.

83. Harnack, p. 12: 'Understanding history means finding the norms by which the phenomena are to be classified.'

84. Holtzmann is very good on this, I, pp. 368ff.; also on several other of the questions mentioned.

85. Although Holtzmann rightly refuses to derive the gospel from the later gnostic systems, nevertheless he, too, considers its world of thought to be influenced and coloured by gnosticism. While agreeing with much of what he says here, I still do not think that he has done enough to make the relationship of the gospel to gnosticism clear. What matters most is making it clear in *historical* terms. It looks as though the evangelist intentionally gave his conception a background of speculative ideas from gnosticism. Or else he means by his book to lead false gnosis back to the truth it contains (II, pp. 381, 386). How can that be imagined? There is also no indication of how terminology and fundamental ideas can betray a gnostic origin and yet the author (in I John) oppose gnosis.

86. To use Holtzmann's appropriate expression, I, p. 363.

87. As with Paul, the task of dealing with the whole more exhaustively can be left to monographs.

88. Consider what impression we would have of the theology of Ignatius if we had from him not letters, but a gospel.

89. Other writers who say nothing about these *erga* will also, of course, have appealed to them in opposing Jews and Gentiles.

90. He saw to the wine at the wedding, not because his mother asked him; he does it of his own accord. He ignores his brothers' challenge to go to Jerusalem (ch. 7), but then sets out of his own accord. He lays down his life of his own free will (10.18) – and so on.

91. The evangelist had no doubt already read his own picture of Christ in the gospels which he knew, and consequently did not feel so acutely as we do how much he (or his like) had given new colours to the traditional picture of Christ. It is equally certain that the gospels he possessed did not satisfy him and were insufficiently clear.

92. They are also very different from the themes of Hebrews, which also has something to say about the humanity of Jesus. Against Holtzmann, II, p. 414.

93. If these suggestions of mine are right, then although the relevant sections of Holtzmann do largely depict the gospel data correctly, nevertheless some things have to be criticized and modified. This point has also to be considered if we are trying to evaluate correctly the relationship of I John to the Gospel. Cf., for example, Holtzmann's statement: 'In any case salvation is more directly tied to a personal relationship with Jesus in the Gospel than in the epistle' – and generally the comment in II, p. 442, n. 3.

94. Am I mistaken in my impression that this is often concealed by the way in which 'the gospel' is paraphrased when it is treated as a factor in the development? By gospel, people do not actually mean what the New Testament calls gospel – the message of the imminent kingdom of God or future salvation – but the quintessence of Jesus' ethical and religious preaching – i.e. primarily the 'law'.

95. Beyschlag can write (I, pp. 24f.): '[The early Christian] doctrinal development has almost no connection at all with the peculiar teaching of the Judaistic period', etc. Compare the whole of this really superficial account. How much more correct he is at II, p. 81.

96. Ibid., pp. 128ff. Cf. on this also the section 'On the Religious Dispositions of the Greeks and the Romans in the First Two Centuries, and Graeco-Roman Philosophy of Religion at that Time', in Harnack, pp. 116ff.

97. In addition to this first task for biblical theology, Deissmann adds two others. To establish, first, the particular individual forms of the early Christian consciousness, and then, secondly, its overall character – i.e. in a kind of systematic summary to get a cross-section and (using the simplest categories, like God, man, sin, Christ, etc.) to show a unity in the variety of the classical witnesses to primitive Christianity. I do not recognize this latter task. This kind of cross-section would only be an abstraction from the real history, and would therefore not make the historical conception any clearer. We are not accustomed to making similar demands for other areas in the history of religion. This is not, of course, to deny that at certain points it is important to define explicitly what they all have in common, although that is not always important. This evidently means that to reproduce 'the particular individual forms of the early Christian consciousness' is not enough.

98. Deissmann, p. 132.

99. The name of the lecture-course will also have to be changed; Krüger, p. 34.

NOTES TO SCHLATTER

1. Schweitzer's review of the 'historical' treatment of the Life of Jesus contains a number of solid observations on this point.

2. This is how Bernhard Weiss sees the task in his *New Testament Theology*.

3. Dalman's *Words of Jesus* should be mentioned in first place here.

4. Even Deissmann's *Light from the East* is not free of the old way of seeing the problem.

5. Thus the question of the semitism of the New Testament is of interest not only to its literary history but also to its theology. The question is how far semitic forms of thought have determined the language of the New Testament.

INDEX OF NAMES